BEYOND DISAGREEMENT

Beyond Disagreement

Open Remedies in Human Rights Adjudication

ARUNA SATHANAPALLY

OXFORD
UNIVERSITY PRESS

OXFORD
UNIVERSITY PRESS

Great Clarendon Street, Oxford, OX2 6DP,
United Kingdom

Oxford University Press is a department of the University of Oxford. It furthers the University's objective of excellence in research, scholarship, and education by publishing worldwide. Oxford is a registered trade mark of Oxford University Press in the UK and in certain other countries

First Edition published in 2012
Impression: 1

British Library Cataloguing in Publication Data
Data available

ISBN 978–0–19–966930–1

Printed in Great Britain by
CPI Group (UK) Ltd, Croydon CR0 4YY

Acknowledgements

The research upon which this book is based was substantially completed as part of my doctorate in law at the University of Oxford. I would like to thank the General Sir John Monash Foundation, the Menzies Foundation, and Balliol College, for their generous support of my research.

My supervisor, Professor Denis Galligan, provided valuable support and advice throughout the DPhil process, and Professor Paul Craig provided helpful supervision of the chapters concerning judicial treatment of declarations of incompatibility in the UK. I would also like to thank my examiners, Professors Sandra Fredman and Francesca Klug, and two anonymous reviewers for their encouragement and thoughtful comments.

I am also very grateful for the unswerving support from my parents, and the excellent advice on drafts provided by Vasudha Sathanapally, Frances Foster-Thorpe and Frances Voon. Lastly, I cannot thank Glenn Goldsmith enough for everything he has done to help me see this work to publication.

Contents

Table of Cases

New Zealand

South Africa

United Kingdom

United States

Table of Legislation

Abbreviations

ATCSA	Anti-Terrorism, Crime and Security Act 2001
DDI	delayed declaration of invalidity
DOI	declaration of incompatibility
ECHR	European Convention on Human Rights
ECJ	European Court of Justice
ECtHR	European Court of Human Rights
GRA	Gender Recognition Act 2004
HRA	Human Rights Act 1998
HRU	Human Rights Unit
ICCPR	International Covenant on Civil and Political Rights
ICESCR	International Covenant on Economic, Social and Cultural Rights
JCHR	Joint Committee on Human Rights
MOJ	Ministry of Justice
MP	Member of Parliament
NGO	non-governmental organization
PTA	Prevention of Terrorism Act 2005
SCC	Supreme Court of Canada
SVGA	Safeguarding Vulnerable Groups Act 2006
TPIM	Terrorism Prevention and Investigation Measure
USSC	United States Supreme Court
VCHRRA	Victorian Charter of Human Rights and Responsibilities Act 2006

Introduction

A. The Point of Departure

The twentieth century saw the remarkable rise of universal human rights as norms governing the actions of States. Heralded into international law by the Universal Declaration of Human Rights and the two principal human rights covenants in the 1960s,[1] the post-Cold War period in particular has seen the expansion of human rights as a language through which claims are made of public, and increasingly private,[2] action. Both the global practice and theory of human rights have moved well beyond the libertarian understandings that characterized natural rights discourse at the turn of the century, to now encompass a richer notion of human freedom.[3] Crucially, human rights are not simply individual rights against interference by the State, but norms understood to govern the social and political conditions of a decent society, a framework for the basic aspects of a dignified life for individuals and groups.[4]

Yet, alongside this expansion of human rights discourse must come the recognition that human rights norms do not always provide clearly delineated claims on public or private actors and there are circumstances when rights need to be balanced against other claims, including other rights. Human rights are broadly worded ethical commitments: with a core that is clearly identifiable and the subject of built-up—often hard-won—consensus over time. However, there remains a great deal of room for argument, persuasion, and disagreement over the boundaries of what they require. Even when given constitutional form as fundamental rights and freedoms

[1] International Covenant on Civil and Political Rights (ICCPR) and International Covenant on Economic, Social and Cultural Rights (ICESCR).

[2] For a forceful critique of the traditional focus of international human rights on government action, see C Mackinnon, 'Crimes of War, Crimes of Peace' in S Shute and S Hurley (eds), *On Human Rights* (Basic Books, New York 1993). See also A Clapham, *Human Rights Obligations of Non-State Actors* (OUP, Oxford 2006) Chapter 1.

[3] For examples see H Shue, *Basic Rights* (2nd edn Princeton University Press, Princeton 1980); T Pogge, *World Poverty and Human Rights* (2nd edn Polity, Cambridge 2008); S Fredman, *Human Rights Transformed: Positive Rights and Positive Duties* (OUP, Oxford 2008).

[4] This can be referred to as a 'political' or 'institutional' conception of human rights (as opposed to a natural rights conception). See J Rawls, *The Law of Peoples* (Harvard University Press, Cambridge MA 1999) 79–82; Pogge (n 3) 50–4; C Beitz, *The Idea of Human Rights* (OUP, Oxford 2009) 96–102; all of whom adopt a political conception of human rights. For a recent review, see K Baynes, 'Discourse Ethics and the Political Conception of Human Rights' (2009) 2 Ethics and Global Politics 1.

in a particular legal system, these rights remain underspecified for the range of circumstances in which they are claimed.

The juridical paradigm of fundamental rights—drawn principally from the US constitutional tradition—understands these rights as circumscribing the powers of the State, enforced by independent courts. This paradigm dominated understandings in the 1960s as to how States would implement at least their civil and political rights commitments.[5] However, fundamental rights, or human rights, generate moral or ethical claims upon the exercise of power, not only legal claims.[6] Human rights *law* gives expression to these ethical claims, but they continue to exist beyond positive law, and allow for criticism of the laws and practices of States inside and outside the courtroom. There is increasing emphasis in human rights theory on how human rights function more broadly as norms which societies use in deliberating and arguing over how to act.[7] Over time, human rights principles provide a framework for societies to reach answers to tricky problems while maintaining the fundamentals of a free and democratic society, ruling out certain answers but not necessarily furnishing a single 'correct' one. As a set of substantive ethical principles, human rights invite deliberation,[8] and support processes of information provision, public argument, and exchange.[9] It is through deliberation that different institutions—courts, lawmakers, policy makers, and civil society—specify what content human rights claims ought to be given, where the boundaries lie and how they ought to develop over time.

Yet, for this reason, even as the acceptance of human rights as ethical principles and their legal protection as constitutional rules has spread, the juridical model of implementing rights has come under criticism for giving judges too much power over matters that are properly the subject of moral and political debate. The idea of 'reasonable disagreement' over rights has been used to criticize judicial protection of rights against the decisions of, in particular, elected legislatures.[10] At the same time, human rights claims that require systematic and positive action challenge the traditional juridical paradigm in which judges stop the State from acting in specific ways by requiring that power be exercised in certain positive ways.

This book takes as its point of departure the three understandings of human rights above: that the scope and application of human rights principles may

[5] It was widely expected that States would incorporate their ICCPR commitments into domestic law, to be enforced by domestic courts. By contrast, most rights under the ICESCR were expected to become priorities for State policy: see Beitz (n 4) 32, 41.

[6] A Sen, 'Elements of a Theory of Human Rights' (2004) 32 Philosophy & Public Affairs 315; Pogge (n 3) 58–9; Shue (n 2) 13–18.

[7] A Sen, *The Idea of Justice* (Penguin, London 2010) 357–9; S Benhabib, *The Rights of Others* (CUP, Cambridge 2004) 178–81; T Risse, 'International Norms and Domestic Change: Arguing and Communicative Behavior in the Human Rights Arena' (1999) 27 Politics & Society 529; J Cohen, 'Minimalism about Human Rights: The Most We Can Hope For' (2003) 12 Journal of Political Philosophy 190.

[8] Sen (n 6) 323.

[9] S Benhabib, *The Rights of Others* (CUP, Cambridge 2004) 176–81.

[10] J Waldron, *Law and Disagreement* (Clarendon Press, Oxford 1999).

generate a range of possible solutions in specific circumstances; that human rights form more than limits on the actions of public bodies and can also call for systematic and positive action; and human rights are not only legal rules, but also broader ethical principles which invite deliberation outside courts as well as within. However, it seeks to step beyond the focus on disagreement evident in existing scholarship and consider how legal protection of human rights can provoke and enhance deliberation on the implementation of human rights principles, in situations of both contestation and cooperation. Concentrating on the remedial side of human rights adjudication—the point where judicial conclusions are translated into practical changes to law and policy—this book examines an innovative approach that seeks to engage legislatures in thinking about and protecting rights, thereby advancing the processes of careful reflection and justification that are central to a healthy democracy.

B. The Subject of this Book

This book makes a targeted intervention into the broader institutional debate of how we implement human rights, by looking at a particular family of remedies in human rights adjudication—employed across the United States, United Kingdom, South Africa, Canada, Australia, New Zealand, and international tribunals—which I term 'open remedies'.

Open remedies in human rights adjudication comprise a range of declaratory mechanisms by which courts communicate their conclusion that human rights have been violated but instead of devising an executory order or invalidating legislation, they invite the other branches of government to decide how to address the identified human rights problem. Where used in relation to *legislation,* these remedies function as 'legislative remand': returning a matter to the legislature for consideration. The shared feature of these remedies is that they explicitly invite the involvement of an institution other than the court in the resolution of a human rights problem. Sometimes referred to in existing scholarship as 'weak remedies', they represent a limited exercise of judicial power, and leave open certain choices for the non-judicial branches of government in translating specific judicial decisions on human rights into general, practical action.

Open remedies have the potential to enlist the other branches of government in making decisions about how to change law and policy in light of human rights principles. They allow courts to identify human rights violations even in situations where the courts are not well placed to design and implement corrective action, and provide space for the non-judicial branches of government to make decisions on the requirements of human rights principles and how these principles are to be balanced against competing ethical claims in prospective action. However, this innovative approach also raises concerns over the proper function of courts and the separation of powers, as well as the remedial effectiveness for victims of human rights violations.

The declaration of incompatibility (DOI)—a remedy provided for in the United Kingdom's Human Rights Act 1998 (HRA) and replicated in a series of similar human rights instruments[11]—is one species of open remedy, and one form of legislative remand. However, it is an especially limited judicial power in its design, because this declaration is purely exhortatory, and generates no legal obligations on the legislature to respond, nor can the courts take any further action should they wish to.

DOIs are particularly interesting from the perspective of comparative human rights law: the structure of this device potentially enlarges the role of the legislature beyond other forms of legislative remand, augmenting the potential benefits, and the potential difficulties, of their use. Non-binding by design, DOIs anticipate the possibility of reasonable disagreement over judicial conclusions on human rights, and for this reason, have been embraced by some who otherwise criticize traditional judicial review.[12] Yet, neither the comparative nor the UK scholarship has situated DOIs in the broader comparative context of other open remedies in fundamental rights adjudication, nor has the practical use of DOIs been systematically examined. Broad brush statements regarding the role of the legislature under the DOI mechanism have ordinarily not been grounded in an examination of what has actually happened after DOIs have been made. At a theoretical level, this lack of attention to the legislative process often accompanies a failure to articulate what conception of democratic decision-making underscores evaluations of different bills of rights.

This book addresses this gap in the current research. At its heart is a systematic study of the operation of DOIs, across courts and legislatures, over the first decade of their use in the UK (2000–10). A distinct normative perspective informs the construction and execution of this project. This is a deliberative democratic understanding of democracy; one in which democratic decision-making involves more than the majoritarian aggregation of private preferences, and requires public reflection and reasoned justification. In the case study, I ask whether, and to what extent, DOIs are a valuable mechanism for implementing human rights within a democracy that seeks to be deliberative.

The book proceeds by establishing, in Part I, two models of how courts and legislatures could interact over DOIs. The DOI has typically been understood as a novel institutional response to the idea of reasonable disagreement over rights—one in which judicial conclusions about what human rights require are merely provisional, and the legislature is given the role of conclusively deciding what interpretation is to be given to the relevant human rights safeguards. This is a model of institutional interaction, or 'dialogue', where judicial review is followed by legislative review (which I refer to as the *dual review* model).

[11] Human Rights Act 1993 (New Zealand); European Convention on Human Rights Act 2003 (Ireland); Human Rights Act 2004 (Australian Capital Territory); Charter of Human Rights and Responsibilities Act 2006 (Victoria).

[12] For instance, CA Gearty, *Principles of Human Rights Adjudication* (OUP, Oxford 2004), F Klug, *Values for a Godless Age: The Story of the United Kingdom's New Bill of Rights* (Penguin, London 2000).

Alternatively, if we look to the experience of open remedies elsewhere—those that do, and those that do not, allow the legislature to disagree with a judicial decision—we see a type of interaction in which courts and legislatures are engaged in an iterative process of adjusting legislation to respect human rights, in which each institution plays a distinct, specialized role. Judges identify the requirements of human rights in the specific cases that come before them, based on legal analysis as well as a factual record. Legislatures then decide how to adjust the general, prospective position of the law in response. Where there is disagreement with judicial decisions, it is through this legislative role that lawmakers can limit the effect of judicial interpretations of rights, rather than through outright refusal to change the law. In this book, this is referred to as the *specialization* model of dialogue.

Constitutional commentators differ over whether the specialization model of dialogue adequately addresses concerns about judges having too much power over the meaning of human rights. Less attention has been paid to why or how we want members of the legislature to be involved in decision-making on human rights. This book argues that we should look at interactions over human rights not simply in terms of decisions but also in terms of deliberation. Across both models—where the legislature decides *whether* to respond to a finding of human rights violation or where the legislature decides *how* to respond to such a finding—there are meaningful legislative decisions to be made, and there may be different levels of engagement with these decisions in the legislative process. We should consider the nature of the reply legislation and the nature of legislative deliberation on rights to fully understand the operation of DOIs in practice and appreciate the strengths and weaknesses of the legislature's involvement.

The UK's experience with DOIs over the ten-year study period indicates that, despite novel features of their design, they operated similarly to other open remedies in practice. Like experience elsewhere, the interaction over DOIs fell into a pattern in which courts and legislatures played distinct and specialized functions: with courts identifying that human rights had been infringed in specific cases, and the legislative process determining how rights were to be accommodated and advanced in legislation and policy. However, the analysis in Parts II and III challenges suggestions that the political branches have simply been dominated by judges and have not played a significant decision-making role. For one, the bulk of DOIs in the early period of the HRA were 'quiet cases': the need to address the identified human rights problem was not controversial within the political arms of government. Disagreement, heavily emphasized in theoretical accounts of dialogue, was not an ever-present feature in the practice of DOIs.

The circumstances in which courts issued DOIs also supported the specialization model in certain respects. The choice to issue a DOI has been a remedial choice, separated as a matter of principle from the merits of the human rights claim. Hence, judges often resorted to DOIs on the grounds that the legislature was better placed to devise remedial measures—rather than because they were faced with a 'hard case'—and issued several DOIs in circumstances where a legislative response was likely (or assured) to be forthcoming. DOIs were also concentrated on particular rights (those related to due process of the law and procedural fairness) and, in roughly half of cases, where there was a clear ECtHR ruling on the point. These factors do not account for all DOIs, and the courts did not eschew making controversial or broad rulings on legislation, but they were nonetheless careful about making interventions into ongoing political debates.

In relation to those DOIs that were controversial, resistance from the political branches of government typically occurred through more passive methods—such as delay, or the reassertion of policy in a new form—than an open refusal to change the law at all. This can be explained in some cases by the fact that open disagreement was not feasible because of the ECtHR dimension to the decisions. But a more important lesson is that the space for political decision-making available in crafting remedial action made it possible to pursue existing policy aims without openly refusing to change the law, making open confrontation less necessary.

On the deeper question of legislative engagement: examples over this period in the UK demonstrate that, because of the wide latitude available in deciding how to address a human rights problem, the executive may propose remedial legislation that raises new human rights and other concerns. Reviewing the executive's chosen response can therefore be an important task for legislative deliberation, even under the specialization model of dialogue. However, careful deliberation on legislative responses to DOIs was ordinarily not well supported either by the parliamentary process in general, or the design of the HRA in particular. Separately, the UK experience illustrates some practical difficulties with making the legislature the first mover in crafting remedial action: in particular, a tendency to neglect retrospective remedies for victims of human rights violations and delay corrective action for long periods.

On select occasions, there was relatively good deliberation on how to address a DOI, such as in relation to the legal recognition of gender change. Yet, other examples, such as in relation to counter-terrorism powers, indicate the difficulties caused by strong executive control over the conditions of deliberation. In particular, the weakness of parliamentary institutions relative to the executive can itself drive minimalist, compliance-oriented debates about legislation which are at odds with the aspirations of a deliberative democracy.

Most interesting from an institutional design perspective was the development of the parliamentary committee entrusted with responsibility for human rights. Over time, this committee moved to engage in sustained consideration of responses to DOIs, and became an avenue for greater accountability and civil society participation. This experience illustrates some ways in which institutional design can support deliberation on human rights.

Overall, this first experiment with DOIs illustrates the potential benefits of the open remedial approach in certain circumstances, yet indicates certain shortcomings in their design from the perspective of fostering deliberation on responsive action. It also suggests reasons to tread carefully in relation to legislative remedies in general. If we are concerned to enhance political deliberation on rights, the UK experience indicates that future efforts would be better directed towards strengthening the institutional foundations of political deliberation—building up processes of reason-giving around rights—rather than further limiting judicial intervention.

C. Chapter Overview

Part I introduces the concept of open remedies in human rights adjudication, and then considers what role the legislature may play where open remedies are used, including how this may work specifically in relation to DOIs. Chapter 1 presents a typology of open remedies in human rights adjudication. It identifies the shared rationales that underpin these remedial strategies as well as the principal concerns they give rise to. Chapter 2 turns to the existing scholarship on the interactions between courts and legislatures over fundamental rights under 'weak-form' review, in order to clarify the two models of how courts and legislatures may interact over open remedies. Chapter 3 then builds on these two models to examine how the legislative decision-making task is performed. It shows how weak-form review is well suited to a deliberative conception of democracy, and draws on this theoretical tradition to build a simple framework to examine legislative engagement in remedial decision-making.

The remainder of the book turns to the detailed analysis of the case study of open remedies in the UK: the leading and dominant example of DOIs. Part II examines the approach that the UK courts have taken towards DOIs. Chapter 4 examines the judicial reasoning that governs the making of a DOI. It considers how the principles governing this remedial choice have been applied in the cases before the courts, and observes that the courts' use of the DOI mechanism aligns the remedy to other forms of legislative remand and in certain respects supports the specialization model of interaction. Chapter 5 asks whether, since DOIs are non-coercive and only exhortatory, courts have been activist in using them to make broad rulings, or to develop a national set of human rights standards which builds on the international minimum provided by the European Convention on Human Rights.

Part III turns to the political response to DOIs made from 2000 to 2010. Chapter 6 examines the pattern of legislative response over the study period and explains two main observations: first, that no DOI has met with refusal to change the law; and second, that most DOIs have excited little attention or debate in the legislature. This chapter also examines the development of the parliamentary JCHR as a site for deliberation on DOIs over the study period. Chapters 7 and 8 ask whether the potential benefits of leaving remedies to the legislature are seen in those select cases where there was a legislative bill dedicated to responding to a DOI, both in terms of the quality of deliberation on how to respond to the issue and the advantages and disadvantages that attach to having remedial action crafted through the legislative process. Chapter 7 examines two examples where reply legislation was given this level of attention in the Houses of Parliament, as well as the ongoing failure to legislate in relation to prisoner voting. Chapter 8 examines the most high-profile DOI in the study period—the *Belmarsh Prisoners*[13] case—and the ensuing institutional dialogue over the control order regime introduced in response to that

[13] *A & Ors v Secretary of State for the Home Department* [2004] UKHL 56.

DOI. Finally, while the focus of this book is the systematic study of DOIs up to the end of the Labour government in 2010, an epilogue considers interesting developments directly after the study period, including the first example of open parliamentary refusal to comply with a DOI, indeed, a DOI that was directly based on an international legal obligation established by a ruling of the ECtHR. Lastly, a short concluding chapter reflects on what lessons we can draw from this study, from the perspective of institutional design.

PART I

TYPOLOGY AND INTERACTIONS

1

Open Remedies in Human Rights Adjudication

1.A. Introduction

Remedies in public law have two generally recognized functions. There is the paradigmatic function of corrective justice, where courts redress the wrong done to the plaintiff. But there is also the systemic function of ensuring that future public action complies with the requirements of the law. In relation to human rights adjudication, where broadly stated yet fundamental norms of public conduct are interpreted and applied, both purposes are important.

Additionally, there is a third potential function that human rights remedies could play. Remedies could be employed in a way that facilitates democratic deliberation beyond the courts as to how best to protect rights and how to balance human rights with other valuable ends. This third purpose may not form part of the mainstream appraisal of the purpose of remedies. However, the remedial phase in human rights adjudication provides a fertile ground for techniques of cooperative constitutionalism, that is, techniques that enlist the other branches of government in implementing constitutional norms. This is not surprising given that it has long been recognized in public law scholarship that the remedial phase is generally the most discretionary and pragmatic aspect of litigation, where a number of purposes and constraints may operate in the circumstances of a given case.[1] It is for this reason that remedies and their enforcement form an important nexus between rights and political realities:[2] a site of negotiation between adherence to principle and pragmatic reliance on institutional comity and cooperation to make rights effective.[3]

This chapter introduces a remedial approach referred to as 'open remedies' in human rights adjudication. First, in section 1.B, I distinguish between the broader

[1] A Chayes, 'The Role of the Judge in Public Law Litigation' (1976) 89 Harvard Law Review; GA Spann, 'Expository Justice' (1983) 131 UPenn Law Review 585. For recent work, see K Roach, *Constitutional Remedies in Canada* (Canada Law Book, Aurora, Ont. 2009) 1-1; I Leigh and R Masterman, *Making Rights Real* (Hart, Oxford 2008).

[2] B Freidman, 'When Rights Encounter Reality: Enforcing Federal Remedies' (1992) 65 Southern California Law Review 735.

[3] C Manfredi, '"Appropriate and Just in the Circumstances": Public Policy and the Enforcement of Rights under the Canadian Charter of Rights and Freedoms' (1994) 27 Canadian Journal of Political Science 435.

concept of weak-form human rights review and open remedies. Weak-form review refers to structural forms of fundamental rights protection that permit the legislature to override, amend, or ignore judicial determinations on what adherence to fundamental rights requires. Open remedies, elsewhere referred to as 'weak remedies' or 'dialogic remedies', are a range of declaratory mechanisms whereby the courts do not provide direct immediate relief to the victim other than a declaration that human rights safeguards have been infringed, leaving corrective action in the hands of the other branches of government either temporarily or indefinitely. Section 1.C examines the variety of such remedies in human rights adjudication. Where these remedies are used in relation to *legislation* that infringes rights, they operate as a form of 'legislative remand', and this may take a coercive or a non-coercive form.

Section 1.D identifies three rationales that may justify the open remedial approach. These rationales demonstrate the conceptual coherence across the spectrum of open remedies. Yet, resort to these remedies also raises concerns about the failure of judges to perform the proper judicial function of upholding the law and providing corrective justice, which I consider in section 1.E.

1.B. Weak-Form Review Considered

The traditional model of the legal protection of fundamental rights has already been referred to as the *juridical* model of implementation. The significant features of this model are that rights are enshrined in a constitutional document and enforced by courts. Where public action, or the law itself, is challenged in the courts and found to violate these norms, then judges are empowered to strike down legislative and executive action, and have access to the full range of public law remedies, such as injunctions and mandatory orders. Through these means, the courts hold the other branches to (their interpretation of) the requirements of human rights principles. The iconic case of this model of fundamental rights protection (though not generally referred to as *human rights* protection) is the United States Constitution and accompanying doctrine of judicial supremacy.[4]

Canada, the UK, New Zealand, and Australia have departed from this model in differing degrees in their attempts to formally protect fundamental rights. Each marks a point in the spectrum between juridical implementation and political

[4] Even in the United States there are competing theories to judicial supremacy over constitutional meaning: 'departmentalist' theories or coordinate theories of constitutional interpretation. For a recent overview see DE Johnson, 'Functional Departmentalism and Nonjudicial Interpretation: Who Determines Constitutional Meaning?' (2005) 67 Law and Contemporary Problems 105. Nonetheless, it remains the case at the federal level that '[d]espite continuing criticism, judicial supremacy is a basic fact about the American constitutional regime. Even its most stringent critics acknowledge that it reflects the popular understanding': D Farber, 'Legislative Constitutionalism in a System of Judicial Supremacy' in RW Bauman and T Kahana (eds), *The Least Examined Branch: The Role of Legislatures in the Constitutional State* (CUP, Cambridge 2006) 432. At a state constitutional level, it is more widely recognized that judicial decisions may be provisional rather than final, given the ease of constitutional amendment in some states: H Herschkoff, 'Positive Rights and State Constitutions: The Limits of Federal Rationality Review' (1999) 112 Harvard Law Review 1131, 1162–3.

implementation, with the latter being where the interpretation and application of fundamental rights norms is left ultimately to the political process.[5] These attempts have variously been described as 'hybrid' bills of rights,[6] 'third-way' bills of rights,[7] 'the Commonwealth model'[8]—and in relation to the UK, Australia and New Zealand in particular—legislative or parliamentary bills of rights.[9]

Early comparative constitutional work by Stephen Gardbaum sought to classify human rights instruments in Canada, New Zealand, and the UK jointly as the *new commonwealth constitutionalism*, arguing that the manner in which fundamental rights were incorporated in these jurisdictions amounted to 'a deliberate rejection of the American model of constitutionalism with its perceived excesses of judicial power'.[10] Gardbaum's analysis emphasized the historical dimension of this common approach. Each bill of rights affirmed a model of parliamentary democracy (the Westminster model) that places the representative legislature, at least symbolically, at the apex of government.[11] According to Gardbaum, the legislature in the Commonwealth tradition is ordinarily understood as the institutional manifestation of popular sovereignty; reflecting the historical triumph of the people against the Crown and a narrow political elite.[12] This is contrasted to the US where, by virtue of its own constitutional history, 'legislatures are not conceived of in the same way as a *distinctive* collective organ of the people'.[13]

The phrase *weak-form review* was coined by Mark Tushnet, who sought, in contrast to Gardbaum's historical approach, to emphasize the conceptual linkages between the different hybrid models.[14] Weak-form review is the mechanism which is employed in each of these instruments to strike a compromise between judicial and political protection of human rights. Judges are empowered to review executive action and legislation for its compliance with fundamental rights and freedoms but judicial powers with respect to the actions of the legislature are weakened in the design of the bill of rights. There are ways in which the judicial decision can be avoided or overridden by

[5] For further discussion of the concepts of political and juridical constitutionalism, see R Bellamy, 'Constitutive Citizenship Versus Constitutional Rights: Republican Reflections on the EU Charter and the Human Rights Act' in T Campbell, KD Ewing, and A Tomkins (eds), *Sceptical Essays on Human Rights* (OUP, Oxford 2001).

[6] J Goldsworthy, 'Homogenizing Constitutions' (2003) 23 Oxford Journal of Legal Studies 483.

[7] F Klug, 'The Human Rights Act—A "Third Way" or a "Third Wave" Bill of Rights' [2001] EHRLR 361.

[8] S Gardbaum, 'The New Commonwealth Model of Constitutionalism' (2001) 49 American Journal of Comparative Law 707.

[9] JL Hiebert, 'New Constitutional Ideas: Can New Parliamentary Models Resist Judicial Dominance When Interpreting Rights?' (2003) 82 Texas Law Review 1963.

[10] Gardbaum (n 8) 710.

[11] The power of this symbolism can be seen in the fact that Australian debates over a bill of rights have seen the regular invocation of the concept of parliamentary sovereignty (see, for instance, the terms of reference of the recent National Human Rights Consultation: <http://www.humanrightsconsultation.gov.au/www/nhrcc/nhrcc.nsf/Page/Terms_of_Reference>) even though all Australian legislatures are subject to binding constitutional review by the High Court of Australia and hence, strictly speaking, are not sovereign or supreme.

[12] Gardbaum (n 8) 740.

[13] Gardbaum (n 8) 741.

[14] M Tushnet, 'New Forms of Judicial Review and the Persistence of Rights- and Democracy-Based Worries' (2003) 38 Wake Forest Law Review 813.

the legislature, without having to amend the constitution itself. The leading example is the Canadian Charter, where judicial review with respect to most rights is weak-form, because the legislature can immunize legislation from judicial review using a power provided by the Charter itself (referred to as the 'notwithstanding clause').[15]

However, there are different types of weak-form judicial review. It is helpful to distinguish different ways in which judicial review may be 'weaker' than the archetype of juridical implementation of rights. There are devices that allow the legislature to *reverse* a judicial decision, techniques that provide for *limited rights*, and devices that provide *open remedies*. One thing that can be noted, from the overview below, is that weaker forms of review are not unique to the new hybrid bills of rights; while they may be provided for in the design of a bill of rights (as hybrid bills of rights do), they may also be developed by judges.[16]

1.B.1. Reversible judicial decisions

There are two ways in which judicial decisions may be reversible. First, the legislature may be able to reinstate the legislation that has been struck down using a power such as the notwithstanding clause. Alternatively, if the courts have protected human rights by presuming that legislation is to be given effect in a rights-compliant way, then the legislature may pass legislation giving express authorization for the conduct or practice that the court considered to infringe rights. This second approach to protecting norms against legislative incursion can be referred to as a clear statement rule or interpretative rule.

In these situations, the court provides resolution in the immediate dispute, in a way that prevents or otherwise remedies the identified violation of rights. (In fact, there may be a similarity between judicial remedies across these two scenarios: techniques such as reading-in, for instance, may be available to judges both in systems where they can invalidate legislation, and in systems where they only have strong interpretive obligations.) The end result is that the law is made to conform to the requirements of fundamental rights, as identified by the court, but that the legislature may act subsequently to change that law.

1.B.2. Limited rights

Alternatively there are techniques and devices whereby fundamental rights themselves are formulated to leave greater room for justified limitations on rights, or for non-judicial institutions to reach their own specifications of what rights require.[17]

[15] s 33 Canadian Charter of Rights and Freedoms 1982.

[16] See M Tushnet, *Weak Courts, Strong Rights* (Princeton University Press, Princeton 2008) 36–42 for an exploration of how techniques of weak-form review exist within US constitutional law.

[17] We will see in Chapter 2.B that a number of Canadian theorists have argued the limitations clause in s 1 Canadian Charter of Rights and Freedoms 1982 is the engine of weak-form review. Tushnet himself (n 14) recognizes incomplete specifications of rights as a variant of weak-form review, referring to Dorf and Sabel's concept of 'democratic experimentalism': see MC Dorf and CF Sabel, 'A Constitution of Democratic Experimentalism' (1998) 98 Columbia Law Review 267.

Judges may limit the scope and application of rights through methods of judicial restraint or deference to lawmakers or members of the government. Alternatively, the structure of the human rights instrument may itself make rights adjudication more sensitive to public policy and resource-based concerns by providing for limitations on rights as are 'necessary in a democratic society' (either generally or for particular rights), or by requiring only progressive implementation of rights. This technique is demonstrated by the specific limitations clauses in the European Convention on Human Rights (ECHR), the generalized limitations clauses in the Canadian and South African bills of rights, and the ICESCR's treatment of social, economic and cultural rights. While these provisions do not provide means for legislatures to reverse or avoid specific judicial decisions, they do allow for a process of reformulation of what rights require and rejustification of limits placed on rights, as will be discussed in more detail in Chapter 2's discussion of theories of institutional dialogue.

1.B.3. Open remedies

A third way in which judicial review may be weakened or restrained is at the remedial stage. Generally speaking, the least obtrusive remedy available to a court is declaratory relief. There are a range of remedies that courts have employed in human rights adjudication that declare an infringement of human rights norms, but leave the choice of means to address that infringement to non-judicial institutions. They include ordinary declaratory judgments (in certain circumstances), legislative remand in the US, delayed declarations of invalidity in Canada and South Africa, and declarations of incompatibility in the UK, Australia, and New Zealand.

Remedial methods of weak-form review have begun to be recognized in the scholarship.[18] Some scholars writing on weak-form review have used the phrase 'weak remedies' to contrast these forms of declaratory relief to 'strong remedies' such as invalidation, reading-in, mandatory orders, and injunctions, which are more directive and more time sensitive.[19] Elsewhere, the same remedies have been referred to by the more favourable term 'dialogic remedies', for they appreciate the role of other institutions in responding to and implementing constitutional norms, contrasting to the view that remedies are solely the preserve of the judiciary.[20]

This book adopts the neutral shorthand of 'open remedies', in preference to the slightly pejorative term 'weak remedies' and the vexed term 'dialogic' (which we will see in the following chapter is a term subject to significant academic debate). This helpfully draws attention to a central feature of these remedies, that they leave

[18] R Dixon, 'Creating Dialogue about Socio-Economic Rights: Strong-Form Versus Weak-Form Judicial Review Revisited' (2007) 5 ICON 391. Likewise, Mark Tushnet refers to weak remedies as one method of weak-form review, including declaratory relief as well as orders which require government officials to formulate plans to eliminate constitutional violations in a reasonable amount of time, (n 16), 248.

[19] Dixon (n 18) 392.

[20] K Roach, 'Constitutional, Remedial and International Dialogues about Rights: The Canadian Experience' (2005) 40 Texas International Law Journal 537, 551.

open to the other branches of government significant choices about how the violation of a fundamental right will be rectified or otherwise responded to. The following section will detail a group of remedies in different systems of human rights review that share this feature.

Thinking of these remedies as 'open', rather than only 'weak', also allows us to broaden out from Tushnet's original emphasis, in his concept of weak-form review, on mechanisms that allow elected representatives to *resist* judicial interpretations of rights. Tushnet argues that the basic idea underpinning weak-form instruments is to 'provide mechanisms for the people to respond to decisions that they believe are *mistaken* that can be deployed more rapidly than the constitutional amendment process'.[21] To Tushnet, each of the hybrid bills of rights achieves this in a different way.

However, by contrast to, say, reversible judicial decisions, the purpose of remedial methods of weak-form review—open remedies—does not necessarily lie in the ability of the legislature to resist or defy judicial decisions that are thought mistaken. As we will see in section1.D, the contestability of judicial interpretations of rights is not the only rationale that underpins these remedial devices. Other concerns, such as institutional capacity or the systemic consequences of judgments, also support judicial recourse to open remedies.

1.C. The Variety of Open Remedies

1.C.1. Declaratory judgments

A declaratory judgment is 'a formal statement by the Court, pronouncing upon the existence or non-existence of a legal state of affairs'.[22] It contrasts to an executory judgment. Where the court employs a declaration, it does not order the defendant to act in any particular way. The leading text on declaratory judgments states that 'a declaration is the least aggressive remedy and therefore the most desirable when a relationship between the parties has to be continued'.[23] In the public law context of regular or continued interaction between public authorities and individuals or groups, declarations can be an especially useful tool. In fact, an important reason for the expansion of declarations into regular use was their entry into public law.[24]

A 'mere' declaration is not devoid of legal effect—it still involves the court delivering a reasoned answer to the controversy between the parties.[25] The significance of a declaratory judgment in fundamental rights adjudication lies in the authoritative interpretation of the law and its application to the dispute before the

[21] Tushnet (n 16) 23 (emphasis added).

[22] I Zamir, H Woolf, and J Woolf, *The Declaratory Judgment* (3rd edn Sweet & Maxwell, London 2002) 1.

[23] Zamir et al (n 22) v.

[24] WG Friedmann, *Law and Social Change in Contemporary Britain* (Stevens and Sons, London 1951) 217–19.

[25] Zamir et al (n 22) 4.

court, resulting in a determination on whether any fundamental right has been violated. By removing any doubt about the state of the law, the declaration can be not only a tool of corrective, but also preventative justice.[26] Even if it is not followed up by a coercive court order, a judicial declaration itself carries significant weight for the parties before the court and for future public conduct.[27] While declarations may be weaker than other orders that a court may make, they may nonetheless be potent in affecting behaviour.

Declaratory relief also lies at the heart of international human rights adjudication.[28] International tribunals ordinarily issue a declaration that a State has or has not violated its international obligations with respect to the complainant.[29] This is an authoritative finding, which establishes the truth of the allegation made against the State and vindicates the victim, but is also the least intrusive remedy that an international tribunal can provide a victim. A declaration alone should lead the State to alter its behaviour, if it is committed to meeting its international obligations.[30] However, the effect of declarations is prospective in this sense and declarations rarely redress the consequences of the harm suffered by the victim; an attribute that I will return to below.

Two examples illustrate how a declaratory judgment may operate in human rights adjudication as an open remedy, putting important remedial choices in the hands of political bodies. The first is the use of declarations in socio-economic rights adjudication. The very first case in which South Africa's Constitutional Court found a violation of a socio-economic provision of the South African Constitution was *Government of the Republic of South Africa v Grootboom.*[31] The case involved a challenge to the government's refusal to provide temporary accommodation to hundreds of evicted squatters. The court held that the government had violated its constitutional obligation to implement reasonable measures to realize the constitutional right of access to adequate housing. This decision was momentous, even within comparative constitutional circles, for demonstrating that the right to housing could be enforced by the courts.

The court's remedial action was entirely declaratory: stating that in order to meet its constitutional obligation of progressive realization, the State must include measures to address the situation of those with no access to housing at all and those living in intolerable conditions; and finding that the housing programme in question failed to comply with this obligation.[32] By contrast to the Cape of Good Hope High Court, which made an order requiring the government to provide certain basic services, the Constitutional Court left the government to devise a housing programme that would meet its constitutional obligations.

26 E Borchard, *Declaratory Judgments* (2nd edn William S Hein, Buffalo, NY 2000) 277.

27 Zamir et al (n 22) 4, who further note that failure to respect a declaration can lead to consequences in any future litigation, and if a defendant ignores a declaration, the claimant may return to the court to seek further relief.

28 D Shelton, *Remedies in International Human Rights Law* (OUP, Oxford 2005) Chapter 7 'Declaratory Judgments'.

29 I will return to this point in section 1.C.4.

30 Shelton (n 28) 256.

31 *Government of the Republic of South Africa v Grootboom* 2001 (1) SA 46 (CC).

32 *Grootboom* (n 31) [99].

Commentators have drawn attention to the range of remedies that were available to the Constitutional Court, such as requiring the government to prepare a plan of action and present it to the court, or ongoing supervision.[33] In relation to supervision, the Constitutional Court observed that the South African Human Rights Commission was entrusted with the duty to monitor the promotion of human rights and would therefore report on the efforts made by the State to comply with the judgment. The court only provided guidance on the proper interpretation of the Constitution, as applied to the existing practice.[34]

Grootboom was one of the earliest cases relating to socio-economic rights decided under the South African Constitution. In the merits phase, the court went some way in affirming the justiciability of socio-economic rights under the Constitution,[35] but held back at the remedial phase from mandating specific State action on the provision of housing. Judges may restrain themselves to declaratory relief when faced with concerns about intrusion into the functions of the other branches of government.[36] However, the aftermath of *Grootboom* demonstrates the importance of institutional cooperation and comity to the effectiveness of declaratory relief. The government failed to act on the declaration in a timely and robust way, either in relation to the situation of the litigants, or in relation to housing policy in general.[37] The absence of any mandated time frame for action proved especially problematic.[38] As a result, the intervention of the court in *Grootboom* came to be criticized as insufficient to compel the government to action.[39]

The second example is the European Court of Human Rights' (ECtHR) use of declarations. Where the ECtHR finds that a State has violated a right protected by the ECHR, it is empowered to provide 'just satisfaction' to the injured party.[40] The court may deny damages to the victim on the grounds that a declaration of wrongdoing is adequate for just satisfaction. The court's stated basis for making this decision is considerations of 'equity': a discretionary blend of factors.[41] Dinah Shelton, in her research into the court's remedial practices, concludes that one of

[33] T Roux, 'Understanding Grootboom: A Reply to Cass Sunstein' (2002) 12 Constitutional Forum 41; K Pillay, 'Implementing Grootboom: Supervision Needed' (2002) 3 Economic Social Rights Review.

[34] Roux (n 33) 51.

[35] 'The question is therefore not whether socio-economic rights are justiciable under our Constitution, but how to enforce them in a given case': *Grootboom* (n 31) [20].

[36] In fact, in the later case of *Minister of Heath & Ors v Treatment Action Campaign & Ors (No 2)* 2002 (5) SA 721 (CC), the government explicitly argued that courts should, because of justiciability concerns, limit themselves to declaratory relief in socio-economic rights cases. The Constitutional Court rejected this suggested remedial principle and demonstrated its willingness to direct the government through use of a mandatory order, at [99], [106], [135]. See M Pieterse, 'Possibilities and Pitfalls in the Domestic Enforcement of Social Rights: Contemplating the South African Experience' (2004) 26 Human Rights Quarterly 882, 894–5.

[37] S Fredman, *Human Rights Transformed: Positive Rights and Positive Duties* (OUP, Oxford 2008) 119; Pillay (n 33).

[38] Pillay (n 33).

[39] Dixon (n 18) 392; Roux (n 33) 51; D Bilchitz, 'Giving Socio-Economic Rights Teeth: The Minimum Core and its Importance' (2002) 119 South African Law Journal 484.

[40] Art 41 ECHR.

[41] Shelton (n 28) 257.

the most significant factors in determining whether damages are awarded is the character of the applicant: prisoners, homosexuals, religious minorities, and legal (as opposed to natural) persons are unlikely to receive damages.[42] Further, the more divided the court is on the decision on its merits, the more likely the majority is to rely solely on a declaration, 'the judges feeling that they have already strained to give a judgment in favour of the applicant'.[43] This example again indicates that resort to declarations may be a form of restraint by judges, who are concerned about how the government in question will react to the court's ruling—cases where there is disagreement amongst judges and cases where the victims are unpopular tend to be the controversial or politically sensitive cases before the court.[44] Shelton is critical of this remedial practice, but accepts that there are pragmatic reasons for this restraint and notes that the use of declarations in politically sensitive cases is a practice that occurs even at the national level, for instance by the United States Supreme Court (USSC).[45] However, beyond unstated pragmatic considerations, there may be principled reasons advanced within judicial reasoning to employ an open remedy, especially in relation to legislation: an approach referred to as legislative remand.

1.C.2. Legislative remand

Thus far, we have considered general declarations and their use in human rights adjudication at the national and supranational level. Legislative remand is a more specific form of declaration, used where a law is declared to violate fundamental rights but the law is not invalidated or otherwise modified.[46] Instead of bringing the law into conformity with constitutional requirements, the court returns ('remands') the question of how the law is to be changed to the legislature itself.

Recent examples of this remedial technique are demonstrated by challenges to marriage laws on the grounds of equality guarantees in the United States and South Africa. In these examples of legislative remand we see, as with general declaratory relief above, the significance of political sensitivity, public reaction, and concerns about judges overstepping their institutional role by making choices as to the way in which the law should change to respect fundamental rights.

The US cases of *Baker v State*[47] and *Lewis v Harris*[48] both involved challenges to marriage laws from same-sex couples on the grounds of equality rights in the respective State constitutions, while the case of *Minister for Home Affairs v Fourie*[49] concerned the equality and non-discrimination provisions in the South African Constitution.

[42] Shelton (n 28) 263. [43] Shelton (n 28) 203.

[44] Shelton (n 28) 203. This finding is based on Shelton's personal interview evidence with judges of the court.

[45] Shelton (n 28) 256.

[46] The phrase legislative remand has sometimes been used loosely. I adopt the same definition as provided in T Jacobi, 'Same-Sex Marriage in Vermont: Implications of Legislative Remand for the Judiciary's Role' (2002) 26 Vermont Law Review 381.

[47] (1999) 744 A.2d 864 (Vermont).

[48] (2006) 908 A.2d 196 (New Jersey).

[49] *Minister for Home Affairs v Fourie* 2005 SA 60 (CC).

Each of these cases shares the following features and hence they can be discussed together. Each judgment held that non-discrimination on grounds of sexual orientation ought to extend to the legal recognition of committed same-sex couples. Each judgment recognized that addressing the discrimination before the court necessitated systematic reform regarding the recognition of same-sex couples, rather than simply addressing the wrong done to the plaintiffs themselves.[50] In each case the court identified two potential routes by which this systematic reform could be achieved: by providing for a civil partnership scheme that afforded the same benefits as marriage, or by extending the institution of marriage itself.[51] Finally, in each case, the choice between these routes was considered (by the majority of the court) to be best left to public and legislative decision-making, in the first instance.[52]

What distinguishes the remedies employed in these cases from pure declaratory relief is that the legislature was given the first chance to correct the infringement of equality rights, but was under some coercion to act. The court in each case indicated that it would provide a remedy if the legislature did not.[53] Specifically, in *Lewis*, the legislature was given a set period to respond;[54] in *Baker*, the court suspended its judgment but remained seized of the matter;[55] and in *Fourie*, the court held that if the legislature did not take action in one year, then the court would read the inclusion of same-sex couples into the existing marriage law.[56]

There are three reasons favouring legislative remand in these cases. The first is that this strategy allowed judges to avoid controversy, given the political sensitivity of making changes to the institution of marriage and the popular contestation over whether equality rights required inclusion into marriage, or simply an extension of the same benefits as married couples, or no action at all. The second is an institutional capacity reason. It was within the tools available to the judges in each case to amend the definition of marriage. Introducing a parallel civil partnership scheme and systematically rolling out equal recognition to marriage and civil partnership would require legislative action. If the court considered that both of these solutions were constitutional, then only the legislature could choose between, and give effect to, *either* solution.

A third reason is that the effective promotion of equality of same-sex couples requires not only changes in the law, but also public acceptance of those changes. The majority judgment in *Fourie*, for instance, was influenced by the extensive public consultation that had been undertaken by the South African Law Reform Commission, which would provide a foundation for legislative decision-making. Justice Sachs noted that, while the law could help establish public norms that are assimilated into daily life, 'the law may not in and of itself eliminate prejudice and stereotyping'.[57] A remedy which invites public and legislative deliberation on how best to respect and protect rights may better support public acceptance of the need

[50] See especially *Fourie* (n 49) [116], [133].
[51] *Baker* (n 47) [225]; *Lewis* (n 48) [19], [224]; *Fourie* (n 49) [140]–[141].
[52] *Baker* (n 47) [197]–[198]; *Lewis* (n 48) [19]; *Fourie* (n 49) [133].
[53] *Baker* (n 47) [11]; *Lewis* (n 48) [19]; *Fourie* (n 49) [118].
[54] *Lewis* (n 48) [11].
[55] *Baker* (n 47) [229].
[56] *Fourie* (n 49) [118].
[57] *Fourie* (n 49) [138].

for change and the nature of change undertaken. To borrow Justice Sach's language, it placed the legislature 'in the frontline' on changes to the law.[58]

It has been suggested that even if the judges were to conclude that there was only one constitutional answer (that is, enacting a remedy that did not involve a choice between different schemes), they may nonetheless consider that greater public acceptance would likely be secured if that conclusion was arrived at through legislative deliberation rather than a court order.[59] In defence of the decision in *Baker v State*, political scientist Tonja Jacobi has argued that legislative remand reduces the chance of public backlash.[60] She contrasts the experience of Vermont, which legislated for civil unions soon after the judicial decision and retained them, to Hawaii, where the Hawaiian Supreme Court's extension of marriage to same-sex couples was quickly reversed by a state constitutional amendment.[61]

1.C.3. Canadian delayed declarations of invalidity

Delayed declarations of invalidity (DDIs),[62] a remedy developed by the Canadian courts in constitutional litigation, are a legislative remand device.[63] There are, however, reasons for considering this remedy as a separate variety of legislative remand. Where this remedy is used in relation to those Canadian Charter rights that are subject to possible legislative override, the delayed declaration of invalidity leaves open the option of avoiding the judicial finding of violation entirely. This is because the legislature can either change the law, or reinstate the law with a 'notwithstanding clause', such that the law is immune from Charter review. Furthermore, Canada's experience warrants separate discussion because of the wide-ranging practice of legislative remand that has built up over the past two decades. Over this period, a body of judicial principles and commentary around DDIs has developed.

The DDI was first used in Canada outside the context of human rights adjudication, in a constitutional challenge to Manitoba's failure to enact all laws in English and French, as required by the Constitution of Canada.[64] Faced with the option of finding all of Manitoba's unilingual laws unconstitutional and invalid—resulting in clear problems for law and order in Manitoba—the Supreme Court of Canada (SCC) delayed the effect of its judgment so that the Manitoba legislature

[58] *Fourie* (n 49) [138].

[59] G Gee and G Webber, 'A Confused Court: Equivocations on Recognising Same-Sex Relationships in South Africa' (2006) 69 Modern Law Review 819, 839.

[60] Jacobi (n 46) 387.

[61] Jacobi (n 46) 405. The civil union legislation was still controversial in the Vermont legislature at the time. However, in 2007, the Vermont legislature legislated to provide for same-sex marriage, making it the first US state to introduce same sex marriage through legislative enactment, rather than court order.

[62] Also referred to as suspended declarations of invalidity.

[63] In fact, the remedy in *Fourie* (n 49) was a delayed declaration of invalidity. This remedy was expressly provided for in s 172 South African Constitution, drawn from the remedial practice of the Canadian Supreme Court.

[64] *Reference Re: Manitoba Language Rights* [1985] 1 SCR 721.

could re-enact all its laws in both languages. In *Schachter v Canada*,[65] the SCC considered use of the DDI in the context of the Canadian Charter and stated that this 'exceptional' remedy, which allowed unconstitutional laws to continue in existence, would only be suitable in a narrow range of cases.[66] These were cases where immediate invalidity threatened public order or the rule of law, or where unconstitutional legislation was under-inclusive and to invalidate the law would disadvantage existing beneficiaries of the law.[67] The court explicitly stated that the choice to issue a DDI ought not rely on considerations of the relative roles of courts and legislatures, beyond these narrow instances of potential disorder.[68]

Had the *Schachter* guidelines been adhered to, DDIs would likely have been a rare occurrence in Canadian constitutional adjudication. However, research into the SCC's remedial practice has identified that, from 1985 to 2003, DDIs were used on at least forty-two occasions,[69] and the guidelines were largely ignored in these cases.[70] The authors observe that the DDI has emerged as an important shift in constitutional remedial practice, growing 'by leaps and bounds . . . verg[ing] on the routine'.[71]

Moreover, the SCC has specifically referred to the legislature's greater competence in crafting remedial action in the circumstances, and used this to justify use of DDIs. In a number of post-*Schachter* cases, the court recognized that there were a variety of solutions that a legislature could adopt to correct the Charter violation and it was better that the legislature was given the first choice between these alternatives.[72] For instance, in the case of *Corbiere v Canada*,[73] which concerned voting rights on indigenous reserves, the court held that denial of voting rights to off-reserve band members violated the Canadian Charter, but that a variety of solutions were possible. The court considered that the legislature was better suited to choose between these possibilities, notably because it would be better able 'to consult with and listen to the opinions of Aboriginal people'.[74] Thus, the court contemplated some public deliberation regarding the choice as to how the law should change.

The Canadian example illustrates steady and regular use of legislative remand in constitutional adjudication. Sujit Choudary and Kent Roach refer to these developments as evincing 'an unannounced but clear shift in the rationale for suspended declarations of invalidity' towards a *shared* responsibility between courts and

[65] [1992] 2 SCR 679. [66] *Schachter* (n 65) [81]. [67] *Schachter* (n 65) [79].

[68] *Schachter* (n 65) [82]. Likewise, in *Baker* (n 47), the State government argued for legislative remand on the grounds of the destabilizing effect of judicial changes. This was accepted as a further reason to employ the chosen remedy, at 225–6.

[69] S Choudary and K Roach, 'Putting the Past Behind Us: Prospective Judicial and Legislative Constitutional Remedies' (2003) 21 Supreme Court Law Review 205, 228–9.

[70] Choudary and Roach (n 69) 232. Hogg et al also observe that only a few DDIs have been used in situations that fit these guidelines: P Hogg, A Thornton, and W Wright, 'Charter Dialogue Revisited or "Much Ado About Metaphors"' (2007) 45 Osgoode Hall LJ 1, 15, 50.

[71] Choudary and Roach (n 69) 226–8.

[72] For a list of these cases, see Hogg et al (n 70) 16. See also B Ryder, 'Suspending the Charter' (2003) 21 Supreme Court Law Review 267, 275.

[73] [1999] 2 SCR 203. [74] *Corbiere* (n 73) [116].

legislatures for assuring that the law complies with constitutional norms.[75] They conclude that the governing principle has become that where a finding of a rights violation leaves open several options for corrective action, legislative deliberation is the preferred process to be employed.[76]

1.C.4. Declarations of incompatibility

Thus far we have considered two varieties of legislative remand: legislative remand where the legislature is required to act to correct the impugned law, or have the court act for it; and legislative remand where the option is open to the legislature to reinstate the impugned law and immunize it from further judicial review.[77] But even in Canada, DDIs can be considered to be coercive: the legislature is not required to respond, but if the legislature fails to respond in any way, this inaction will trigger eventual judicial correction of the law (ordinarily invalidation). If the legislature wishes to retain the impugned legislation, it still must take positive action in the allowed time frame.

Declarations of incompatibility (DOIs) are a recent remedial innovation that builds on the characteristics of declaratory relief and legislative remand, and are the primary subject of this book. DOIs should be understood as a *non-coercive* variety of legislative remand. Unlike coercive legislative remand, the legislature is not required to respond to a DOI, and if it does not, no further action is taken by courts. First introduced under the UK's Human Rights Act 1998 (HRA), this remedy was subsequently introduced in the New Zealand Human Rights Act 1993 by amendment in 2001, the Irish European Convention of Human Rights Act 2003, and the Australian Capital Territory Human Rights Act 2004. The same remedy, although named a 'declaration of inconsistent interpretation', was included in the Victorian Charter of Human Rights and Responsibilities Act 2006. A judicially created DOI also exists under the New Zealand Bill of Rights Act 1990. Hence, the DOI mechanism is a universal feature of the statutory model of human rights protection. The mechanism enjoys continued support, with consultations on a British Bill of Rights[78] and an Australian Charter of Rights and Freedoms[79] both recommending a system of review of legislation that included a DOI mechanism.

DOIs under all of these instruments need to be understood in the context of the statutory model of judicial review of legislation. The HRA forms the template for the other schemes of review. With respect to primary legislation, the Act places an interpretative duty upon UK courts to construe legislation in a way that is

[75] Choudary and Roach (n 69) 233.

[76] Choudary and Roach (n 69) 227–8.

[77] The latter form is specific to review under the Canadian Charter, in relation to the rights to which the notwithstanding clause applies.

[78] JCHR, *Twenty-Ninth Report 2007–08: A Bill of Rights for the UK?* (2008) HL-165, HC-150, 100, 117 (21 July 2008).

[79] National Human Rights Consultation Committee (Australia), *National Human Rights Consultation Report* (September 2009), available at <http://www.humanrightsconsultation.gov.au/www/nhrcc/nhrcc.nsf/Page/Report> 299–303.

compatible with human rights norms 'so far as it is possible to do so'.[80] However, if the court is satisfied that the legislation is *incompatible* with human rights, it may then make a declaration to that effect. Unlike a general declaration in public law, it is not expected that the government will comply with a DOI by, for instance, refraining from reliance on a provision declared incompatible with human rights. Rather, the HRA clearly states that law subject to a DOI remains valid and in force, indefinitely.

The ability to disagree with a judicial decision that legislation infringes human rights norms and allow the legislation to remain in place is not unique to DOIs. This formal possibility also exists when DDIs are used in Canada, as I noted above. The differences between DOIs and coercive legislative remand are as follows. First, the law will only change if the legislature acts to change it. Not only does the legislature have the power to decide whether and to what extent to respond; any legislative inertia or inaction falls in favour of the rights violation *not* being addressed. Second, this remedy has been introduced in the design of the human rights instrument *as an alternative* to giving judges the power to invalidate legislation. Hence, courts do not have the option under any of these instruments to invalidate legislation on the basis of human rights norms, either immediately or in the future.

There is also an important difference *within* the group of statutory bills of rights. The UK HRA and the Irish ECHR Act both incorporate the ECHR into municipal law. It was noted above that declaratory relief is central to international human rights adjudication: international tribunals are not empowered to modify domestic law, but can declare the state of national law to violate international law. Changes to law and practice must come from national institutions. Prior to the incorporation of the ECHR, this was the task of the executive and the legislature in the UK. DOIs mimic this process at the domestic level, by identifying a violation of human rights norms but leaving correction to the political branches of government. Furthermore, the UK and Irish statutory instruments are not entirely separated from binding, judicially enforced human rights obligations. Further recourse to the ECtHR is available if the legislature fails to act, and the rulings of that court are binding as a matter of international law. This differentiates DOIs in the UK and Ireland from the remaining countries: DOIs in Australia and New Zealand are the weakest across the spectrum because no further recourse is available.[81]

The statutory model of human rights protection in all these countries adjusts the status of human rights norms from the inviolable status of traditional constitutional rules, to a prioritized status within the municipal legal system. The formal model specifically contemplates that the legislature may choose not to act on a judicial finding that human rights norms have been/are being infringed. The following chapter will turn to the literature that theorizes this approach to human rights protection. For the immediate purpose of situating DOIs within the field of open

[80] s 3(1) HRA.

[81] There may still be recourse to UN human rights complaints mechanisms, but these can only result in non-binding recommendations from, for instance, the Human Rights Committee.

remedies, one can see that DOIs expand the possible choices of the legislature beyond other forms of legislative remand.

The differences between DOIs and other open remedies, let alone traditional 'strong' constitutional remedies, give rise to a series of questions as to whether and how this remedy will be employed by courts and how it will be received by the political branches. In the following section, I turn to the common rationales supporting the use of open remedies, and the principal objections to them. The even more permissive design of DOIs could be understood to hold greater promise than other open remedies, or greater peril. The full answer to these questions, however, requires examination of how these formal differences play out in practice, rather than conceptual and doctrinal analysis alone.

1.D. Shared Rationales for Open Remedies in Human Rights Adjudication

The range of open remedies described in section 1.C share the following basic characteristics. The court makes a finding that there has been a violation of a fundamental right or freedom, but leaves remedial or corrective action to the other branches of government, either on a temporary or indefinite basis. Drawing from the discussion in 1.C, there are three rationales that could support recourse to these types of remedies: judicial restraint in view of the contestability of certain decisions as to what fundamental rights protection requires; the different institutional capacities of courts and legislatures to design and give effect to remedial action; and the promotion of democratic deliberation.

1.D.1. Contestability and judicial restraint

Judicial interpretations of rights may be contestable. I have noted that human rights norms are general ethical principles, which may give rise to a range of possible specifications. Defining what is and is not permissible public action or inaction in view of, say, a constitutional guarantee of equality may be a difficult task, open to disagreement and dissensus. Even apart from questions of interpretation, upholding the rights of deeply unpopular individuals or groups may provoke public outrage. Open remedies can function as a form of judicial restraint in these circumstances. In fact, the use of open remedies may comprise a form of 'decisional minimalism', that is, leaving certain controversial questions undecided.[82] For example, Gil Kujovich argues that this is precisely how legislative remand was used in *Baker v State*. By characterizing the choice between extending marriage to same-sex couples or creating a parallel institution with equal rights and benefits as a *remedial* choice, the Vermont Supreme Court 'avoided what appeared to be the central

[82] C Sunstein, 'Foreword: Leaving Things Undecided' (1996) 110 Harvard Law Review 4.

issue'.[83] By giving this choice to the legislature, the court negotiated a difficult political situation.[84]

The idea that decisions on rights are contestable, as we will see in the following chapter, has particularly animated the design of statutory bills of rights. The explicit limitation of judicial power to a DOI instead of granting judges powers of severance or invalidation sees remedial restraint introduced into the *structure* of the human rights instrument, rather than as a matter of judicial discretion.[85] The White Paper to the UK Human Rights Bill made clear the intention to limit judicial power and ensure that 'Parliament [remains] competent to make or unmake any law of its choosing and no court may question the validity of any Act it passes.'[86] This position was justified both on the grounds that the legislature possessed a democratic mandate to make important decisions by virtue of being (partly) elected; as well as by the suggestion that the judiciary did not desire powers of invalidation and the attendant controversy and conflict with Parliament that this would entail.[87] Similar justifications have been advanced in the Australian context.[88]

1.D.2. Legislative remedial capacity

Yet, as we have seen in the overview of open remedies, these remedies have a usefulness beyond being a technique to deal with the contestation and controversy over human rights decisions. Across both the declaratory remedies that allow for lawful defiance by the other branches of government, and those that do not, legislative decision-making on responsive action can be complementary to the role of the courts. In certain circumstances, the legislature may be better equipped to make remedial decisions. Three such situations can be suggested.[89]

First, as we have seen in section 1.C, there may be two or more solutions that the court considers would satisfy the requirements of fundamental rights guarantees, for instance, where a violation of equality rights involves a benefit conferred on one particular group, but not another. Equality can be ensured by either providing the benefit equally to both groups, or by removing it altogether (that is, levelling up or levelling down). The law permits both courses of action, and the choice between them is therefore a matter for political deliberation. Legislative deliberation on responsive action may thereby complement the judicial process of identifying that legislation has violated the right to equal treatment.

Second, where a judicial decision affects not only the parties to the case, but a large number of people, such that the finding of violation demonstrates the need for

[83] G Kujovich, 'An Essay on the Passive Virtue of Baker v State' (2000) 25 Vermont Law Review 93, 95.

[84] Jacobi argues that the decision demonstrates prudential self-restraint in the political circumstances: see (n 46) 387.

[85] As we will when examining DOIs in the courts, this does not remove judicial discretion but rather displaces to a different type of remedial choice.

[86] GB Home Office, *Rights Brought Home: The Human Rights Bill* (Cm 3782, 1997) [2.13].

[87] GB Home Office (n 86).

[88] See *National Human Rights Consultation Report* (n 79).

[89] These three situations are not mutually exclusive.

systematic changes to law and policy, then a legislative remedy may be appropriate. Certain powerful remedial techniques, such as reading-in, or mandatory orders, allow judges to modify legislative schemes, but the legislature can completely rewrite laws and comprehensively direct the executive as to public policy.

Third, the right being invoked may engage positive duties on the part of the State. If correcting the infringement of rights requires positive action, then action from the other branches of government is necessary. One of the basic features of contemporary human rights, stated in the introduction, is that modern human rights practice makes demands of all branches of government, and the realization of human rights requires positive legislative and policy action as well as duties of restraint. Certain positive duties entail wide-ranging legislative and policy initiatives, even those which attach to classic civil rights such as the right to a fair trial, or the right to be free from inhuman and degrading treatment.[90]

There are different ways in which judicial orders can be constructed in the event of a need for positive action.[91] For instance, litigation in the US over prison conditions that amounted to 'cruel and unusual punishment' prohibited by the Constitution has produced elaborate mandatory orders and ongoing judicial supervision over public bodies.[92] A declaratory remedy is the gentlest way of dealing with positive duties: mandating (or in the case of DOIs, supporting) action, but not prescribing the form that the action ought to take, nor prescribing a timetable or reporting requirements. A declaratory remedy can pave the way for a remedy from the legislature itself, and limit accusations of judicial intrusion into the policy-setting functions of the elected organs of government.

In particular, an open remedial strategy may be an alternative route to deal with concerns over positive duties, preferable to weaker articulations of the rights themselves.[93] The availability of open remedies may allow for more robust articulations of what human rights require, because courts do not need to absorb concerns about their ability to devise a remedy into the process of determining the question of whether rights have been violated.

However, in all of these situations, we need to be careful with the argument that the legislature is better equipped to devise remedial action. This rationale presumes a high degree of institutional comity and cooperation: a willingness and ability of the legislature to embark, *bona fides*, on deciding how best to correct the identified human rights infringement. A number of examples in the US civil rights arena, and the *Grootboom* example above, demonstrate that a cooperative attitude and prompt

[90] C Scott and P Macklem, 'Constitutional Ropes of Sand or Justiciable Guarantees? Social Rights in a New South African Constitution' (1992) 141 UPenn Law Review 1, 46–56.

[91] For a discussion of the variety of techniques used in South Africa and Canada, see G Budlender and K Roach, 'Mandatory Relief and Supervisory Jurisdiction' (2005) 122 South African Law Journal 325.

[92] WA Fletcher, 'The Discretionary Constitution: Institutional Remedies and Judicial Legitimacy' (1982) 4 Yale Law Journal 635; D Horowitz, 'Decreeing Organizational Change: Judicial Supervision of Public Institutions' [1983] Duke Law Journal 1265.

[93] Dixon (n 18) 391–2.

response may not follow from a declaration.[94] Institutional choice arguments based on institutional capacity are always *relative*.[95] So, if legislatures are not willing or able to embark on remedial action with due care and deliberation in practice, then we need to adjust accordingly our evaluations of which institution is best equipped to provide remedial action, and what the relative roles of courts and legislatures ought to be.

1.D.3. Promoting deliberation

A third possible rationale can be advanced, not drawn from the reasoning of judges, but from the perspective of constitutional design. This rationale is not directed towards limiting judicial power but rather towards the potential for judicial decisions on fundamental rights to provoke democratic deliberation on the ethical commitments of the polity and how best to realize them. The following chapters, which discuss the role of the legislature in responding to a judicial decision, will introduce the deliberative turn in democratic theory and argue that weak-form review is, at a conceptual level, well tailored to a deliberative democracy.

Deliberative democrats focus on the possibility of deliberation leading to the transformation of attitudes and preferences, rather than taking these matters as given. By returning the question of how the law can better reflect our fundamental commitments to the political process, open remedies invite deliberation, rather than removing questions from political decision-making. Binding or coercive forms of legislative remand invite deliberation on how best to respond, while non-coercive DOIs also open space for deliberation on whether the impugned legislation is in fact unacceptable, or whether the judicial conclusion is mistaken. This deliberation occurs with the benefit of the government's justification for the existing law in open court, and the documented experiences of those who have been adversely affected by the law.

Taken together, these three rationales furnish reasons for judges to use open remedies in particular circumstances, and provide justification for the inclusion of open remedial devices within the structure of a bill of rights. They demonstrate the shared coherence to open remedies as devices within human rights adjudication. However, there are also common objections that have been launched against open remedies, to which I now turn.

1.E. The Judicial Function and Objections to Open Remedies

Above I differentiated between reversible judicial decisions and open remedies on the grounds that, where open remedies are used, the successful plaintiff does not

[94] For a discussion of how the North American and South African courts have responded to lack of cooperation, see Budlender and Roach (n 91).

[95] N Komesar, *Imperfect Alternatives: Choosing Institutions in Law, Economics and Public Policy* (University of Chicago Press, Chicago 1997) 22.

receive any tangible remedy from the court other than a declaration vindicating their claim. In the case of legislative remand, rights-infringing legislation continues in effect. This can be criticized as a departure both from the dispute resolution task that courts ought to fulfil as well as from the corrective function of judicial remedies. Orthodox ideas about the role of courts give rise to two types of objections to open remedies: first (and particular to legislative remand), that judges are stepping outside the judicial function by making decisions beyond simply resolving the controversy between the parties; and second, that judges are neglecting the victims before the court. I argue herein that the first of these objections is misplaced; however, the second objection deserves attention.

The various open remedies are either a creature of equitable discretion, or, even if created by statute, *exercised* as a matter of discretion. The objections below do not necessarily suggest that open remedies should *never* be used; rather, they are factors that may weigh against the use of this discretionary power. In the examination of DOIs in the courts, I will return to these objections, and consider whether they affect the way judicial powers have been exercised.

1.E.1. Overstepping the judicial function

The dispute resolution model of adjudication dictates that the role of the court is to interpret the law to resolve a concrete dispute between the parties. The court is not to consider prospective or general reform of the law, nor give opinions beyond what is required for the resolution of the controversy between the parties. The law in this sense is bipolar, self-contained, and party controlled.[96]

Legislative remand does not achieve this purpose—in fact, it leaves the law in place despite finding it to violate fundamental rights. Particularly when justified by a broader need for systemic reform, this may be criticized for departing from the proper function of the court. For instance, the reason given in the Canadian case of *Schachter* for very limited use of DDIs was that they not only allowed unconstitutional law to remain in place, but they intruded on the role of the legislature by forcing an issue onto its agenda.[97]

Insofar as the fulfilment of human rights obligations does require prospective and systemic action, this objection is difficult to sustain. We have seen that, where positive action is needed for human rights obligations to be met, returning the matter to the legislature is a restrained approach in comparison with other remedial options, such as invalidation, reading-in, or judicial supervision of executive bodies.

This leads us to a more general response to this type of objection to remedies in public law, namely, that the dispute resolution model of adjudication is ill suited to the role of courts in constitutional adjudication, particularly the role of higher courts. A privatized, retrospective approach to adjudication can be contrasted to Abrahm Chayes's public law model of adjudication. Here, remedial decision-making is

[96] Chayes (n 1) 1282–3. [97] *Schachter v Canada* (n 65) [81] (Lamer J).

not conceived as compensation for a past wrong in a form logically derived from the substantive liability and confined in its impact to the immediate parties; instead it is forward looking…often having important consequences for many persons including absentees.[98]

Others have drawn attention to the fact that the court may, particularly in constitutional law cases, engage not only in dispute resolution and corrective justice, but in *expository* justice, giving meaning to broad public and constitutional values by applying them to concrete situations, and thereby providing useful information to the other branches of government in the future.[99] This prospective, regulative function of remedies makes good sense where litigation affects the actions of public bodies beyond the case at hand, in future interactions with individuals or groups. For example, a decision that the regime of public housing is discriminatory, or otherwise violates a right of access to housing or a right to a family life, is highly likely to affect others beyond the parties to the legal challenge. This effect is not incidental, but in fact a vital part of the function of public law (including human rights law/constitutional law) in holding public bodies to account, before an independent court, for their exercise of power.

DOIs in particular have been accused of overstepping the judicial function, given that they are designed to be exhortatory and do not generate any legal obligations. Some commentators argue that they are effectively advisory opinions, rather than authoritative judicial rulings.[100] An advisory opinion is a device whereby judges may issue non-binding opinions on the constitutionality of law or policy on the request of the legislature. Neither the United States Supreme Court nor the Australian High Court will provide them, on the grounds that such opinions depart from the proper judicial function.[101] (That said, many courts do provide advisory opinions, including the Supreme Court of Canada, and many State supreme courts in the US.)

Even if one were to accept that advisory opinions are objectionable, the criticisms made of advisory opinions are not directly applicable to DOIs. Advisory opinions

[98] Chayes (n 1) 1302.

[99] Joanna Miles argues that the HRA is best fit to an expository, rather than corrective, model of rights enforcement: J Miles, 'Standing under the Human Rights Act 1998: Theories of Rights Enforcement and the Nature of Public Law Adjudication' (2000) 59 Cambridge Law Journal 133. See also Spann (n 1).

[100] This argument was prominent in the Australian debates over the introduction of a statutory bill of rights: see *National Human Rights Consultation Report* (n 79) 327–8; M McHugh, 'A Human Rights Act, the Courts and the Constitution' (Paper presented at the Australian Human Rights Commission, Sydney, 5 March 2009). It has also been levelled against the ACT and Victorian bills of rights: D Dalla-Pozza and G Williams, 'The Constitutional Validity of Declarations of Incompatibility in Australian Charters of Rights' (2007) 12 Deakin Law Review 1. In 2011, a majority of the High Court of Australia held that DOIs were outside the federal judicial power conferred by the Constitution, implying that such declarations could be made by State courts but could not be reviewed by federal courts: *Momcilovic v The Queen & Ors* [2011] HCA 34. A minority of the court held that the power to issue such declarations was constitutionally invalid altogether, for it impaired the institutional integrity of the Victorian Supreme Court to exercise this type of non-judicial power.

[101] *Muskrat v United States* (1911) 219 US 346, 361–2 (USSC); *Re Judiciary and Navigations Acts* (1921) 29 CLR 257 (High Court of Australia).

have been objected to, by scholars and judges, because of the *abstract* nature of review, not because they are non-binding.[102] DOIs, by contrast, do not emerge from abstract review, but rather a concrete case where a victim alleges a human rights violation on the basis of facts before the court. The principal criticism of advisory opinions therefore does not apply, in substance, to DOIs.[103]

1.E.2. Neglecting the victim

The second objection to open remedies is that by leaving remedial action to the other branches of government, courts are neglecting the paradigmatic function of remedies, which is corrective justice. This is a narrower version of the previous objection: the problem is not that courts are performing a broader function than corrective justice, only that, in doing so, this remedy may fail to redress the harm done to the claimant, who has successfully made out a human rights violation. This objection applies not only to legislative remand, but also to declaratory relief in relation to executive action.

For instance, the leading account of remedies in international human rights law is firmly critical of the ECtHR's preference for 'mere declarations' as overlooking, or at least de-emphasizing, the wrongful harm done to the victim before the court.[104] Shelton argues that it would be better practice for the court to determine the nature and scope of redress, or order restitution if possible, in order to avoid the danger that the victim will be left without a tangible remedy.[105] She states that 'the denial of damages or other remedies should be exceptional because a violation of human rights is *ipso facto* an infringement of the individual's moral dignity and demands a personal remedy, not simply a prospective change in law or practice'.[106] Similarly, DDIs have been criticized by Canadian scholars for neglecting the victim before the court. Choudary and Roach, who favour these remedies as providing for institutional balance and democratic dialogue, nonetheless express concern that a singular focus on prospective change can leave victims without redress, because new legislative measures are not retrospectively applied to them.[107]

It would be too strong to apply Shelton's arguments to all cases in which open remedies are used. The claimants themselves may be seeking prospective changes to the law, or they may be seeking the provision of services or some other remedy that the court cannot design by itself. Moreover, Shelton's argument loses sight of the

[102] In the US: F Frankfurter, 'A Note on Advisory Opinions' (1923–4) 37 Harvard Law Review 1002. In Australia: *Bass v Permanent Trustee Co Ltd* (1999) 198 CLR 334 [45].

[103] The decision in *Momcilovic* (n 100) did not turn on an analogy between DOIs and advisory opinions per se, rather on the definition of a 'matter' with respect to which judicial power could be exercised under the Australian Constitution.

[104] Shelton (n 28) 259–63. The argument has also been made specifically in the case of continuing violations of human rights: L McGregor, 'Are Declaratory Orders Appropriate for Continuing Human Rights Violations? The Case of Khadr v Canada' (2010) 10 Human Rights Law Review 487.

[105] Shelton (n 28) 259–63. [106] Shelton (n 28) 257.

[107] Choudary and Roach (n 69) 210–11.

fact that the outcome of a human rights case may affect many others beyond the litigants before the court. Hence, courts may face 'multiple and sometimes conflicting goals when they devise . . . remedies',[108] and it may even be impossible for the court to address the harm to the victim fully or immediately.[109]

Nonetheless, it may sometimes, or indeed often, be the case that redress to the victim is sacrificed in the name of the rationales considered in the previous section. In the case of DOIs, it is important to note that, because of the design of statutory bills of rights, law which is incompatible with human rights remains valid. The victim has therefore not suffered from an illegality. Hence, where courts employ a DOI, the victim is not entitled to redress as a matter of law though the Minister and/or the legislature may choose to provide redress. In Chapter 3, and again in Chapter 7, I will examine this remedial aspect of the HRA more carefully as it has the potential to affect how judges use DOIs, as well as affect our evaluation of whether the HRA is, ultimately, a well-designed human rights instrument.

1.F. Conclusion

The variety of declaratory remedies discussed in this chapter are different devices, operating in different legal orders. But they share a certain feature, which allows them to be categorized as open remedies within human rights adjudication. In each instance, the judicial remedy is limited to a declaration of the finding that human rights have been infringed, with any further remedial action being left to the other branches of government, for a set period of time, or indefinitely.

This chapter has considered a series of rationales that may justify either recourse to this type of remedy by judges in particular cases, or its inclusion within the structure of a human rights instrument. It has also considered objections to open remedies on the basis that they depart from the traditional dispute resolution and corrective justice functions of courts. Open remedies may therefore, at an abstract level, be considered promising on certain grounds; perilous on others. But, if we are interested in enlisting institutions other than courts in crafting action to protect rights, and if we understand that human rights norms are open to reasonable disagreement, then this method of human rights implementation merits attention.

The research undertaken in this work is directed to one species of open remedy—the DOI—in the one jurisdiction that to date has built up significant experience with this remedy. I will refer to this as a case study, but the reader should note what type of case study this is. We have seen in this chapter that DOIs share some similarities with other open remedies, but also important differences in design. They are most similar to DDIs in Canada, but even here significant differences remain. DOIs are therefore not a *representative* case study. Rather, the purpose of the study is to assess this particular experiment with open remedies, and

[108] Roach (n 1) 1-1. [109] Roach (n 1) 3-1.

assess the significance of these novel aspects of institutional design in practice. Crucially, this assessment relies not only on the design of the remedy, or even its use by courts, but what happens *afterwards*. This brings us to the question of what possible types of institutional interaction may occur where DOIs are employed, and how this relates to the type of institutional interaction that may occur where other open remedies are employed.

2

The Role of the Legislature

2.A. Introduction

The previous chapter introduced the field of open remedies in human rights adjudication: a range of declaratory remedies employed by courts that invite the legislature to formulate remedial action after a finding of a human rights violation. This chapter asks what type of role the legislature might play relative to the courts when open remedies are employed.

Section 2.B examines the extent to which the 'new dialogue scholarship' is useful in understanding the possibilities for institutional interaction resulting from open remedies. We will see that there are two divergent understandings of dialogue advanced in this scholarship, each of which translates to a different type of interaction between courts and legislatures. The first understanding of dialogue (*the specialization model*) is a process of adjustment of legislation between courts and legislatures, with each institution playing its own distinct, or specialized, role. The role of the courts is to decide the application of human rights norms to the specific cases before them, while the role of the legislature is to decide *how to respond* to judicial identification of a human rights violation in terms of changes to law and policy.

By contrast, the second understanding (*the dual review model*) posits that 'genuine' dialogue exists only where judicial conclusions on human rights compliance are not treated as authoritative and binding, but rather provisional and open to disagreement, so that the legislature can be fully engaged in interpreting fundamental rights safeguards. Here the role of the legislature is more expansive, as it ought to first review *whether to agree and respond* to the judicial opinion that human rights have been violated.

Where the dialogue metaphor has been applied to delayed declarations of invalidity (DDIs), it has been employed in the first sense above. However, in 2.C, I observe that where dialogue has been used to describe the institutional interaction supported by DOIs, it has ordinarily been used in the second sense above. The non-coercive character of DOIs has been justified as a way of dealing with the contestability of rights issues and a way of allowing the legislature to decide on the protection given to human rights, with provisional judicial input. As a matter of design and structure, DOIs have been viewed as a mechanism through which courts propose their opinion to Parliament, for its agreement or disagreement.

However, the specialization model of dialogue provides an alternative way for DOIs to operate: compelling remedial action but allowing the legislature to decide on the nature of that action. In fact, the specialization model is reinforced by traditional understandings of fundamental rights and the authoritativeness of judicial decisions. It is the dual review model that is the more radical vision for the operation of a bill of rights. While the structure of statutory bills of rights permits this vision, we need to look beyond structural features to the operation of the bill of rights, to understand what type of interaction occurs in a given legal system, in practice.

This chapter concludes by identifying a notable gap in the existing dialogue scholarship, namely, a tendency to focus on legislative output rather than interrogate the role and processes of the legislature itself. This leads to the task of Chapter 3, which seeks to develop a greater understanding of legislative engagement in human rights decision-making.

2.B. The New Dialogue Scholarship

The traditional conception of constitutional human rights is that these supreme values are secured against the decisions made by representative political institutions, delimiting the powers of those institutions. Courts uphold these constitutional boundaries to political action, justified variously as the limits to legitimate action by the legislature or the preconditions for the exercise of self-government (rights are treated as pre-political or apolitical).[1] Consequently, a great deal of theoretical scholarship has been dedicated to how courts ought to fulfil this role. The role of legislatures in relation to fundamental rights is far less theorized.[2]

However, over the past decade, there has been a surge in interest in legislative constitutionalism and forms of human rights protection that involve courts *and* legislatures in determining the boundaries to legitimate political action. Three pieces of scholarship have been especially influential. First, in 1997, Peter Hogg and Alison Bushell presented an account of the first fifteen years of the Canadian Charter which described the protection of human rights in Canada as a system of 'dialogue' between courts and legislatures, rather than judicial supremacy.[3] Second, in 1999, legal philosopher Jeremy Waldron gave sustained attention to the legitimacy of legislative decisions on rights in his book, *Law and Disagreement*.[4] Third,

[1] J Habermas, 'Three Normative Models of Democracy' in S Benhabib (ed), *Democracy and Difference* (Princeton University Press, Princeton 1996) 22; M Koskenniemi, 'The Effect of Rights on Political Culture' in P Alston (ed), *The EU and Human Rights* (OUP, New York 1999) 101–2; R Dworkin, *Taking Rights Seriously* (Harvard University Press, Cambridge MA 1978) xi.

[2] For a recent attempt to redress this imbalance in the scholarship, see RW Bauman and T Kahana (eds), *The Least Examined Branch: The Role of Legislatures in the Constitutional State* (CUP, Cambridge 2006).

[3] PW Hogg and AA Bushell, 'The Charter Dialogue between Courts and Legislatures (Or Perhaps the Charter of Rights Isn't Such a Bad Thing after All)' (1997) 35 Osgoode Hall Law Journal 75.

[4] J Waldron, *Law and Disagreement* (Clarendon Press, Oxford 1999). See also J Waldron, 'A Right-Based Critique of Constitutional Rights' (1993) 13 Oxford Journal of Legal Studies 18.

in 2001, Stephen Gardbaum drew attention to what he referred to as 'the new commonwealth model of constitutionalism': a model of human rights protection that consciously preserves the ultimate role for the legislature in deciding the level of protection given to constitutional rights.[5] These works have given rise to a large body of scholarship, renewing what many believed was the well-worn debate over judicial supremacy on questions of constitutional rights,[6] and exploring the role of the legislature in defining what rights require and how they are to be balanced against each other and other public policy goals (*legislative rights review* being useful shorthand to describe this activity).[7]

In particular, the burgeoning work on institutional 'dialogue' over the meaning and limitation of constitutional rights has focused on the *interaction* between courts and legislatures. This body of work is therefore a natural starting point for thinking about how to analyse and critique the role that the legislature plays where open remedies are used.

2.B.1. The meaning of dialogue

The use of the metaphor of dialogue to describe the operation and structure of the Canadian Charter spurred wide-ranging use of the concept amongst judges, legislators, and academic commentators, in Canada and beyond. The concept of dialogue has come to be ubiquitous across the literature concerning weak-form review, furnishing the main language through which weak-form review is theorized and justified. The diffusion of this terminology is understandable. Apart from its strong positive connotations, the idea of dialogue over rights takes us beyond an either/or debate over courts and legislatures, suggesting that we can constructively engage both institutions in human rights protection, rather than relying on one institution alone.[8]

This turn in constitutional thought and scholarship has also been valuable in moving away from strict and often artificial notions of the separation of powers between courts and legislatures which suggest that the role of courts is to apply the law, not make law, because the latter involves making political choices. A strict separation of legislative and judicial functions is difficult to sustain in relation to the protection of fundamental rights. Decisions over what human rights require—their scope and justifiable limitations—certainly involve political and ethical questions. The important matter is how best to protect these rights despite the fact that they

[5] S Gardbaum, 'The New Commonwealth Model of Constitutionalism' (2001) 49 American Journal of Comparative Law 707.

[6] Each has subsequently revisited their original argument in light of this debate: see P Hogg, A Thornton, and W Wright, 'Charter Dialogue Revisited or "Much Ado About Metaphors"' (2007) 45 Osgoode Hall LJ 1; J Waldron, 'The Core of the Case against Judicial Review' (2006) 115 Yale Law Journal 1346; S Gardbaum, 'Reassessing the New Commonwealth Model of Constitutionalism' (2010) 8 ICON 167.

[7] JL Hiebert, 'Interpreting a Bill of Rights: The Importance of Legislative Rights Review' (2005) 35 British Journal of Political Science 235.

[8] The term may then displace some of the debate to which institution should have the final word, as we will see below.

cannot be easily allocated to one branch of government or the other.[9] Dialogue scholarship in all its varieties accepts an overlap and interaction between the role of courts and legislatures concerning the protection of fundamental human rights.

That said, across the body of work promoting and critiquing institutional dialogue, the metaphor has been used to describe a wide variety of different interactions between courts and legislatures, and different understandings of the scope of the judicial and legislative roles.[10] Further, accounts of dialogue may be *empirical*, describing the actual interaction of courts and legislatures under a particular system of judicial review of legislation; or *normative*, advancing a form of interaction that is considered to address objections to judicial review and/or provide a guide for how courts ought to exercise their judicial review powers.

Moreover, the positive connotations of the dialogue metaphor have provoked a battle over what 'genuine' dialogue is, as commentators seek to claim the metaphor for what they believe is a desirable constitutional system (and dispute whether the empirical claims of others deserve the label). This definitional debate risks being an unhelpful distraction from the underlying normative and empirical arguments over how courts and legislatures share the task of protecting rights.[11]

This chapter proceeds on the basis that it is useful to think of dialogue as having a 'thin', shared meaning across its different uses, where the term signifies some institutional interaction over the meaning and protection of fundamental rights. This leaves open significant questions on the nature of the role of the legislature, and how judges ought to treat legislative decisions on rights. These questions are answered in different ways by a range of substantive or 'thick' accounts of dialogue. Rather than seeking to advance any particular substantive theory of dialogue, the purpose of this section is to discern, amongst these various accounts, two ideal-types of interaction, the *specialization* model and the *dual review* model, each of which gives the legislature a different role and each of which addresses a different normative concern about strong-form judicial review.

2.B.2. The new dialogue literature

Alexander Bickel is generally credited for having first conceived of a dialogue between courts and legislatures over the protection of constitutional rights.[12] Bickel's concept of dialogue did not rely on any formal relaxation of judicial supremacy over constitutional interpretation, and drew on his analysis of judicial

[9] A Guttman, 'Foreword: Legislatures and the Constitutional State' in RW Bauman and T Kahana (eds), *The Least Examined Branch: The Role of Legislatures in the Constitutional State* (CUP, Cambridge 2006) ix.

[10] R Dixon, 'Creating Dialogue about Socio-Economic Rights: Strong-Form Versus Weak-Form Judicial Review Revisited' (2007) 5 ICON 391, 393–4. See also C Bateup, 'The Dialogic Promise' (2006) 71 Brooklyn Law Review 1109.

[11] For this reason, it has been suggested that using a more prosaic, value-neutral term, such as institutional interaction, might reduce the fierceness of the debate: L McDonald, 'Rights, "Dialogue" and the Democratic Objections to Judicial Review' (2004) 32 Federal Law Review 1.

[12] AM Bickel, *The Least Dangerous Branch: The Supreme Court at the Bar of Politics* (2nd edn Yale University Press, New Haven 1986).

behaviour within a system of judicial supremacy. Bickel identified, and advocated, various judicial techniques of avoidance and restraint ('passive virtues') as effectively leaving space for legislative decision-making. What was important about Bickel's work is that he conceived of the development and application of constitutional principles as a *cooperative* venture between courts and legislatures, and appreciated only a *partial* separation of powers, rather than rigid compartmentalizing of judicial and legislative functions.[13]

From the 1990s, it was argued that the metaphor of dialogue, employed in the US context, was in fact more appropriate to the system of rights protection provided by the Canadian Charter. Hogg and Bushell introduced a new definition of dialogue between courts and legislatures that crucially related to the way in which judicial powers over legislation were constructed, stating that

> where a judicial decision is open to legislative reversal, modification or avoidance, then it is meaningful to regard the relationship between the Court and the competent legislative body as dialogue.[14]

This new account stressed that legislatures in Canada participated in dialogue about fundamental rights through the ordinary processes of legislation (what the authors referred to as 'legislative sequels' to judicial decisions),[15] rather than through more onerous processes such as constitutional amendment or judicial appointment.[16] Hogg and Bushell advanced the empirical claim that, in most cases where the Canadian Supreme Court invalidated legislation, the decision was promptly followed by fresh legislation, and these responses demonstrate that 'there is usually an alternative law that is available to the legislative body and that enables the legislative purpose to be substantially carried out, albeit by other means'.[17] As part of the structural features of dialogue, they included the notwithstanding clause provision of the Canadian Charter, which (in relation to most Charter rights) allowed the legislature to override the judicial decision and re-enact the original law if it so chose, though they recognized that in practice, this provision was rarely used.[18]

Hogg and Bushell's account of court–legislature interaction signals the start of what can be referred to as the 'new dialogue literature', a body of work concerned with interaction between courts and legislatures, within a system where judicial review is weakened as a matter of the structure of the bill of rights. What proved provocative about their work was their bold suggestion (later retracted)[19] that, in light of their empirical findings of dialogue between courts and legislatures, the

[13] Bickel (n 12) 25. [14] Hogg and Bushell (n 3) 79. [15] Hogg and Bushell (n 3) 82.

[16] Cf. Friedman's concept of dialogue in the United States, which includes these methods. Friedman's concept of dialogue extends over a longer time-period, including public debate, political elections, and judicial appointment, and thereby involves a far wider range of actors than simply courts and legislatures (including the media, the public, and government officials): B Friedman, 'Dialogue and Judicial Review' (1993) 91 Michigan Law Review 577, 653–8.

[17] Hogg and Bushell (n 3) 80.

[18] Hogg and Bushell (n 3) 83.

[19] The authors subsequently stated that the phenomenon of dialogue that they described made it more difficult to sustain the anti-majoritarian objection to the Charter, rather than answering it directly. Hogg et al (n 6) 4.

critique of the Canadian Charter based on democratic legitimacy could not be sustained.[20] This triggered fierce criticism of the theoretical and methodological underpinnings of their claims.[21] However, Hogg and Bushell were successful in directing attention beyond the theoretical debate over democratic legitimacy of judicial review to what was actually happening after judicial decisions, and how legislatures can and do respond to them.[22]

It is in the ensuing debate over what would qualify as 'dialogue' that we see two different strands of normative reasoning about court–legislature interaction emerge. The first strand, beginning with Hogg and Bushell's account but growing in sophistication, is concerned with the objection that judicial review removes matters from the consideration of the political branches and thereby frustrates the policies chosen by the elected institutions of the State. Here, it is argued that under a system of dialogue, judicial decisions on rights are met with legislative accommodation and adjustment in devising new legislation, such that legislative objectives are not frustrated, but greater attention is paid to fundamental rights.

By contrast, the second strand of reasoning, evident in the criticism of Hogg and Bushell's work, is concerned with avoiding a judicial monopoly on determining what constitutional rights require; that is, the scope of the rights and when limitations on rights are proportionate.[23] Here, it is argued that a system of dialogue is one in which both courts and legislatures engage in the interpretation of what rights require,[24] where judicial decisions on fundamental rights are not definitive, but rather, the legislature is to evaluate whether it agrees, or disagrees, with the court. We can refer to this type of interaction by the shorthand *dual review,* for it envisages a judicial opinion followed by legislative consideration. For example, one prominent set of Canadian critics have argued that 'genuine' dialogue only occurs where the legislature is not placed in a position of hierarchical inferiority to the courts, and can advance its own interpretations of what Canadian Charter rights require.[25]

This second vision of dialogue appears to be formally satisfied by mechanisms that maintain parliamentary supremacy over what level of protection is given to constitutional rights, such as the notwithstanding clause in the Canadian Charter and the non-binding status of DOIs. However, advocates of this model are concerned that disagreement with judicial interpretations is a *realistic* and *viable* route available to legislatures;[26] else these new constitutional innovations are mere

[20] Hogg et al (n 6) 105.

[21] C Manfredi and JB Kelly, 'Six Degrees of Dialogue: A Response to Hogg and Bushell' (1999) 37 Osgoode Hall LJ 513; FL Morton, 'Dialogue or Monologue' [1999] (April) Policy Options 23; J Waldron, 'Some Models of Dialogue between Judges and Legislators' (2004) 23 Supreme Court Law Review 7; C Manfredi, 'The Unfulfilled Promise of Dialogic Constitutionalism' in T Campbell, J Goldsworthy, and A Stone (eds), *Protecting Rights without a Bill of Rights: Institutional Performance and Reform in Australia* (Ashgate, Aldershot 2006).

[22] McDonald (n 11) 24.

[23] See n 21. See also G Huscroft, 'Rationalizing Judicial Power: The Mischief of Dialogue Theory' in JB Kelly and C Manfredi (eds), *Contested Constitutionalism* (UBC Press, Vancouver 2009).

[24] Manfredi and Kelly (n 21); Morton (n 21); Manfredi (n 21); Huscroft (n 23).

[25] Manfredi and Kelly (n 21) 521.

[26] Manfredi and Kelly (n 21) 524; M Tushnet, 'New Forms of Judicial Review and the Persistence of Rights- and Democracy-Based Worries' (2003) 38 Wake Forest Law Review 813, 831.

formalities of constitutional structure, little different in practice from a traditional system of judicial interpretative supremacy.[27]

To those who believe in dual review as 'true' dialogue, Canada's experience with judicial review is no such thing, rather it is a 'monologue' where courts determine how rights are to be interpreted and applied, and legislatures comply.[28] Parliament has very rarely used its power under section 33 to advance an independent decision on whether legislation is unacceptable, and the power to override judicial decision is considered to be deeply unpopular.[29] Hence, it is argued that judicial interpretations of what rights require are effectively supreme:

> The Charter is the Court's to interpret, so much so that for many there is no distinction between the Court and the Charter itself: the Charter's vaguely worded rights and freedoms are supposed to mean whatever the Court says they do.[30]

(a) Dialogue as specialization

Later accounts of dialogue in the Canadian and comparative literature have grown in sophistication in light of this debate over how 'dialogue' differs from legislative compliance with judicial decisions. A series of 'thick' conceptions of dialogue have emerged that are more considered than Hogg and Bushell's account, both as empirical accounts of the Canadian Charter[31] and normative aspirations for comparative constitutional law.[32]

Those writing in this vein share the belief that rights can often be accommodated by legislatures while still pursuing policy aims, without resort to override powers. This is either because of provisions that allow for the imposition of proportionate limits on rights, or because of judicial deference to legislation modified in response to judicial decisions.[33] They also identify the role of courts as something more specific and limited than simply deciding what constitutional rights mean in general and in the abstract. Drawing on this work, we see a type of interaction in

[27] For a similar emphasis on political culture, rather than structure (though not advocating legislative interpretative supremacy) see D Dyzenhaus, 'Are Legislatures Good at Morality? Or Better at it than the Courts?' (2009) 7 ICON 46.

[28] Morton (n 21) 26.

[29] P Russell, 'The Charter and Canadian Democracy' in JB Kelly and C Manfredi (eds), *Contested Constitutionalism* (UBC Press, Vancouver 2009) 293 cites studies of public opinion to this effect.

[30] Huscroft (n 23) 64. Likewise, use of the metaphor by Canadian Supreme Court judges equally indicates the view that courts determine the content of the constitutional standards, and while a range of laws may meet these standards, it is always for the court, in the final analysis, to determine whether a law actually does so: LB Tremblay, 'The Legitimacy of Judicial Review: The Limits of Dialogue between Courts and Legislatures' (2005) 3 ICON 617, 647–8.

[31] K Roach, *The Supreme Court on Trial: Judicial Activism or Democratic Dialogue* (Irwin Law, Toronto 2001); K Roach, 'Dialogic Judicial Review and its Critics' (2004) 23 Supreme Court Law Review 49.

[32] Dixon (n 10); R Dixon, 'The Supreme Court of Canada, Charter Dialogue, and Deference' (2009) 47 Osgoode Hall LJ 235; G Webber, 'The Unfulfilled Potential of the Court and Legislature Dialogue' (2009) 42 Canadian Journal of Political Science 443.

[33] Roach, *The Supreme Court on Trial* (n 31); Dixon, 'The Supreme Court of Canada, Charter Dialogue, and Deference' (n 32).

which courts and legislatures both play roles in applying human rights norms; however each institution has a *different* role to play. These roles are complementary to each other, and therefore this vision of interaction is akin to a division of labour, or *specialization*, across courts and legislatures.

For instance, in the leading account of dialogue in Canada, Kent Roach has argued extensively that Canada's system of constitutional review is dialogic in its structure, but that dialogue is driven by the provision in the Canadian Charter that all rights within it may be limited 'as demonstrably justified in a free and democratic society'.[34] There is place for outright disagreement in Roach's account, through the use of section 33,[35] but this is not the focal point of institutional interaction over fundamental rights. Rather, legislatures respond to judicial decisions by deciding *how* to modify legislation (maybe only in minor ways) and advancing a new justification as to why any limitations on rights are proportionate. This may include introducing new evidence as a matter of the legislative record, or including a preamble stating the legislature's view.

Under this approach, courts engaged in human rights review play a role that will not otherwise be played by legislatures: namely, placing uncomfortable issues on the legislative agenda that legislatures would rather ignore; and testing the preferences of the legislature in a different forum.[36] Legislatures may face different types of legislative 'blind spots'.[37] Lawmakers may fail to recognize that the law could be applied in a rights-infringing way, or fail to anticipate its effect on particular groups of people, or may fail to perceive how rights claims can be accommodated without much or any cost to legislative objectives.[38] Additionally, there are 'burdens of inertia' in the legislative process, such that rights-infringing laws may remain on the statute books by omission and delay, not driven by principled justifications or resource concerns.[39] The role of the court is to get the legislature to revisit its commitment to the status quo. The legislature can then, should it choose, narrow and limit the effect of judicial decisions through subsequent legislation.[40] Popular preferences may be vindicated through subsequent legislation which is similar to impugned legislation, but the process will be characterized by fuller consideration and better awareness of the consequences of legislative choices because of the courts' contribution.[41] In particular, a requirement that limitations on rights be proportional to a pressing social need requires the government to adduce a justification, and evidence, before the court, as to why legislation strikes an appropriate balance; which is more than may be demanded of the government by the legislature.

In this model of dialogue as specialization, there is a reflexive or iterative process of adjustment of legislation between courts and legislatures. By focusing on how courts and legislatures may play complementary, rather than directly competing

[34] Roach, *The Supreme Court on Trial* (n 31) 236.
[35] Roach, 'Dialogic Judicial Review and its Critics' (n 31) 63.
[36] Roach, 'Dialogic Judicial Review and its Critics' (n 31) 52. [37] Dixon (n 10) 402.
[38] Dixon (n 10) 402. [39] Dixon (n 10) 402–3. [40] Dixon (n 10) 407.
[41] Roach, 'Dialogic Judicial Review and its Critics' (n 31) 54.

roles, these theories tell us not to expect that in all or even most instances in which courts find laws to violate rights, they are disrupting a *considered* legislative position. Legislatures may then respond through more tailored legislation, better evidence for why limitations on rights are necessary, or a clearer statement of justification for legislative choices.

(b) Delayed declarations of invalidity and dialogue

Numerous commentators have now identified open remedies as instruments of dialogue in Canada.[42] Delayed declarations of invalidity (DDIs) have been considered to exemplify dialogue to those who conceive of dialogue as specialization, because courts leave a role for legislatures in devising the responsive action, rather than immediately correcting the impugned law. The legislature is given the role of determining how the judicial decision is to be accommodated, or advanced, in general, prospective legislation. While DDIs may compel the legislature to address an issue that it might otherwise choose to ignore, the judicial decision may leave the legislature a wide latitude for response. Roach specifically identifies DDIs as one of the new structural features that comprise dialogue in Canada: they give the legislature the chance to expand the terms of the debate and enact more comprehensive and creative remedies than the courts could devise.[43] Here we see the division of functions quite clearly: courts determine human rights violations on the basis of knowledge of how the law has operated in a concrete case; while legislatures consider how to translate that determination into better tailored general rules, in the future.

DDIs also give the legislature the opportunity to avoid the judicial decision entirely, because by reinstating the original legislation with a section 33 'notwithstanding' statement attached, the legislature can reassert its legislation before the judicial invalidation ever has effect. However, in line with the declining emphasis on the use of section 33 to openly disagree with judicial decisions, this point has received little attention.[44]

(c) Structure and political culture: a return to dialogue as dual review

Theorists who conceive of dialogue as specialization have been sceptical of the desirability of a form of institutional interaction where legislatures can choose whether to respond to judicial decisions.[45] In their accounts, it is ultimately for

[42] Dixon (n 10); K Roach, 'Sharpening the Dialogue Debate: The Next Decade of Scholarship' (2007) 45 Osgoode Hall LJ; Hogg et al (n 6).

[43] Roach (n 42) 176–7. Hogg et al argue that the Canadian Supreme Court's widespread use of its remedial discretion in this way signals the importance of the dialogue rationale in guiding Charter review: Hogg et al (n 6) 14–18.

[44] Cf. Huscroft, who mentions this possibility but is disappointed that the use of DDIs occurs purely at the discretion of the courts: see n 23, 72–3.

[45] Roach, 'Dialogic Judicial Review and its Critics' (n 31) 93–4; Dixon (n 10) 404.

judges to decide the question of whether a given legislative choice respects fundamental rights when challenged. For those interested in new forms of judicial review for their potential in introducing judicial perspectives, but not giving judges interpretative supremacy over rights, the end result of these normative accounts of dialogue, as well as their empirical examples from Canada, may be disappointing. Judges remain the final arbiters of constitutional meaning.[46]

The continuing tendency to overlook this ambition of weak-form review—to question the primacy and finality of judicial opinion—has been recently challenged by Gregoire Webber as overlooking the potential of constitutional dialogue as a way to displace the interpretative supremacy of judges.[47] Webber's theoretical work marks a resurgence of the second strand of thinking about dialogue as dual review, that is concerned with reasonable disagreement over what rights mean and the role for legislatures in deciding what interpretation human rights are to be given. Under Webber's theory of dialogue, the potential of interaction over human rights is epistemological, and dialogue is a dialectical process of movement towards eventual inter-institutional agreement on their meaning (synthesis). In this process, the court advances its interpretation of rights through judgments, while the legislature acts through legislative enactments. To Webber, rights are only set out 'in contours . . . a framework to be fleshed out organically'.[48] Webber sets out a system in which both courts and legislatures can be partners in interpreting rights, if we see constitutional meaning as open-ended, and understand that both judicial decisions and legislation are stand-alone actions specifying the content of rights, but always contingent on subsequent action from the other branch.[49]

Webber's dialogue as dialectic, by contrast to many of the other accounts, is not primarily concerned with structural arrangements. He argues that structures can at most create a framework that allows dialogue, but it is up to courts and legislatures to each take responsibility for developing constitutional meaning. In the aftermath of a judicial decision, the legislature should reassess if its legislation is reasonable, and should either clarify its position, adopt the court's position, or adopt some other position.[50] Depending on the attitude taken by different institutions, a formal structure may be needed to end the debate between institutions, such as section 33 of the Canadian Charter; but Webber suggests that what is fundamentally required is 'a certain political culture', and a disposition by the legislature to take responsibility for developing constitutional meaning.[51]

The idea that institutional interaction is not simply about the structure or form of constitutional review, but also about the behaviour and attitudes of judges and politicians towards their constitutional roles, refocuses our attention on the importance of empirical investigation of assertions of dialogue or otherwise. We must

[46] Russell (n 29). See also Webber (n 32); M Tushnet, *Weak Courts, Strong Rights* (Princeton University Press, Princeton 2008) 52–60.

[47] Webber (n 32) 446.

[48] Webber (n 32) 448.

[49] Webber (n 32) 452. See also G Webber, *The Negotiable Constitution* (CUP, Cambridge 2009).

[50] Webber (n 32) 456.

[51] Webber (n 32) 455.

look *beyond structure* to practice; and look beyond the mere fact of a legislative sequel, to how legislators understand their role, and the courts' role, in relation to fundamental rights.

2.C. Dialogue and Declarations of Incompatibility

The development of statutory bills of rights in the United Kingdom and Australia has been strongly influenced by the idea of shared responsibility for rights across courts and the political branches of government.[52] The British Labour Party was mindful of the Canadian Charter's compromise, and New Zealand's interpretative Bill of Rights Act 1990, when it decided in the 1990s to support human rights legislation. Yet, the design of the HRA, and subsequent statutory bills of rights which follow its model, made important modifications to the Canadian position. Courts are directed to interpret legislation compatibly with human rights, 'so far as it is possible to do so'.[53] But where the court finds legislation to be incompatible with rights, any remedial action must come from the legislature; and since the court's decision does not mandate corrective action, no response is necessary. This makes it easier for legislatures to avoid judicial decisions, as there is no need to legislate in order to prevent the judicial decision from taking effect.

David Feldman has explained this further weakening of judicial review compared to the Canadian Charter on the pragmatic grounds that allowing judges to strike down legislation (even with a legislative override option) 'was anathema to representative democrats' in the Labour Party; and by the fact that it would have posed drafting difficulties.[54] However, the position taken by the HRA has also been understood as responding to concerns that judicial review under the Canadian Charter was too strong, and that the legislative override created too much of a hurdle for the legislature to respond if it disagreed with the courts.[55] Certainly, within the comparative constitutional accounts of weak-form review, the HRA is understood to provide for a less robust alternative to the Canadian Charter.[56] It has even been described as a 'conversational model', too weak to support institutional dialogue, by those who conceive of dialogue as specialization.[57] Yet, for those who are interested in advancing the dual review model of dialogue, the DOI may provide a more promising design of human rights remedy, in view of the failure of section 33 of the Canadian Charter to become an accepted tool for legislatures.

Within the UK context, a number of theorists and constitutional lawyers have directed their attention to how the courts ought to exercise their new powers under

[52] JL Hiebert, 'Parliamentary Bills of Rights: An Alternative Model?' (2006) 69 Modern Law Review 7.

[53] s 3(1) HRA.

[54] D Feldman, 'The Human Rights Act and Constitutional Principles' (1999) 165 Legal Studies 165, 169.

[55] F Klug, *Values for a Godless Age: The Story of the United Kingdom's New Bill of Rights* (Penguin, London 2000) 165–6.

[56] Tushnet (n 46) 27–30; Roach, 'Dialogic Judicial Review and its Critics' (n 31) 49.

[57] Dixon (n 10) 404.

the Act, some of which employ the language of dialogue,[58] while others choose to address the institutional division of labour under the HRA without recourse to the term.[59] Yet, across these accounts we see a similar divergence to the debates in Canada, this time arising around the two routes available to judges under the Act: the 'reading down' power and the DOI.

Some commentators have taken a normative approach to the HRA that fits well with the dual review model of dialogue, and they argue that the DOI is the instrument of dialogue under the HRA, because by using it judges give their opinion of what human rights require, but leave the final decision on principle to the legislature.[60] This understanding of DOIs is premissed on the idea that the interpretation of human rights is essentially a political or moral exercise, and for this reason, choices on what rights mean in the event of controversy ought to be taken by representative institutions, not courts. Like their Canadian counterparts, their ideal of institutional interaction over human rights is the dual review model where the legislature has the final word; the power to agree, modify, or disagree with judicial decision. So, for instance, Tom Campbell argues that DOIs ought to be understood as 'only provisional determinations of what it is that the human rights asserted in the ECHR require us to do',[61] leaving the final determination to the legislature.

However, not all commentators in the UK believe this to be the correct understanding of the relative roles of courts and legislatures. Others adopt the more traditional approach that the determination of human rights compatibility is for the courts in the final instance, and any evaluations of compatibility by the executive or legislature are only predictions of a matter that solely a court can determine.[62] This approach results in some discomfort with the design of DOIs, because they do convey the impression of being merely provisional by virtue of being non-binding. For example, Tom Hickman argues that dialogue as dual review (which he calls 'principle-proposing dialogue') reduces judicial decisions to 'mere opinions' and reduces judges from arbiters of rights, and 'repositions them in the forum of ordinary politics, not providing a check or balance, but a counsel'.[63]

Instead, where normative thinking about the HRA has been underpinned by a vision of courts and legislatures each playing their own specialized role, it has

[58] Klug (n 55); R Clayton, 'Judicial Deference and "Democratic Dialogue": The Legitimacy of Judicial Intervention under the Human Rights Act' [2004] PL 33; T Hickman, 'Constitutional Dialogue, Constitutional Theories and the Human Rights Act 1998' [2005] PL 306; D Nicol, 'Law and Politics after the Human Rights Act' [2006] PL 722; A Young, *Parliamentary Sovereignty and the Human Rights Act* (Hart, Oxford 2009).

[59] CA Gearty, *Principles of Human Rights Adjudication* (OUP, Oxford 2004); D Feldman, 'Institutional Roles and Meanings of Compatibility under the Human Rights Act 1998' in H Fenwick, R Masterman, and G Phillipson (eds), *Judicial Reasoning under the Human Rights Act* (CUP, Cambridge 2007); A Kavanagh, *Constitutional Review under the UK Human Rights Act* (CUP, Cambridge 2009).

[60] T Campbell, 'Incorporation through Interpretation' in T Campbell, K Ewing, and A Tomkins (eds), *Sceptical Essays on Human Rights* (OUP, Oxford 2001) 99–102; Nicol (n 58) 747.

[61] Campbell et al (n 60) 99.

[62] For example, stating 'these are matters of law, not politics... Authoritatively deciding on compatibility is the prerogative of the judicial branch': Feldman (n 59) 98–9, 102–3.

[63] Hickman (n 58) 309–10.

focused on the other power available to the courts in relation to legislation: reading down. In Hickman's preferred approach to dialogue, courts ought to draw the legislature's attention to the concrete application of general laws, allowing the legislature room to pursue political goals, but in accordance with the requirements of principle determined by the courts.[64] He sees the reading down power under the HRA as the appropriate mechanism to trigger this type of dialogue, and argues that DOIs are only appropriate for legislation that is truly worthy of scorn, or for practical administrative reasons when legislation needs to be seriously redrafted.[65] Likewise, Alison Young argues that, faced with the types of rights questions that courts are best suited to answer (protection of minority rights and the protection of long-standing principles are her main examples), courts ought to use their reading down power. DOIs ought instead to be used in relation to the types of rights questions that legislatures are best suited to answer (cases where it is reasonable to disagree, it is suggested).[66] Here, as above, DOIs are seen to perform a provisional role, rather than necessarily resolving questions over rights compatibility.

In Australia, the adoption of the HRA model has been justified precisely on the grounds of this provisional status of DOIs. In fact, in light of concerns that the name of the remedy was too pejorative for its purpose of only indicating the court's *opinion* that legislation was incompatible, the name was changed in Victoria to a declaration of inconsistent interpretation.[67] By 2009, the HRA model was widely referred to in Australian debates as 'the dialogue model', premissed on the idea that it only allowed courts to state their opinion to their public and the legislature that legislation violated fundamental rights.[68]

So in the statutory bill of rights context, we see the continuation of the two schools of thought about institutional interaction. One school is animated by a normative vision of judges identifying the requirements of human rights in specific cases, followed by legislative adjustment and accommodation, while the other school is focused on a normative vision of judicial review followed by legislative review in which judicial interpretations are open to disagreement. What is interesting for our purposes is that, across the scholarship, DOIs have been understood as an instrument fitted to dialogue as dual review, not dialogue as specialization. As a matter of design and structure, DOIs have been considered to be a way in which courts indicate their opinion to the legislature, for its agreement or disagreement; whether or not commentators then go on to see this as desirable or undesirable.

[64] Hickman (n 58) 319. [65] Hickman (n 58) 327.

[66] Young (n 58) 129–31. Gearty proposes a similar approach, where judges ought to use a DOI as a form of deference: Gearty (n 59).

[67] The chair of the Consultation Committee that led to the adoption of the Victoria Charter has stressed that the change in language is intended to emphasize not that the law is incompatible but that the courts have taken a contrary view to Parliament in interpreting the meaning of the right or its limitation: G Williams, 'The Victorian Charter of Rights and Responsibilities: Origins and Scope' (2006) MULR 880, 902–3.

[68] National Human Rights Consultation Report (Australia), chapter 11 'The dialogue model' [11.1] (September 2009), available at <http://www.humanrightsconsultation.gov.au/www/nhrcc/nhrcc.nsf/Page/Report>. This reflected the terminology widely adopted by those making submissions.

But this need not be the case. The previous chapter concluded that DOIs lie on a spectrum of open remedies in human rights law, and these remedies share rationales that go beyond simply allowing for disagreement from the legislature. Albeit non-binding, the DOI is a type of legislative remand. The cooperative vision of courts and legislatures playing specialized and complementary roles—where a DOI is appropriate not because an immediate human rights decision is contestable, but because the legislature may be better placed to devise a response—is equally open to DOIs.

2.D. Two Models of Court–Legislature Interaction

We have seen two potential types of interaction between courts and legislatures in the new dialogue scholarship. Each can be considered to be a valuable form of constitutionalism, though responding to *different* normative aspirations for the protection of rights in a democracy. Where dialogue is understood as each institution playing its own specialized function, complementary to the other institution, this theory responds to the concern that judicial protection of human rights removes these matters from political consideration. Here it is suggested that judicial protection of human rights results in a reflexive process of adjustment of legislation and an ultimately more carefully tailored legislative pursuit of political objectives. Dialogue as dual review—judicial review followed by legislative agreement or disagreement—responds to the deeper philosophical objection to giving judges the power to specify what human rights require, because these are broad norms subject to reasonable disagreement.

These two theories of dialogue support two different models for how DOIs may operate in practice. Under the specialization model, the specific judicial decision on the incompatibility of legislation is treated as authoritative, and the role for the legislature is not to second-guess the court's decision, but rather to decide what responsive action is required, and how/to what extent to change the impugned laws. Under the dual review model, judicial decisions are not understood as authoritative interpretations of what rights require, hence the role for the legislature in the aftermath of a declaration is broader, not only to decide *how* to respond, but *whether* to respond.

It should be emphasized that these models are based on 'ideal-types' of interaction,[69] that is, each type of 'dialogue' is an idealized description of how political institutions may behave. Their heuristic value lies in guiding our examination of institutional behaviour (that is, an anterior framework for analysis), not in coinciding with reality precisely. In practice, we may see institutional interaction deviate

[69] 'Ideal-typical' models are a technique commonly used in qualitative or sociological research: see, F Collin, 'Idiographic Theorizing and Ideal-Types: Max Weber's Metholodology of the Social Sciences' (1995) 30 Danish Yearbook of Philosophy 37. For discussion of the use of an ideal-type as a model, see NJ Smelser, J Wright, and PB Baltes, *International Encyclopedia of Social & Behavioral Sciences* (Elsevier, Oxford 2001) 7139–42.

from either or both of these types. Significant deviations may alert us to the importance of factors that presently sit outside this modelling.[70]

Nor should it be assumed that the specialization model is unique to particular structures of weak-form review. In fact, it can credibly be argued that the claim that strong-form review in the US removes constitutional rights matters from political consideration is a vast overstatement, and in fact, the normal state of affairs is a process of reflexive adjustment of legislation across courts and legislatures.[71] As we will explore further in 3.C, the structure of judicial review in strong-form or weak-form systems may be far less important than the discursive power of judges over understandings of human rights.

Just as, with experience of the Charter, Canadian scholarship moved away from section 33 as the vehicle for institutional interaction and looked to how legislatures respond in other ways, the statutory bills of rights scholarship also needs to look beyond the formal power to refuse to respond to DOIs. The previous chapter's discussion of the rationales underpinning open remedies, and the understanding of DDIs in the Canadian context, indicate that the dual review approach to dialogue is not the only way to understand the usefulness of DOIs. Even if legislatures respond as a matter of course, we need to look at the nature of their response; and how pursuit of policy is reconciled with the judicial decision.

2.E. Sidestepping Legislative Reality: Two Concerns

This final section turns to a notable lacuna in the new dialogue scholarship concerning the role of the legislature: for all this new-found interest in legislatures and their role in relation to giving general human rights norms precise content, commentators have generally failed to give any sustained attention to the legislative process or legislative deliberation.

This feature of the existing scholarship is significant for two reasons. First, as I identify in this section, it generates dissonance between certain normative arguments about *why* we want to involve legislatures in decisions on rights and accounts within political science scholarship of the role of legislatures in relation to law-making. Political scientists are strongly sceptical of the significance of the legislature, as opposed to the executive, to law-making. This gives rise to important practical questions about the capacity and willingness of legislatures to engage with human rights. Dialogue literature has by and large sidestepped these questions by

[70] For example, in Part III we observe the phenomenon of passive resistance to judicial decision through delay; something that neither ideal-type includes.

[71] Huscroft argues that Hogg and Bushell's distinction between Canadian and US constitutional rights review is based on a mischaracterization of the US system, Huscroft (n 23) 75; see also Gardbaum (n 6) 16, who argues that the difference between s 1 Canadian Charter and the different levels of scrutiny developed by the US constitutional jurisprudence is a matter of degree.

defining the participation of legislatures in dialogue solely in terms of legislative output, not legislative process.[72]

The second significance is that the lack of theoretical interest in deliberation suggests implicit acceptance of a majoritarian and aggregative conception of democratic decision-making, through the election of political party candidates into the legislature, where the government's decisions are understood as 'democratic' because they, albeit indirectly, represent the majority of voters. It overlooks significant developments in political theory towards more deliberative understandings of what democracy means. The following chapter challenges this oversight, arguing that weak-form review is conceptually well fitted to a deliberative democratic approach, and using this approach to build on the analytical framework developed in this chapter.

2.E.1. Dissonance over legislatures and law-making

(a) Reasons to value legislative decisions on rights

Justifications within constitutional law and theory for giving the legislature an important, or even the primary, role in relation to constitutional rights typically break down into two types of reasons. The first reason emphasizes the democratic legitimacy of legislative decisions; the second, the institutional capacity of legislatures to make good decisions on the scope and balancing of rights.

Jeremy Waldron's theoretical work on legislatures has been influential in terms of furnishing reasons why legislatures are valuable sites of decision-making on rights. His original account centred on how the legislative process respects the equal right to participation of all voters, by combining the principles of equal representation, equal voting in the legislature, and decision-making by majority vote. This was advanced as a 'rights-based' reason to respect legislative decisions on rights as more legitimate than judicial decisions on rights, because the right to participation is the 'right of rights'.[73] By contrast, the more typical democratic legitimacy argument advanced for legislative decision-making is that democratic representatives are accountable to the polity through regular, competitive elections.[74]

[72] There is a small collection of recent work on parliamentary scrutiny of legislation, which does not always use the terminology of dialogue, but is concerned with how legislatures deal with human rights issues in the course of law-making. This literature has focused on legislative rights review prior to any judicial decision (D Feldman, 'The Impact of Human Rights on the UK Legislative Processes' (2004) 25 Statute Law Review 91; JL Hiebert, 'Parliament and the Human Rights Act: Can the JCHR Help Facilitate a Culture of Rights?' (2006) 4 ICON 1; F Klug and H Wildbore, 'Breaking New Ground: The Joint Committee on Human Rights and the Role of Parliament in Human Rights Compliance' [2007] EHRLR 231) and in the absence of a bill of rights (J Uhr, 'The Performance of Australian Legislatures in Protecting Rights' in T Campbell, J Goldsworthy, and A Stone (eds), *Protecting Rights without a Bill of Rights* (Ashgate, Aldershot 2006)). These empirical accounts, particularly in relation to the UK JCHR will be drawn upon in the analysis in Part III.

[73] Waldron, 'A Right-Based Critique of Constitutional Rights' (n 4).

[74] Jane Schacter refers to this as the 'accountability axiom': JC Schacter, 'Political Accountability, Proxy Accountability and the Democratic Legitimacy of Legislatures' in RW Bauman and T Kahana (eds), *The Least Examined Branch: The Role of Legislatures in the Constitutional State* (CUP, Cambridge 2006).

It can also be argued that legislatures will make better decisions in light of the specific features that equip legislatures to deal with the ethical and policy dimensions of fundamental rights. This argument for a role for the legislature is a relative one: based as much on institutional limitations of the courts as institutional strengths of the legislature. Asserted limitations of courts are said to relate to the limited number of decision-makers; their lack of expertise and experience in particular areas of social policy; the reliance of judges on the parties and evidence before them; and Lon Fuller's famous argument of the weakness of courts to deal with 'polycentric' questions: problems which comprise a complicated web of interdependent relationships.[75]

In addition to his rights-based argument, Waldron claims that legislatures are better equipped to engage in the interpretation of bills of rights because legislatures are superior at the *type of reasoning* required to deal with the moral issues that bills of rights give rise to—they can address moral issues 'directly, on the merits . . . mostly undistracted by legal doctrine or precedents'.[76] Janet Hiebert also justifies hybrid bills of rights on the basis of the institutional capacity of the legislature.[77] She acknowledges the potential benefit of hearing judicial perspectives on fundamental rights, but raises concerns about judicial capabilities to make decisions on necessity and proportionality. To Hiebert, the *proportionality analysis* involved in deciding on the justified limitation of rights 'bears more resemblance to a policy analysis than a legal analysis'.[78] She argues that judges do not have the resources to assess the various dimensions of complex social issues, nor can they claim particular expertise in relation to social problems.[79] Similar claims are made that legislatures are better placed than courts to deal with matters that have significant resource implications.[80]

These are general assertions about the incapacities of courts—not empirically grounded, comparative claims—and are therefore open to question.[81] However, my immediate purpose is not to interrogate the incapacities of courts, but the claimed capacities of the legislature. What concrete features of the legislature are these claims of superior institutional capacity based upon?

[75] NW Barber, 'Prelude to the Separation of Powers' (2001) 60 Cambridge Law Journal 59, 75–9; LL Fuller, 'The Forms and Limits of Adjudication' (1978) 92 Harvard Law Review 353.

[76] J Waldron, 'Judges as Moral Reasoners' (2009) 7 ICON 2, 19.

[77] Specifically, see Hiebert (n 7) 238–9.

[78] JL Hiebert, 'Parliament and Rights' in T Campbell, J Goldsworthy, and A Stone (eds), *Protecting Human Rights: Instruments and Institutions* (OUP, Oxford 2003) 233–4.

[79] J Hiebert, *Limiting Rights* (McGill-Queens, Kingston 1996).

[80] C Scott and P Macklem, 'Constitutional Ropes of Sand or Justiciable Guarantees? Social Rights in a New South African Constitution' (1992) 141 UPenn Law Review 1, 23–4 summarize these claims and present a detailed critique of the assertion that courts cannot/should not deal with questions with resource implications in relation to social rights.

[81] Nor should it be assumed that courts cannot be made better at doing these things; the judicial process may be structured to better suit, say, polycentric disputes or social policy questions. For example, S Fredman, *Human Rights Transformed: Positive Rights and Positive Duties* (OUP, Oxford 2008) chapters 4 and 5, considers ways in which the judicial process can be structured to better deal with positive rights; see also Scott and Macklem (n 80) 137–47.

The following possibilities can be suggested:

(a) the representative and amateur nature of the legislature, making it the best institution to make decisions where there is no technically correct answer or the options available are incommensurable;[82]

(b) the fact (or assumption) that the legislature engages in public debate and reflects the diverse range of political viewpoints in the polity allows it to weigh up competing views in society;[83]

(c) the social policy information that Parliament has, via the executive, as well as via communication with constituents and interest groups, and the wide range of backgrounds and expertise of parliamentarians. Barber, for instance, argues that the size of legislative chambers makes it likely that a number of people will bring some understanding and expertise to the issue being debated.[84]

These features point to the legislature having its own strengths in reviewing issues of principle and policy raised by legislation relative to the other, more technically specialized and less representative, branches of government. However, once we break down the reasons to value legislative decisions in this way, we begin to encounter the problem of dissonance between this normatively oriented depiction of the legislature as a valuable decision-maker, built from the idea of a large assembly of elected representatives, and accounts of legislatures in political science scholarship.

(b) Legislatures in political science

Weak-form review in Canada, the UK, Australia, and New Zealand involves parliamentary government in the Westminster model. In contrast to a system that separates executive and legislative power, such as the US, in a Westminster system of government, the executive and the legislature are closely linked. The Prime Minister and Cabinet are composed of members of the legislature and chosen by the party that obtains the majority of seats in the lower house. Typically referred to as the government, the Cabinet is also the head of the executive, comprising the heads of the various government departments.

Political scientists concerned with legislatures in parliamentary systems have long disputed the idea of the legislature as lawmaker.[85] The overwhelming majority of legislation is drafted and introduced by government departments. The government typically has control over the parliamentary timetable, as well as strong structures to ensure votes are in place where needed. Insofar as decisions of principle are being expressed in the form of legislation, we need to query *whose* decisions these are. Empirical accounts of Westminster parliaments suggest most legislation represents decisions made by members of the executive, often with little or no change being made by elected representatives outside Cabinet.[86]

[82] Barber (n 75) 87. [83] Waldron (n 4). [84] Barber (n 75) 84–5.

[85] P Norton, *Parliament in British Politics* (Palgrave Macmillan, New York 2005) 3.

[86] I Loveland, *Constitutional Law, Administrative Law and Human Rights: A Critical Introduction* (4th edn OUP, Oxford 2006), 129–33; Russell (n 29) 299; A Petter, 'Look Who's Talking Now:

Accounts of Parliament in constitutional theory and political science in Westminster democracies are often dissonant: that is, while constitutional theory emphasizes the role of the legislature as the lawmaker,[87] political science generally places legislation very low in the functions of the legislature. Moreover, where constitutional theory conceives of democratic legislatures as underpinning the legitimacy of the laws which govern the polity—what makes the law 'democratic'—political scientists are more likely to see legislatures as playing a role of outward legitimation for the power effectively exercised by the executive. For instance, Packenham's influential 1970 study of the functions of legislatures placed the decision-making functions of legislatures at the bottom of the list in terms of priority, and considered the manifest legitimation of the system of government provided by the regular meeting of the legislature, and the recruitment, socialization, and training functions of the legislature to be far more important.[88] In the UK, Australia, and Canada, the lower house of Parliament (the representative house) has been described by leading commentators to behave as an 'electoral college', suggesting its primary function is to choose and uphold the government of the day.[89]

The description of the relationship between the accounts of the legislature in constitutional theory and political science as *dissonant*, rather than contradictory, is deliberate. Political scientists' accounts of the legislature have a different focus, characteristically descriptive and concerned with coercive power, but not with the normative status of legislation or what checks should be placed on legislation.[90] Furthermore, even if there is little involvement of the legislature itself in the majority of legislation, this should not be taken to determine the question of what role legislatures play specifically in relation to legislation that implicates fundamental constitutional principles such as human rights safeguards. Rather, the importance of including this alternative understanding of legislatures is that it encourages us not to unquestioningly accept theoretical claims as to what legislatures are good at, or better at than courts; and to take seriously the matter of executive dominance of real-world legislatures.

Nor should we immediately accept that since legislatures do not make law, or focus primarily on legislation, we should relegate legislatures to being a formal rubber stamp. For one, legislatures do not have to *make* law for the arguments made

Dialogue Theory and the Return to Democracy' in RW Bauman and T Kahana (eds), *The Least Examined Branch: Legislatures in the Constitutional State* (CUP, Cambridge 2006) 525.

87 Dawn Oliver has aptly described this as the myth of the centrality of Parliament: D Oliver, 'The Modernisation of the United Kingdom Parliament' in J Jowell and D Oliver (eds), *The Changing Constitution* (OUP, Oxford 2004).

88 R Packenham, 'Legislatures and Political Development' in A Kornberg and L Musolf (eds), *Legislatures in a Developmental Perspective* (Duke University Press, Durham NC 1970).

89 V Bogdanor, 'Britain: The Political Constitution' in V Bogdanor (ed), *Constitutions in Democratic Politics* (Gower, Aldershot 1988) 56 (United Kingdom); Uhr (n 72) 45 (Australia); Russell (n 29) 299 (Canada, as well as more general trends in parliamentary democracies towards executive control). AV Jennings considered that every vote in the House of Commons was a vote of confidence in the government, not a vote on the merits of the legislative or policy proposal: AV Jennings, *The British Constitution* (3rd edn CUP, Cambridge 1950) 81.

90 Schacter (n 74) 49, 72. Political scientist Philip Norton criticizes the tendency of political science to focus on coercive power, and make claims that the legislature is in decline solely on this basis: Norton (n 85) 9–11.

by constitutional theorists concerning the institutional capacity of legislatures to have any force. Legislatures in parliamentary systems are not well equipped to devise policy and draft law; properly understood their function in relation to legislation is one of assent and review.[91] Based on this, we can add some precision to these arguments on legislative capacity. It is in performing this *review* function in relation to legislation that affects fundamental rights that legislatures may bring the benefits of diversity of perspectives and expertise to evaluate legislation (what I have referred to earlier as legislative rights review). The legislative process can thereby contribute to the public justification of the exercise of legislative power,[92] even if legislatures do not themselves set the legislative agenda or draft law.

Lastly, Parliament is not a unitary concept. It can refer to the executive acting with the formal assent of Parliament, commanding its political control over legislative power. It can also refer to either chamber of bicameral legislatures or some component of the legislature, such as a parliamentary committee or working group, acting independently of the executive.[93] There may be different levels of executive control over these various components.

Overall, rather than foreclose consideration of the role of the legislature in relation to laws that affect human rights, the dissonance in the existing scholarship invites us to take a closer, more empirically sensitive look at legislative deliberation.

2.E.2. Moving beyond majoritarian preference aggregation

Yet, this is not how the literature discussed in this chapter has dealt with dissonance between constitutional theory and political science. In his work on legislatures and fundamental rights, Waldron expressly sets aside the empirical accounts of legislatures. He argues that political science has failed to provide a helpful normative account of the legislative process.[94] Waldron makes clear that his account is a normative ideal vision, 'a rosy picture' in contrast to the 'cynicism' of political science, because it is useful for jurisprudence to have such an account in order to understand the prescriptive force of legislation.[95]

Because of this limited analysis of a hypothetical ideal legislature, Waldron's arguments should be applied with care to the broader normative project of justifying particular constitutional designs, and in particular, rejecting strong-form judicial review of legislation produced by *real-world* legislatures. Once we move from the terrain of legal philosophy's 'rosy pictures' to the question of how we

[91] Norton (n 85) argues that a parliament should be understood as a *law-affecting* body rather than a law-making body, one which exerts persuasive rather than coercive power. See also A Tomkins, 'What is Parliament For?' in N Bamforth and P Leyland (eds), *Public Law in a Multi-Layered Constitution* (Hart, Oxford 2003) 54–5; Feldman (n 59) 94.

[92] D Dyzenhaus, 'Deference, Security and Human Rights' in L Lazarus and B Goold (eds), *Security and Human Rights* (Hart, Oxford 2007) 130.

[93] Uhr (n 72) 43.

[94] Waldron, *Law and Disagreement* (n 4) 28–9. In response to criticism, Waldron elaborates all the assumed conditions in his normative account of legislatures in Waldron (n 6).

[95] Waldron, *Law and Disagreement* (n 4) 32.

ought to design human rights protection in reality, questions over the extent to which legislatures are actually engaged in the legislative process become important. The attributes of elected legislatures upon which legislative constitutionalism is justified in theory may not be especially relevant to the formulation of legislation in practice.

Dialogue literature has generally sidestepped questions over the capacity and willingness of legislatures to engage with human rights. This has been done by defining the participation of legislatures in dialogue solely in terms of legislative *output*, not legislative process.[96] In his otherwise nuanced account of dialogue, Webber explicitly recognizes that he is bracketing out debates over the legislature's engagement in law-making:

> Even if a bill is conceived exclusively by the executive and the public service, legislation is the action of the legislature. And while the executive may control a majority of Parliament, legislation is passed in the legislature's name. For the purposes of this essay's argument, this delimited dialogue will be the focus.[97]

In fact, Roach specifically includes a Cabinet-dominated legislature as a necessary component in his account of dialogue. The fact that the government controls a majority in the legislature, and the workings of party discipline, allow for quick reply legislation in the aftermath of a judicial decision.[98] Roach acknowledges that these very same features are responsible for reduced accountability of the government's legislative choices, but states that responding to judicial decisions would be too difficult in a system such as the US system.[99] This is the only alternative he considers; he does not explore the idea of a parliamentary system with strong legislative rights review and more robust accountability processes.[100]

At an empirical level, looking at legislative deliberation can reveal a 'largely unmapped dimension' to dialogue literature within the legislature itself.[101] At the theoretical level, the literature on hybrid bills of rights and institutional dialogue has given us cause to reflect more carefully on ways to address the counter-majoritarian difficulty with judicial review. However, major accounts of dialogue have been unreflective about the conception of democracy and democratic decision-making that underpins their interest in cooperative constitutionalism, and weakening judicial powers of review legislation. Either implicitly or explicitly,

[96] This is common to Hogg and Bushell's account as well as the accounts of critics such as Manfredi and Kelly, and Webber; and in the UK, accounts of Hickman, Clayton, and Young.

[97] Webber (n 32) 445.

[98] Roach, 'Dialogic Judicial Review and its Critics' (n 31) 65–6.

[99] Roach, 'Dialogic Judicial Review and its Critics' (n 31) 65–6.

[100] This stance does produce tension in Roach's work. He also states in favour of weak-form review that popular preferences can still be vindicated through reply legislation, however with the added benefit of 'fuller deliberation and debate': 'Dialogic Judicial Review and its Critics' (n 31) 54. He specifically argues that democracy should be measured not simply by legislation, but by the 'tenor of democratic debate': ibid 89. These statements sit uncomfortably alongside an executive-dominated legislative process with strong party discipline.

[101] Uhr (n 72) 42.

the new dialogue literature has largely remained grounded in a majoritarian or aggregative conception of democracy where legislation is taken to represent the majority will, criticism of the representative character and accountability of legislatures are overlooked,[102] and democratic deliberation is not accorded much significance. The following chapter begins to address this oversight.

[102] Petter (n 86) 525–6. The idea that legislation reflects majority will itself remains deeply problematic, as the extensive political science scholarship on legislative accountability shows. Schacter (n 74) provides an excellent analysis of this work.

3

From Dialogue to Engagement

3.A. Introduction

While concerned with the legislature, the new dialogue literature has so far not recognized or accounted for the deliberative turn in democratic theory, and has not given sustained attention to legislative deliberation. This chapter explains the deliberative conception of democracy and argues that weak-form review is a good conceptual fit to this understanding of democracy. Deliberative democrats do not take 'democratic decision-making' as a given, rather the project of democratization is a continuous project of enhancing the authenticity of democratic control. Weak-form review is a promising institutional design approach for this project insofar as it may advance the accountability and justification of public action.

Thinking about the interactions between courts and legislatures as a deliberative (as opposed to majoritarian) democrat has two concrete implications. First, it directs attention beyond the mere fact of legislation to the legislative process, and whether judicial decisions can promote greater reflectiveness in the legislature. Second, we can draw on accounts within deliberative democracy scholarship to construct normative standards against which real-world legislatures can be evaluated.

There are two principal challenges to using judicial review to foster legislative deliberation. The first challenge, with which we are already familiar, is executive dominance of the legislative process, such that there is not meaningful deliberation in the legislature. The second danger is the inverse of the argument that having judges contribute reasoned decisions on human rights compatibility enriches deliberation. Sceptics suggest that one of the perverse effects of judicial review is judicial dominance over political debate, such that legislative engagement with human rights is reduced to predicting what judges will consider to be human rights compliant ('compliance-oriented' rights review), diverting deliberation away from what is the correct or most legitimate course of action.

Considering the extent to which the legislature is engaged in deliberation on human rights in response to a DOI adds an additional dimension to the analysis undertaken in this book. Under either the specialization model or the dual review model of court–legislature interaction there may be different levels of legislative engagement in responsive deliberation.

The final section of this chapter examines a factor that potentially affects deliberation on, and interaction over, human rights, namely, the implications of international human rights obligations for the role of the domestic legislature.

International human rights law does not preclude legislative engagement in developing and elaborating what human rights require. Nonetheless, this is one factor that may promote the specialization model of interaction, and even compliance-oriented legislative rights review.

3.B. Applying the Deliberative Turn in Democratic Theory

3.B.1. The deliberative turn in democratic theory

In the 1990s, a body of political theory emerged questioning majoritarian theories of democratic decision-making based around the aggregation of private preferences and personal attitudes, instead focusing on the communicative or discursive aspects of public decision-making in modern democracies.[1] The idea of a *deliberative democracy*[2] provides a fresh intervention in the theoretical debate over counter-majoritarian protection for fundamental individual rights.

Deliberative democracy theory is a normative political theory that rejects the idea of politics as merely the aggregation of private interests, while still recognizing that in a modern democracy there is no single, shared conception of the common good (that is, there is value pluralism). It takes a different approach to the task of democratic decision-making in a pluralist society to aggregative accounts of democratic decision-making, by emphasizing public decision-making through discussion and reflection, not simply voting and majority rule.

Under aggregative accounts of democracy, the political process is designed to produce a compromise between a plurality of private views, and is made legitimate by the governing principle of majority rule. Political behaviour is seen in a similar way to market behaviour insofar as voters act on given, private preferences.[3] Deliberative democrats challenge this view on the grounds that preferences are not given and static, but capable of transformation through public and rational discussion. Moreover, these preferences are not purely a private matter, because a citizen is asked to make choices between laws and policies that differ in how they affect other people.[4] Deliberative democrats believe that the democratic will is not simply the aggregation of existing preferences but the outcome of preferences that are subject to reasoned argument in the public sphere.[5]

[1] For two critical overviews of this turn in scholarship, from different perspectives: J Dryzek, *Deliberative Democracy and Beyond: Liberals, Critics, Contestations* (OUP, Oxford 2000); RE Pildes, 'Competitive, Deliberative, and Rights-Oriented Democracy' (2004) 3 Election Law Journal 685.

[2] The idea was also referred to early on as 'discursive democracy' (J Dryzek, *Discursive Democracy* (CUP, Cambridge 1990)), but 'deliberative democracy' has become the dominant terminology.

[3] J Elster, 'The Market and the Forum: Three Varieties of Political Theory' in J Bohman and W Rehg (eds), *Deliberative Democracy* (MIT Press, Cambridge MA 1997) 10; J Habermas, *Between Facts and Norms* (MIT Press, Cambridge MA 1996) 272–3.

[4] Elster (n 3) 10.

[5] See J Cohen, 'Procedure and Substance in a Deliberative Democracy' in S Benhabib (ed), *Democracy and Difference* (Princeton University Press, Princeton 1996); A Gutmann and DF Thompson, *Democracy and Disagreement* (Belknap Press, Cambridge MA 1996); CR Sunstein, *Designing Democracy: What Constitutions Do* (OUP, Oxford 2001).

Foundational to deliberative democratic thought is Jürgen Habermas's attempted philosophical reconciliation of liberal democracy (with its emphasis on private autonomy, and limiting government from encroaching onto the private sphere and individual rights) and civic republicanism (with its emphasis on public autonomy, collective self-government, and popular sovereignty).[6] Habermas argues that individual rights and popular sovereignty are internally linked, based on the fact that private autonomy and public autonomy (or self-government) are mutually enabling (the *co-originality* of private and public autonomy). Advocates of rights-based constitutionalism have convincingly argued that judicial protection of human rights is not antithetical to democracy: the protection of rights enables democratic processes.[7] At the same time, civic republicans have argued that freedom ought not to be reduced to negative liberty against the interference of the state, but rather the positive freedom which is facilitated by the collective ability to govern and shape society.[8] In Habermas's account, neither individual rights nor collective self-government takes priority, rather they are internally related and symbiotic.[9]

Even apart from the idea that certain rights provide the preconditions for the exercise of self-government, it should also certainly be recognized that there is no such thing as a 'public will' that floats free of constitutional structures. Rather, the public voice is something that is constructed and supported by institutional structures.[10] Even the voice of the 'majority' can be constructed in different ways, depending on how one defines the extent of the polity, constituencies, the electoral system, and the rules by which legislators deliberate and vote.[11] Hence, we can constantly strive towards a greater authenticity of democratic decision-making processes, rather than easily identifying that we have done so already.

Deliberative democrats understand democracy as an open-ended project, not a congratulatory description of existing liberal democratic states: the process of democratization does not just mean the spread of liberal democracy to new parts of the world, but a continual striving towards more authentic democratic control in all democratic states.[12] This understanding of democratization captures deliberative democracy's impetus for institutional innovation and experimentalism. Deliberative

[6] Habermas (n 3), see especially chapter 3: 'Contributions to a Discourse Theory of Law and Democracy'. See also K Günther, 'Law, the State and Discourse Theory (Droits, Etat et Théorie de la Discussion)' (2007) 6 Raison Publique 129, for a defence of the co-originality thesis.

[7] For one classic account of this argument, see JH Ely, *Democracy and Distrust: A Theory of Judicial Review* (Harvard University Press, Cambridge MA 1980).

[8] For a recent statement of contemporary republicanism, see R Bellamy, *Political Constitutionalism: A Republican Defence of the Constitutionality of Democracy* (CUP, Cambridge 2007). For an overview of the 'Republican Revival' in the United States, see *Special Issue: The Republican Revival* (1987–8) 97 Yale Law Journal.

[9] Habermas (n 3) 104, 121–3.

[10] A Sathanapally, 'Between the People and the Constitution: The Constitutional Role(s) of the Legislature' (The Social Foundations of Constitutions, Foundation for Law, Justice and Society, Oxford 2009), available at <http://www.fljs.org>; J Webber, 'Democratic Decision-Making as the First Principle of Contemporary Constitutionalism' in RW Bauman and T Kahana (eds), *The Least Examined Branch: The Role of Legislatures in the Constitutional State* (CUP, Cambridge 2006).

[11] Webber (n 10) 413.

[12] Dryzek (n 1) 28–9.

democrats are keen to enhance the deliberative capacity of state institutions but also support the existence of multiple public spheres, rather than conceiving of a unified public will institutionalized in a single state structure. This approach to democracy emphasizes the inclusion of multiple perspectives in public deliberation, and the use of alternative sites where these perspectives can be developed and deliberation can be fostered, as well as points of access or entry of multiple perspectives into governmental institutions.

Weak-form judicial review in general, and open remedies in particular, are one such innovation. Below it is argued that, even though deliberative democrats have generally not opposed strong-form judicial review, weak-form review is a good fit to this tradition's approach to human rights and democratization. Weak-form review has the potential to advance the processes of reason-giving that are central to a deliberative democracy, and support the entry of alternative points of view into political decision-making. In turn, the idea of deliberative democracy makes conceptual sense of weak-form review as a principled alternative and more than a 'halfway house' or trade-off between the opposing traditions of juridical and political constitutionalism.

3.B.2. Deliberative democracy and weak-form review

Deliberative democrats have generally been sanguine about strong-form judicial review, or have openly supported it.[13] That judicial review may come at the expense of the power of legislatures is generally not a matter of concern.[14]

It is not entirely surprising that the counter-majoritarian objection has little resonance for those who approach democracy in deliberative, rather than majoritarian, terms. Deliberative democrats do not ordinarily see the official political process as conveying a common public will, nor do they believe that democratic decisions are best made by simply identifying the preferences of the majority. Hence, they are understandably less likely to consider judicial review to be 'undemocratic'.

Indeed, there are good reasons for deliberative democrats to support judicial review on fundamental rights grounds. This can provide an entry point into the public sphere for previously excluded claims, provide an alternative avenue for civil

[13] J Knight, 'Constitutionalism and Deliberative Democracy' in S Macedo (ed), *Deliberative Politics: Essays on Democracy and Disagreement* (OUP, New York 1999). This is particularly the case in the Rawlsian strand (typically American) of deliberative democracy theory, where judicial reasoning is taken to exemplify public reasoning: J Rawls, *Political Liberalism* (Columbia University Press, New York 1993) §6; see critical discussion by Dryzek (n 1) 14–17. The notable exception is Cass Sunstein, who has linked judicial minimalism to the project of supporting a deliberative democracy: C Sunstein, 'Beyond the Republican Revival' (1988) 97 Yale Law Journal 1539; Sunstein (n 5). Another recent exception is E Ghosh, 'Deliberative Democracy and the Counter-Majoritarian Difficulty: Considering Constitutional Juries' (2010) 30 Oxford Journal of Legal Studies 1 (who suggests that constitutional juries of lay people, rather than courts, ought to deliberate on and decide on constitutional rights matters).

[14] This aspect of the literature is observed by Uhr and Ghosh, both of whom attempt to apply deliberative democratic theory to political institutions in Australia: J Uhr, *Deliberative Democracy in Australia: The Changing Place of Parliament* (CUP, Cambridge 1998) 7; Ghosh (n 13) 2.

society actors to engage with the State, and subject the exercise of State power to the need for *reasoned justification*. In fact, critical theorists within the school of deliberative democracy have focused on the potential of civil society in advancing the project of democratization and have been less interested in, if not hostile to, official State channels of public decision-making (legislatures and executive bodies).[15] This draws from the emphasis within Habermas's early work, which was critical of the instrumental and non-deliberative nature of official State institutions and looked instead to alternative public spheres.[16]

However, in *Between Facts and Norms*, Habermas turned to address 'legally institutionalized procedures of democratic deliberation and decision-making' within his theory and clarified that legislatures do play a vital role in a deliberative democracy, as one component of a complex society.[17] Over time, greater attention has begun to be paid to how the notion of a deliberative democracy can be applied to the official institutions of the State, and how this relates to the protection of fundamental human rights. Two important themes arise here.

First, unlike liberal constitutionalists, deliberative democrats do not generally accord primacy to human rights for the sake of rights-bearers, but rather for the sake of securing a space for, and enabling participation in, democratic deliberation.[18] For instance, Habermas argues that human rights inscribed in the law are a major support for moral and political discourse.[19] Likewise, Seyla Benhabib has stressed the role of human rights norms in supporting complex processes of public argument, deliberation, and exchange through which rights claims are contested and contextualized.[20] She argues that these processes ('democratic iterations') can take place in the courts, legislatures, civil society, and the media.[21]

Second, human rights have a dual legal and ethical character and deliberative democratic theory accepts this ethical aspect as a matter for political deliberation. In the words of Rainer Forst, 'human rights constitute the inner core of any justified social structure without being concrete regulations that the legal system must simply mirror'; the polity must determine their content through deliberation.[22] In particular, the indeterminacy of human rights norms, and the scope for disagreement over fundamental norms, have been recognized by deliberative democrats as generating debates over which there *ought* to be reasoned deliberation. Klaus

[15] Dryzek (n 1) 22.

[16] Dryzek (n 1) 22–3, with reference to J Habermas, *Structural Transformation of the Public Sphere* (Polity, Cambridge 1989).

[17] Habermas (n 3) 170–3. Habermas considers that legislatures may not be the *primary* site for deliberation, given the importance of civil society and mobilized groups in the polity, at 184–6. Uhr (n 14) 8–9, draws together Habermas's statements on the legislature.

[18] Dryzek (n 1) 26. Likewise, Joshua Cohen argues that human rights are a 'terrain for deliberation and argument', playing a practical role in focusing debate on the basic conditions of membership in a political society: J Cohen, 'Minimalism about Human Rights: The Most We Can Hope for' [2003] (Spring) 12 Journal of Political Philosophy 190, 195.

[19] Dryzek (n 1) 25.

[20] S Benhabib, *The Rights of Others* (CUP, Cambridge 2004) 176–81.

[21] Benhabib (n 20) 179.

[22] R Forst, 'The Basic Right to Justification: Toward a Constructivist Conception of Human Rights' (1999) 6 Constellations 35, 48. See also Benhabib (n 20) 180–1.

Günther, for example, notes the 'notorious indeterminacy' of human rights in terms of their present and future application as especially due to their abstract nature in respect of whom rights are directed against, which rights ought to be protected, and what the limits of rights are.[23] He argues that human rights need to be understood as binding democratic discourse, but also being reproduced through reinterpretation and re-implementation by different actors over time.[24]

American theorists Gutmann and Thompson address the juridical model of human rights more directly: they question the orthodoxy in the US that courts are the forum for principled decision-making on rights, and that the primary function of legislatures is to register the actual preferences of the people and do not need to justify their decisions on principle.[25] Their work translates the ideas underpinning deliberative democratic theory into a set of ideals for, inter alia, legislatures to address principled disagreement. They argue that by making democratic processes more deliberative, 'citizens stand a better chance of resolving some of their moral disagreements and living with those that will inevitably persist, on terms that all will accept'.[26]

So, within deliberative democracy theory, human rights protections support deliberation (including as a source of friction that challenges institutionalized power), yet, simultaneously, the requirements of human rights principles are themselves a subject on which there ought to be deliberation and room for contestation. This position is well aligned to weak-form judicial review. At the theoretical level, weak-form review provides one way to institutionalize fundamental rights as prioritized claims within political processes, constitutive of democratic government; while at the same time ensuring that these norms—and disagreements over what they require—are not enforced 'against' the actions of a reflective and deliberative polity. By allowing, or inviting, a role for the legislature as well as courts, hybrid bills of rights leave space for the process of reinterpretation and re-implementation of human rights across courts and legislatures.

Moreover, hybrid bills of rights also introduce a clear ethical code for political decision-making; providing a structure for principled justification of legislative decisions. By providing for judicial feedback on whether legislation has met these ethical standards, judicial review can refocus legislative attention on matters of principle. Cass Sunstein points to this potential for constitutional judicial review to energize democracy and promote deliberation by adding to electoral accountability a requirement for reflectiveness and 'a general commitment to reason-giving'.[27]

At a more practical level, weak-form judicial review can function as an access point for alternative viewpoints and groups into the institutions of government. Judicial review can provide one source of friction that allows views formulated outside the institutions of the State, in civil society, to seek entry. Günther uses anti-discrimination guarantees as the classic example of how human rights can operate as 'door openers' to those who have been excluded and treated unfairly, and

[23] Günther (n 6). [24] Günther (n 6).
[25] Gutmann and Thompson (n 5) 45–6. [26] Gutmann and Thompson (n 5) 51.
[27] Sunstein (n 5) 'Introduction'.

can be used to demand justification for discrimination, expanding to more types of discrimination over time.[28]

In fact, legislatures have been criticized as poor deliberative forums because of 'group polarization' in party-based politics, as well as because of social influences on politicians.[29] This makes it important to expand otherwise limited argument pools, as well as to provide enclaves within which those whose views are marginalized in mainstream institutions can participate, and provide avenues for these views to be brought into contact with mainstream decision-makers. Institutions that provide checks and balances on legislative power can therefore be justified as promoting better decision-making by introducing heterogeneous viewpoints:

> An appreciation of group polarization helps show why a constitutional democracy takes steps to protect deliberation within enclaves, ensure that those within enclaves hear alternative views and ensure that those outside enclaves are exposed to what the enclaves have to say. It is self-insulation that can cause serious trouble . . .[30]

Open remedies, which draw the attention of the legislature to a human rights problem and require the legislature to devise an appropriate solution, provide one example of an institutional design that works against self-insulation in the legislature.[31] Groups and individuals who are marginalized in mainstream political fora may have access to courts, and weak-form review enlists courts in putting claims that courts find meritorious on the legislative agenda.

Weak-form judicial review, in its treatment of human rights and the powers of judges, can thus be seen as a promising institutional innovation from the perspective of supporting a deliberative democracy. The corollary of this argument is that a deliberative conception of democracy helps make theoretical sense of a system of human rights protection that limits the power of judges to decide on the protection given to rights. Under an aggregative conception of democracy, a hybrid bill of rights that gives the legislature the final word looks like a compromise between the protection of rights *against* majorities and majority rule. This compromise enlists courts in protecting constitutional rights but ultimately deals with the counter-majoritarian difficulty by allowing the majoritarian political process the final word on the protection of rights.

But rather than being seen as a compromise between rights protection and pure majoritarian government, the above analysis indicates that weakening judicial review can represent a principled alternative that is valuable in its own right. If we value not just the final decision rules in a democracy, but the deliberative process by which we reach decisions, then weak-form review is a promising method of human rights protection—one which supports human rights protection against majorities yet invites representative institutions to engage in principled deliberation on what rights require.

[28] Günther (n 6) 7. [29] Sunstein (n 5) 37–8. [30] Sunstein (n 5) 36.

[31] In fact, Sunstein has argued elsewhere that clear statement rules, identified as a type of weak-form review in Chapter 1, support political deliberation on fundamental rights by requiring full democratic debate by the legislature before allowing rights to be put at risk: C Sunstein, 'Non-Delegation Canons' (2000) 67 University of Chicago Law Review 315.

In some quarters, the literature on court-legislature interaction has begun moving towards this principled alternative by drawing attention to the fact that legislatures have generally performed poorly in demanding reasons from the executive with respect to action that could implicate rights and evaluating those reasons carefully.[32] A deliberative approach to democracy theoretically grounds the desire for reasoned justification and considered legislation by not endorsing action which the government of the day simply believes to be popular, expedient, or politically savvy to be authentically democratic. Section 3.B.3 considers what adopting this theoretical approach means in terms of examining the practical operation of the legislative process.

3.B.3. Examining legislative deliberation: a further dimension to institutional interaction

Thinking about institutional dialogue over human rights as a deliberative democrat has two concrete implications. First, it directs us to look beyond the mere fact of a legislative reply, and the formal assent of Parliament by majority vote, to the processes that lead to that legislation. Second, since legislatures' treatment of fundamental rights has only recently attracted the interest of constitutional scholars, there is little by way of existing standards by which to evaluate legislative behaviour. Deliberative democracy furnishes a normative ideal against which democratic institutions can be evaluated.[33] Sunstein clarifies that:

> [The] belief in deliberation is aspirational and critical rather than celebratory and descriptive. It is a basis for evaluating political practices. Modern republicans do not claim that existing systems actually embody republican deliberation. The republican commitments may reveal that actual deliberation, and purportedly deliberative processes, are badly distorted.[34]

However, the challenge of assessing the practice of real-world institutions is that any normative standard must not be pitched entirely beyond what is reasonably achievable. If the criteria of analysis in this book were developed on the basis of, say, an ideal speech situation (where power politics are removed), these criteria would not yield much that is useful other than affirmation that real-world legislatures fail to operate as ideal deliberative spaces. In *The Idea of Justice*, Amartya Sen contrasts the

[32] Janet Hiebert, for example, has been careful to draw a distinction between executive decision-making on what the Charter requires, and parliamentary evaluation of human rights in her empirical work: J Hiebert, *Charter Conflicts: What is Parliament's Role?* (McGill-Queens University Press, Montreal 2002). David Dyzenhaus has developed the concept of the culture of justification, and has called for greater attention to the failure of legislatures to demand reasons from executives: D Dyzenhaus, 'Are Legislatures Good at Morality? Or Better at it than the Courts?' (2009) 7 ICON 46; D Dyzenhaus, 'Aspiring to the Rule of Law' in T Campbell, J Goldsworthy, and A Stone (eds), *Protecting Human Rights: Instruments and Institutions* (OUP, Oxford 2003) 209.

[33] Above we discussed the normative standard, or 'rosy picture' that Jeremy Waldron develops for legal philosophy. Here, Waldron's standard is challenged by an alternative view that does not share his purpose of justifying the formal structures of majority vote and representative democracy.

[34] Sunstein, 'Beyond the Republican Revival' (n 13) 1549.

pursuit of 'perfectly just institutions' to normative scholarship directed to 'advancing justice' in a realizable way, from where we are now.[35] Similarly, we can contrast the task of theorizing about ideal deliberation to the inquiry appropriate to advancing deliberative outcomes in existing societies, or in our case, legislatures. Hence, our standards of analysis need to be not only normatively grounded, but also realistic. Being realistic does not mean a passive acceptance of the status quo,[36] or limiting the continual striving towards greater democratization. Rather, it begins with a recognition of the need to build a bridge between current institutions and institutional aspirations; a need to devise tangible and realizable first steps towards a more deliberative democracy.

Below are the elements which guide the evaluation of legislative deliberation in this book, tailored to the context of political responses to court rulings on fundamental rights. The central thread to them is the idea of public reflectiveness on the implications of law and policy and reason-giving for incursions into fundamental rights. They draw from the work of Guttman and Thompson,[37] Sunstein,[38] and John Uhr[39] in distilling the main features of deliberation in official state institutions, and legislatures specifically.

These elements of deliberation focus the examination of legislative responses to DOIs in Part III. They are not in the nature of a checklist to be 'met' or 'not met'.[40] Rather, they direct attention along certain practical dimensions of the legislative process. These are:

1. *Time*. The most basic element of good deliberation in legislatures is time to consider legislative proposals.[41] This includes the actual time for debate and notice given of any legislation proposed. This may be the first hurdle facing good deliberation in the legislature, particularly if control of the legislative agenda and timetabling are in the hands of party leaders.

2. *Public justification*. Second is the demand for public justification of legislative conduct. This is elsewhere described as the requirement of publicity.[42] There are three things required here. Deliberation should be conducted publicly, prior to legislative choices being made. Justifications given for conduct (and challenges made) need to be public-regarding not self-interested.[43] (The requirement of publicity is a partial safeguard against self-interested reasons because legislators are unlikely to openly rely on such reasons.) Finally, the information required to evaluate justifications should be made public.[44]

3. *Diversity of views*. In order for legislative deliberation to be meaningful, there must be a diversity in the pool of viewpoints or arguments that enter the deliberative assembly.[45] The DOI is itself a viewpoint from an alternative forum (the courts), and has the potential to work against self-insulation in the legislature

35 A Sen, *The Idea of Justice* (Penguin, London 2010) 8–10.
36 This is also noted by Uhr (n 14) xiv.
37 Guttman and Thompson (n 5).
38 Sunstein (n 5).
39 Uhr (n 14).
40 Uhr (n 14) 221.
41 Uhr (n 14) 223–4.
42 Gutmann and Thompson (n 5) 95–127.
43 Gutmann and Thompson refer to this as the requirement of reciprocity: (n 5) 52–94.
44 Gutmann and Thompson (n 5) 95.
45 Sunstein's work (n 5) chapter 1 provides an examination of the importance of diversity in group decision-making situations as well as the dangers of deliberation amongst enclaves of like-minded

(including the blind spots and burdens of inertia discussed in Chapter 2). The question is whether this viewpoint gets the attention of members of the legislature, whether it presents compelling reasons, and whether it functions as a 'door-opener' for those affected by the impugned law. Additionally, we can look to whether representations from constituents and views from civil society groups enter into legislative consideration of what response to take.

4. *The ethical aspect of human rights.* The above are general elements concerning the legislature's performance of its review function. Human rights charters provide for a set of rights possessed by each member of the polity, and when public action impacts upon these prioritized norms, these charters typically provide a framing for the justification of that impact, for instance, that a right to free exercise of religion may be limited in a manner proportionate to a pressing social need.

As discussed above, the position of deliberative democrats is that human rights are not merely concrete regulations for the legal system to uphold, but the core democratic principles providing a structure for principled justification of the exercise of power. This requires that the ethical reasons for the interpretation, limitation, and development of human rights norms be open to deliberation in the legislature, rather than human rights being treated solely as legal conclusions expounded by judges. Section 3.C addresses this element as it applies to legislative deliberation on DOIs in further detail.

5. *Openness to change in viewpoint.* One important consequence of generating realistic standards of analysis is that the above criteria do not include any requirement for decision-making by consensus. A common misunderstanding amongst critics of deliberative democracy is that such a democracy requires decision-making without recourse to bargaining or voting.[46] Yet those deliberative democracy theorists who direct their attention to institutions of official decision-making, such as Guttman and Thompson, and Uhr, openly recognize that even after deliberation there may be enduring disagreement, and that bargaining and voting are appropriate to resolve that disagreement.[47]

But this does not mean that deliberation is 'mere talk'. The final criterion of deliberation is openness amongst participants to the possibility of changing their viewpoints.[48] In an ideal deliberative forum of equals, this would refer to the openness of each participant to change their mind. However, in the case study

people. Though not a deliberative democrat, Waldron emphasizes the importance that proposals face dissent and a wide range of voices are heard: J Waldron, 'Legislating with Integrity' (2003) 72 *Fordham Law Review* 373, 383–4. See also Uhr (n 14) 226–7.

[46] Pildes, in surveying major criticisms of deliberative democratic theory, notes that much criticism has been misplaced in this way: Pildes (n 1).

[47] Gutmann and Thompson (n 5) 71; Uhr (n 14) 12–13. Feminist theorists sympathetic to deliberative democracy have argued against consensus even as an ideal goal, stressing the importance that a deliberative democracy is not universalist and accepts difference: see especially IM Young, 'Communication and the Other: Beyond Deliberative Democracy' in S Benhabib (ed), *Democracy and Difference* (Princeton University Press, Princeton 1996).

[48] T Risse, 'International Norms and Domestic Change: Arguing and Communicative Behavior in the Human Rights Arena' (1999) 27 Politics & Society 529.

context of a partisan parliament in the Westminster system, this criterion needs to be tailored. The effectiveness of legislative review generally relies on the extent to which the responsible Minister is open to making or accepting amendments in light of parliamentarians' concerns.

The above is a reasonable set of standards by which to assess legislative engagement in response to DOIs. This provides an additional level of inquiry in the analysis of court–legislature interaction, going beyond aggregative notions of the democratic process to include how the exercise of power is considered and justified, and the way in which viewpoints from the courts enter and challenge official processes of decision-making.

Yet, opponents may still argue that this type of evaluative framework is too idealistic. Even deliberative democrats have been sceptical about the capacity for deliberation within official political structures of decision-making. There are two further responses to such criticism. First, even if it may be unworkable to expect careful and deliberate law-making across *all* matters of government, we are concerned here with that subset of laws which affect fundamental pre-commitments—the basic conditions of a just society—and have been officially brought to the attention of the legislature on these grounds.[49] Human rights are prioritized ethical claims that give rise to the obligation of careful and deliberate public action,[50] and would not be expected to be a major issue for the majority of laws and regulations before the legislature in a liberal democratic state.[51] Second, ultimately, criticism that deliberative democracy is too idealistic only supports the need to explore and test these ideas through real-world research.[52] Insofar as seemingly promising institutional design fails to bring about better deliberation, this may teach us where we should focus our energy if we are to better support deliberation over the long term.

3.C. Instability and Compliance-Oriented Rights Review

I have already identified that a major challenge to independent deliberation in the legislature on human rights is executive dominance over the legislative process and the concomitant limitation of involvement by members of the legislature to voting on party lines. We ought to consider a second possible challenge to legislative deliberation on rights in the aftermath of a judicial decision, namely, *judicial* dominance. It has been suggested that, instead of promoting reflectiveness on

[49] See discussion in Introduction, section A.

[50] For instance, Amartya Sen has stated that 'the induced obligations (from human rights) primarily involve the duty to give reasonable consideration to the reasons for action and their practical implications': A Sen, 'Elements of a Theory of Human Rights' (2004) 32 Philosophy & Public Affairs 315, 319.

[51] The fact that only a minority of laws give rise to substantial human rights questions is illustrated by the sifting exercise and reporting rates of the parliamentary JCHR in the UK. See JCHR, *Twenty-Third Report 2005–06*, HL Paper 239, HC 1575 (4 August 2006) Appendix 1, Table 2.

[52] For an account of the two-way relationship between normative and empirical scholarship, in the context of deliberative democracy, see C Zurn, *Deliberative Democracy and the Institutions of Judicial Review* (CUP, New York 2006) 8–9.

rights, judicial review may have the perverse effect of limiting and distorting political debate.

This section considers the claim that judicial opinions on rights will overpower alternative understandings of rights, even if they are not formally supreme. The concern of one set of critics of weak-form review is that formal limitations on judicial power will not necessarily prevent judicial dominance because human rights discourse privileges judges' viewpoints in political debate. The fear is that consideration of rights in the legislature will not be deliberation on what legislators think is the correct, or most legitimate, course of action in terms of human rights and other values. Rather, legislative rights review will mimic judicial rights review, concerned primarily with legality and seeking to anticipate future judicial review.

These suggestions give rise to three concrete questions. First, to what extent is this challenge different from an objection to judicial input at all, that is, rejecting the very premiss of weak-form review? Second, what is suggested to drive the dominance of judges even in a system where judicial powers are weaker? Third, what type of criteria would indicate compliance-oriented legislative rights review, if we are to assess this challenge to deliberation in a given case study?

3.C.1. A methodological debate or disappointed absolutism?

It is useful to begin with a methodological debate in the new dialogue literature that illustrates the seeds of the debate regarding judicial influence over the exercise of legislative power. In Hogg and Bushell's account of dialogue, all legislative replies signified participation in dialogue, for two reasons. First, their idea of dialogue was concerned with the *structure* of the Canadian Charter in sections 1 and 33 and this ensured that every decision to comply with a judicial decision was a *choice* on the part of Parliament (at least where it related to a right that was open to legislative override). Second, Hogg and Bushell considered that dialogue would sometimes result in inter-branch agreement, and straightforward compliance signified such agreement. By contrast, critics argued that legislative sequels must constitute some positive exercise of judgment other than simple compliance to constitute genuine dialogue.[53] On the first point, critics were less concerned with structural or formal power and more with effective power.[54] On the second point, critics argued that compliance often did *not* signify agreement on the part of democratic representatives. Instead, compliance resulted because, it was claimed, the existence of an adverse judicial decision changes the landscape of politics on the issue and makes it very difficult for a legislature to gather the necessary votes for change[55] or because of a lack of public acceptance of the legitimacy of the override provision.[56]

[53] C Manfredi and JB Kelly, 'Six Degrees of Dialogue: A Response to Hogg and Bushell' (1999) 37 Osgoode Hall LJ 513, 520.

[54] See Chapter 2 n 26 and accompanying text.

[55] FL Morton, 'Dialogue or Monologue' [1999] (April) Policy Options 23, 25–6.

[56] C Manfredi, 'The Unfulfilled Promise of Dialogic Constitutionalism' in T Campbell, J Goldsworthy, and A Stone (eds), *Protecting Rights without a Bill of Rights: Institutional Performance and Reform in Australia* (Ashgate, Aldershot 2006) 249–51.

While this was presented as a methodological challenge to empirical claims of dialogue, in fact, these arguments trigger a deeper debate about judicial influence. Roach argues in response to critics that, ultimately, Canadian state and federal governments can enact legislation if they want to, as a result of the Cabinet-dominated legislative system. If they decide not to due to a lack of public support—because the public trusts the judgment of the courts—then it is the electorate's right to trust the courts.[57] Similarly, Jeffrey Goldsworthy argues, with reference to the UK, that in instances where it is not politically feasible to ignore a DOI, this does not mean that judges have overridden the democratic process; rather, 'the democratic process will determine what's politically feasible'.[58] But this is precisely the objection from critics: that the electorate will end up trusting the courts rather than deciding these issues through political fora, even where these are issues characterized by reasonable disagreement.

Part of this debate about judicial influence is disagreement over the very project of weak-form judicial review. One may believe that judges have nothing unique to contribute to political debates over rights.[59] (Indeed, one may not even believe in human rights as useful political principles.[60]) If so, *any* judicial influence over political debates on rights is a distortion. Hence, part of the objection from Manfredi, Morton, and others can be explained as secondary criticism, stemming from initial disagreement over involving the courts at all. For the purposes of this chapter, this can be set aside; I have already argued in 3.B that some judicial protection for rights is beneficial in a *deliberative* democracy. Judicial review subjects State power to the demands of justification, and provides an alternative entry point for individuals and groups to engage with the State. In reaching their conclusions, judges are able to contribute information and public reasons for the conformity or nonconformity of State action with a set of fundamental principles, and can thereby advance the ongoing iteration over the meaning of human rights across all institutions of society.

However, another strand of the judicial dominance objection is concern over the quality of political debate, and the possible perverse effect of legalizing human rights. If we are concerned to promote deliberation, then this type of objection deserves attention. Critics who raise the prospect of judicial dominance in debates over rights require us to clarify what role we want judicial opinions to play in legislative deliberation. We ought to be alert to the possibility that legislative rights review

[57] K Roach, 'Dialogic Judicial Review and its Critics' (2004) 23 Supreme Court Law Review 49, 90–1.

[58] J Goldsworthy, 'Judicial Review, Legislative Override and Democracy' in T Campbell, J Goldsworthy, and A Stone (eds), *Protecting Human Rights: Instruments and Institutions* (OUP, Oxford 2003) 268.

[59] J Waldron, 'Judges as Moral Reasoners' (2009) 7 ICON 2; T Campbell, 'Incorporation through Interpretation' in T Campbell, K Ewing, and A Tomkins (eds), *Sceptical Essays on Human Rights* (OUP, Oxford 2001) 99–102, 88–92.

[60] The classic example being Bentham's utilitarian claim that the purpose of State action was to promote the greatest good for the greatest number of people, and fundamental rights were 'nonsense upon stilts'. See Dworkin's discussion in R Dworkin, *Taking Rights Seriously* (Harvard University Press, Cambridge MA 1978) (introduction).

may amount to applying past judicial decisions and predicting future legal decisions by courts. Is this a satisfactory form of deliberation in the aftermath of a DOI?

This type of legislative rights review can have its benefits. For one, if judicial decisions are strongly influential, then this suggests that we can have a working mechanism of judicial review, where the legislature devises new legislation that complies with judicial decisions, while retaining the formal supremacy of democratic institutions, that is symbolically valuable and may function as a safety valve in deeply controversial cases. Second, a legislative process oriented towards compliance with judicial standards has the benefit of preventing human rights violations from occurring in the first place, rather than being addressed retrospectively, on a case-by-case basis. The majority of legislation will not be subject to judicial review, so legislative rights review can expand the reach of human rights law to all measures passed by the legislature.[61]

However, if judicial decisions are influential based on judicial authority alone, this may compromise democratic deliberation. It may divert the concern of deliberation away from the quality of reasons offered, and what is the best or most legitimate course of action, to simply what the existing law dictates; stifling debates over competing conceptions of the good.[62] Judicial dominance over political understandings of rights may also compromise our ability to draw on the posited institutional strengths of the legislature as a deliberative forum: its internal diversity; its lay character; and its ability to engage in debates on the merits, to draw from broad sources of information, and to deal with polycentric issues. Legislatures are not institutions designed to determine legal questions, but rather institutions designed to be able to make broader decisions on behalf of the polity. So, for instance, under the specialization model, the use of open remedies is supported on the grounds of enlisting the legislature in deciding how best to respond to a judicial decision, but if legislative deliberation is dominated by concerns about legality and future judicial opinions, then the open remedial approach may fail to draw much benefit from involving the legislature.

Second, judicial dominance may compromise human rights themselves, as they are reduced to their minimum content, as elaborated by judges. While human rights discourse has been considered to have the capacity to promote deliberation, for example by providing door openers for excluded groups, even human rights advocates have been concerned that once these rights are given concrete legal form, they may become 'petrified', and lose their transformative potential.[63] An example might be where the right to health under a bill of rights is given an enforceable minimum content by courts, but judicial decisions on this minimum content are

[61] JL Hiebert, 'Interpreting a Bill of Rights: The Importance of Legislative Rights Review' (2005) 35 British Journal of Political Science 235, 243.

[62] M Koskenniemi, 'The Effect of Rights on Political Culture' in P Alston (ed), *The EU and Human Rights* (OUP, New York 1999) 99, 102–3. A similar concern is that political debates will become 'subsumed' or 'hijacked' by debates over constitutional rights that are couched in jargon and inaccessible to most people: Goldsworthy (n 58) 271.

[63] K Günther, 'The Legacies of Injustice and Fear: A European Approach to Human Rights and their Effect on Political Culture' in P Alston (ed), *The EU and Human Rights* (OUP, New York 1999) 142–3; Koskenniemi (n 62) 99, 110, 114.

then used within political debate as barriers to further, more expansive claims of what the right to health requires. Moreover, enumerated rights may be limited, and hence some rights (typically civil and political rights) may overpower other rights which are not included in the human rights instrument.[64]

So even if we believe that judges can contribute something valuable to debates about rights, the goal of engaging the legislature in the protection of human rights is not simply to use the legislature as a forum to apply and anticipate judicial opinions on what human rights require and judicial elaborations of how rights can be protected and advanced. However, the possibilities of judicial dominance above are speculation, and we may be sceptical of them: is it plausible that judicial decisions on rights will come to dominate legislative deliberation in this way?

3.C.2. The drivers of 'judicialized' rights review

The argument that legislative consideration of rights generally amounts to an exercise in predicting judicial decisions has been supported by empirical examination of how legislatures approach constitutional issues in systems with strong-form review. Alec Stone-Sweet's theory of the judicialization of politics is the major exposition of the idea that regular use of a third party, such as courts, to decide on norms governing a society mutates relations between political actors.[65] There are two principal mechanisms at work. First, the censure and disruption caused by an adverse judgment leads legislators, in the interests of policy stability, to anticipate judicial decisions. Second, political actors—particularly opposition parties—strategically employ arguments concerning legality in the political process, driving the absorption of legal norms into political discourse. The introduction of judicial review of legislation therefore encourages self-limitation amongst legislators to comply with legal standards, and alters the nature of debate to focus on legal compatibility of controversial legislation.[66]

However, the applicability of Stone-Sweet's theory to systems of weak-form review can be questioned. The theory was developed in the context of abstract constitutional review in France and Germany, which allowed opposition parties to counter government proposals through constitutional challenge. This is not possible in a system of concrete constitutional review. The impetus provided by risk aversion and a desire for policy stability do remain in the context of concrete constitutional review. For instance, studies of the United States Congress also support the idea that where legislatures engage in debate over constitutionality, these debates are oriented towards anticipating judicial review and dominated by lawyers.[67] However, if we are interested

[64] S Fredman, *Human Rights Transformed: Positive Rights and Positive Duties* (OUP, Oxford 2008) 96–8 discusses how privileging duties of restraint may undermine the fulfilment of positive duties.

[65] A Stone-Sweet, 'Judicialisation and the Construction of Governance' (1999) 31 Comparative Political Studies 147.

[66] M Shapiro and A Stone-Sweet, *On Law, Politics and Judicialization* (OUP, Oxford 2002) chapters 1 and 3.

[67] See K Whittington, N Devins, and H Hicken, 'The Constitution and Congressional Committees: 1971–2000' in RW Bauman and T Kahana (eds), *The Least Examined Branch: Legislatures in the*

in the case of DOIs, they do not disrupt policy stability. Judges do not have the final word and judicial decisions can be avoided. Why would this structure of review give rise to debates overly concerned with future compliance before a court?

The same desire for risk aversion may emerge in a weak-form system of review if, as a matter of political reality, judicial decisions do have to be complied with. Mark Tushnet has advanced the hypothesis that weak-form review is 'unstable': that formal mechanisms that preserve parliamentary sovereignty may not be significant in practice, and hence weak-form systems will come to replicate the behaviour of strong-form systems.[68] The principal empirical support for his thesis is the failure of the legislative override in Canada to be a viable option for legislatures. However, rather than advance *generalizable* reasons why the structure of weak-form review is unstable, Tushnet's argument is based on a series of political factors particular to Canada that rendered section 33 deeply unpopular.[69]

Others have suggested that a country's political culture may be such that human rights are treated as matters over which judges are the authoritative interpreters, not matters for political consideration (again citing Canada as an example).[70] Hence, it could be that the dominant discourse about rights—the implicit understandings in the language of rights—privileges judges, and directs people to look to courts for determinate answers. Another possible speculation has been that the phenomenon of reliance on judicial decisions may have less to do with active trust in courts and more to do with *distrust* in representative politics and structures for political decision-making.[71]

We should also consider the role that judicial behaviour may play in supporting rich debate on the requirements of human rights or, alternatively, minimalism and a technical legal debate. If judges choose to publish 'black letter' judgments focused on precedent and statutory interpretation without also including broadly accessible discussion for why the state of the law is or is not compatible with human rights, then they may not provide a set of reasons that are helpful or convincing in broader political debate. If judges are highly deferential, and refrain from rigorous evaluation of human rights compatibility, then they may become partners in a minimalist approach to human rights across all institutions.

Overall, however, the research is in need of more careful analysis of the idea of judicial dominance over political debate. Ultimately, this is an empirical question, and needs to be explored by actual reference to political deliberation if we are to move beyond speculation and assertions about the power that judges wield over

Constitutional State (CUP, Cambridge 2006), which also surveys other major studies in addition to the authors' own.

[68] M Tushnet, 'New Forms of Judicial Review and the Persistence of Rights- and Democracy-Based Worries' (2003) 38 Wake Forest Law Review 813.

[69] M Tushnet, *Weak Courts, Strong Rights* (Princeton University Press, Princeton 2008) 57–8.

[70] G Webber, 'The Unfulfilled Potential of the Court and Legislature Dialogue' (2009) 42 Canadian Journal of Political Science 443, 461 (referring to political culture); Roach, 'Dialogic Judicial Review and its Critics' (n 57) 97 (referring to popular understandings of rights and court rulings).

[71] P Russell, 'The Charter and Canadian Democracy' in JB Kelly and C Manfredi (eds), *Contested Constitutionalism* (UBC Press, Vancouver 2009) 294; Goldsworthy (n 58) 274.

human rights discourse. In particular, the existing scholarship has not considered the potential interplay between legal and non-legal uses of human rights-based arguments. We should be careful not to assume that 'political culture' is a monolithic entity that treats human rights or judicial decisions in only one way. This brings us to the third and final question: if we are to empirically evaluate the question of judicial dominance over political debate, how is this to be done?

3.C.3. Assessing compliance-oriented review

On the basis of what was identified as judicial *dominance* (and not simply judicial influence) in 3.C.1, the following features of legislative deliberation indicate what can be referred to as *compliance-oriented* review. First, human rights are treated by members of the legislature as external limits on the exercise of legislative power, the content of which is ultimately determined by courts. Second, political debate is directed towards compliance with human rights law and seeks to anticipate future judicial review.

That said, we are ultimately concerned with the possible effect of debates about legality *overwhelming* debates about legitimacy, and human rights-based motivations being *reduced* to the minimum needed to comply with judicial decisions. We must not assume that taking judicial opinions seriously and making an independent judgment are mutually exclusive. We should be alert to two further possibilities when judicial opinions are employed in debate, which are indicia of *judicial influence*, not judicial dominance. First, members of the legislature may agree with judicial reasons and conclusions on the merits, and advance judicial opinions to add support to their argument on the best thing to do. This may be indicated by the use of both arguments on the law and arguments on the merits to support the same position. Second, members of the legislature may treat judicial opinions as authoritative findings on a basic minimum of rights protection, rather than an exhaustive statement of what rights require. This is more difficult to assess, but may be indicated by members of the legislature making ethical arguments about rights which go beyond the requirements laid forth by courts.

The criteria above are not suggested to be watertight tests for analysis of debates. Rather they are questions around which to orient qualitative analysis of deliberation in the legislature. Ultimately, case studies of legislative debate deliver impressions of how judicial standards are employed and how they are appreciated, as conveyed in the language of debate.[72]

Furthermore, when examining political deliberation in the context of the HRA it is important to be alert to the significance of the ECHR and the ECtHR. The idea that the rights in the HRA are ultimately a matter for judicial interpretation may be

[72] Goldsworthy (n 58), who advances a theoretical argument on judicial dominance (what he refers to as the 'consequentialist objection to judicial review'), but recognizes that evaluating whether this occurs in practice will necessarily '[depend] on sociological evidence that is inevitably impressionistic' (at 274).

strengthened by the belief that, in Europe, it is ultimately for the ECtHR to decide what human rights require. It is to this feature of the Act that we now turn.

3.D. The International Legal Dimension

Legal scholarship on institutional roles in relation to fundamental rights ordinarily refers to constitutional rights rather than international human rights. These are matters of municipal law and scholars in this field are ordinarily constitutional lawyers or comparative constitutional lawyers. Comparative constitutional scholars were quick to claim the HRA as a new hybrid bill of rights. However, it is also an instrument delicately woven around international human rights law.

In a dualist national legal system, municipal and international law are two separate legal orders: questions of what the law requires within the municipal system are distinct from questions of what international law requires of the State. In practice, this division is not a strict one. In some dualist legal systems, reference is had to unincorporated international law in certain circumstances.[73] In the UK, prior to the enactment of the HRA, rights under the ECHR could be cited as a guide to statutory interpretation and within administrative law.[74] However, as a formal matter, international legal obligations must be incorporated into the domestic legal order to be applied in domestic courts.[75]

It has been suggested that to see the HRA as providing for dialogue between the different branches of national government is to 'misconstrue the HRA and the position of national authorities under the [European Human Rights] Convention'.[76] It has been further suggested that the HRA should be understood as a statute implementing international treaty obligations rather than a bill of rights.[77] This argument is supported by the fact that the HRA was introduced by the government at the time as incorporating the ECHR and ensuring that British people did not need to go to Strasbourg to make a human rights complaint.[78]

Clearly, the international legal dimension of the HRA has implications for court–legislature interaction and the possibilities for legislative engagement. The

[73] Y Shany, 'How Supreme is the Supreme Law of the Land?' (2006) 31 Brook Journal of International Law 341.

[74] See M Hunt, *Using Human Rights Law in English Courts* (Hart, Oxford 1997).

[75] For discussion see H Steiner, P Alston, and R Goodman, *International Human Rights Law in Context* (3rd edn OUP, Oxford 2007) 1096–7.

[76] R Masterman, 'Interpretations, Declarations and Dialogue: Rights Protection under the Human Rights Act and Victorian Charter of Human Rights and Responsibilities' [2009] PL 112.

[77] C Warbick, 'The European Convention on Human Rights and the Human Rights Act: A View from the Outside' in H Fenwick, R Masterman, and G Phillipson (eds), *Judicial Reasoning under the Human Rights Act* (CUP, Cambridge 2007) 25–6.

[78] GB Home Office, *Rights Brought Home: The Human Rights Bill* (Cm 3782, 1997) [1.14]–[1.19]. However, the position of one of the main architects of the Act, Lord Irvine, has been that the Act was intended for the UK courts to develop a national set of human rights, respectful of the ECHR institutions but not designed merely to apply international legal standards domestically: Lord Irvine of Lairg, 'A British Interpretation of Convention Rights' (Lecture at University College of London Judicial Institute, 14 December 2011).

existence of international human rights obligations does not preclude a role for domestic legislatures in evaluations of the meaning or application of rights. We should not assume that the existence of the ECtHR necessarily makes the HRA effectively a court-centred system in which judicial interpretations are supreme. However, the interplay between these two bodies of law is nonetheless a relevant factor in the operation of DOIs. The ECHR dimension of the HRA may support the specialization model of interaction, as well as affect the nature of political debate on human rights.

3.D.1. The relationship between municipal and international human rights

It is useful to begin by considering what implications international human rights law has for national systems in general before considering the specific case of the ECHR. Does international human rights law furnish correct answers to questions on what human rights require? Certainly, the international human rights architecture provides a general, *minimum* standard of rights, to which all states are held. However, the universalist underpinnings of the post-Second World War human rights regime result in human rights being employed against all types of States: States with vastly different systems of government and circumstances of development and social cohesion (or lack thereof). It can hardly be expected that the scope and content of these rights as protected by law and practice can be consistent across such a range of contexts, just as it cannot be expected that rights will maintain the same meaning over time. Countries may also differ in the way in which different rights are balanced against each other. A State might decide that certain rights are especially important, or conversely cannot be protected, in its system of government and may make reservations and derogations accordingly.

Ultimately, international human rights law provides a number of basic principles but the adjudication of those standards by international tribunals does not remove the need for precision of those standards in national law.[79] In some cases, there will be a clear answer furnished by international law, but not usually in cases that turn on distinct matters of national law and practice. The cases where international human rights law will fail to provide clear answers are the more fraught questions in human rights law: clashing rights cases, the ambit of positive State duties, the nature of equality rights, and proportionate limitation of rights in light of public policy goals. Here States are left considerable latitude, and this provides space for dialogue between national courts, legislatures, and civil society. The international system of human rights protection is best understood as a *pluralist* system in which

[79] For a detailed analysis of the relationship between national and international institutional arrangements, see GL Neuman, 'Human Rights and Constitutional Rights: Harmony and Dissonance' (2003) 55 Stanford Law Review 1863. For the argument specifically in relation to the ECtHR, see S Grosz, J Beatson, and P Duffy, *Human Rights: The 1998 Act and the European Convention* (1st edn Sweet & Maxwell, London 2000) 2.01–2.08.

multiple institutions—national, regional, and international—engage in the task of interpreting, protecting, and advancing human rights.

The Strasbourg system in fact provides a good illustration of this argument, albeit on a smaller scale.[80] Chapter 5 will argue that the ECtHR is properly understood as a subsidiary system of human rights protection to national systems. The ECtHR has developed specific doctrinal devices to deal with issues of diversity, most notably, the 'margin of appreciation' doctrine that allows for a degree of variation amongst different States on the grounds of national conditions. The ECHR institutions also operate in the face of considerable practical limitations and without the executory powers of national courts.

Once we recognize that there is room for deliberation in a national context in specifying the content of human rights, there is no automatic reason why this exercise needs to be undertaken solely by judges. Certainly, it is not a requirement of international human rights law that human rights must be protected through judicial elaboration of what rights require.[81] Hence, the path is open, in principle, to have multiple institutions responsible for protecting rights and participating in the precision of international human rights guarantees into specific legislative and policy contexts.

But even if the international human rights system is *permissive* of a degree of national variation, and hence does not preclude national elaboration of what human rights require, this does not mean that a given State will engage in this further elaboration. Instead concerns about human rights may be focused on only achieving the basic minimum required for international legal compliance. If so, the scope for political deliberation on rights may be much reduced.

3.D.2. The challenge of an international legal compliance approach

Prior to the introduction of the HRA, Andrew Clapham raised a possible pitfall in developing a Bill of Rights 'cloned from one or more international instruments', with specific reference to the ECHR.[82] He argued that the judges of the ECtHR treated these rights as progressive standards, and looked to a European consensus when developing what the ECHR rights require. However, there was a danger that these minimums would be used as evidence of the content of the rights at stake; whereas national authorities ought to give rights *maximum* protection at the national level. He concluded that, were the UK to develop a human rights instrument based on the ECHR:

80 See N Krisch, 'The Open Architecture of European Human Rights Law' (2008) 71 Modern Law Review 183.

81 Victims need to be provided with an effective remedy under international and regional human rights instruments, but this need not to be a judicial remedy. See D Harris and others, *Law of the European Convention of Human Rights* (2nd edn OUP, Oxford 2009) 557–60.

82 A Clapham, 'The European Convention on Human Rights in the British Court: Problems Associated with the Incorporation of International Human Rights' in P Alston (ed), *Promoting Human Rights through Bills of Rights: Comparative Perspectives* (OUP, New York 1999) 147.

> [T]here ought to be institutional possibilities to ensure that the human rights debate remains a lively national one. If human rights dilemmas are easily exported to far-away international tribunals one loses the chance to make Governments accountable and have a real democratic debate in society.[83]

In an afterword, examining how the HRA had in fact incorporated international human rights, Clapham was approving of the design of the DOI and the treatment of Strasbourg jurisprudence, noting that it 'neatly avoids any impression that national and international decisions have a different hierarchical status'.[84]

However, the structure of the Act does not necessarily guard against the prospect that, in practice, the Act is viewed by the various branches of government as an instrument to ensure that national laws comply with Strasbourg jurisprudence and to avoid adverse judgments from the ECtHR in the future, *and no more*. The international legal dimension of the Act has the potential to propel the UK towards a particular version of the specialization model of dialogue, where DOIs are treated as mandating action, not because of the moral force and perceived wisdom of judicial decisions but because of the fact, or perception, that judges are simply declaring what is required as a matter of international law. This can be considered a variant on the specialization model, where the DOI is effectively an alert of an international law violation. This would not preclude a role for the political branches, but the relevant space for decision-making would be how to respond, or whether to delay and await a definitive decision—and formally binding obligation to change the law—from Strasbourg.

Moreover, in relation to legislative deliberation, this international dimension of the Act may support an approach to human rights as a technical legal evaluation based on the minimum standards of ECHR compliance. (That is, a variant on the judicial dominance concern, except with the relevant judges being not only, or even principally, national judges.) This opens up a further dimension for examination in the case of DOIs: how have the different branches of government approached the international dimension of the Act in practice? It is important to consider this factor particularly in the courts (which I do in Chapter 5), because judicial appreciations of what human rights compatibility means set the stage for institutional interaction over DOIs.

3.E. A Framework for the Examination of Declarations of Incompatibility

Part I has provided a framework for the analysis and critique of the operation of DOIs in the UK. Chapters 2 and 3 have explored what role the legislature might play under a system of open remedies, which invite the legislature to respond after a judicial finding of a human rights violation. Chapter 2 developed two models of court–legislature interaction over DOIs, drawing from debates in the new dialogue

[83] Clapham (n 82) 147. [84] Clapham (n 82) 151.

scholarship. This chapter has argued that it is important to look beyond the existing notions of dialogue to the engagement of the legislature in responsive action. Deliberative democracy furnishes an aspiration for how we treat human rights and conduct democratic decision-making, and we ought to consider whether the innovations of weak-form judicial review help to drive the legislature towards this aspiration.

This adds an additional dimension to the analysis in this book: do we see reflective deliberation occur on the response to DOIs, whether the objective of that deliberation is to devise remedial action, or to review the correctness of the judicial decision? At one extreme, the response to a judicial declaration may be devised by the executive with no more than the formal assent of the legislature. Or we may see relatively good political deliberation within the legislature on the response to be taken. A further alternative form of legislative rights review is not deliberative in the sense understood by deliberative democrats, but rather is oriented towards compliance with judicial standards of human rights. The current state of the scholarship invites empirically grounded, case-study work to shed light on these possibilities in a given context. This is the task of Parts II and III.

PART II

DECLARATIONS OF INCOMPATIBILITY IN THE COURTS

4

The Criteria for a Declaration of Incompatibility

4.A. Introduction

In Chapter 1 we saw that amongst a range of open remedies, DOIs are the weakest in formal legal status. They are a non-coercive form of legislative remand. The differences in the design of the HRA compared to traditional bills of rights have, as we saw in Chapter 2, led to an expectation that DOIs are different from coercive or mandatory remedies, more akin to judicial advice that the law infringes human rights, leaving the other branches to decide whether they agree. Part II of this book (Chapters 4 and 5) addresses the question of how the UK courts have used the innovative, non-coercive, declaratory power given to them by the HRA. Have they been willing to use it, and what rules have they developed to guide its use?

Any consideration of the judicial use of DOIs must be accompanied by consideration of sections 2 and 3 HRA. Sections 2–4 provide the foundation for the HRA's complex form of judicial review of primary legislation.[1] It is a form of judicial review that provides courts with *two* avenues for dealing with legislation which, read literally, could violate human rights. It also connects the judicial elaboration of protected human rights to a body of international human rights law. Both these dimensions have implications for the division of labour between courts and legislatures under the HRA.

This chapter examines how, and to what extent, courts have exercised their power to issue a DOI, by examining the criteria that have developed in the jurisprudence. It begins with one possible reading of the HRA's provisions relating to primary legislation (sections 3 and 4), in which the interpretative duty is a clear statement rule—that is, a requirement that incursions into rights be clearly stated in statute—and the DOI is a soft-power replacement for the power to invalidate legislation. This is referred to as a 'clear statement plus' method of human rights protection: a means by which certain norms are given *prioritized* status in a constitutional system, without being given an absolute priority over legislation. Accordingly, the legislature decides to what extent these norms will be protected, against judicial opinion if it so chooses.

However, in practice, the UK courts have developed the interpretative duty not as a clear statement rule but as a power to correct legislation, albeit a *partial* one. The choice between section 3 and section 4 has thus emerged as type of remedial

[1] Hereafter, 'legislation' will be used to mean primary legislation unless stated otherwise.

choice, with the limits of judicial powers of correction forming the basis for the use of a DOI. This chapter examines the limits of section 3, which are the prima facie criteria for issuing a DOI. It also considers whether concerns about providing an effective remedy to the litigant may discourage judicial use of the DOI remedy.

The analysis in this chapter provides the starting point to understanding the operation of DOIs across courts and the legislature. We see that the process of reasoning leading to a DOI shares important parallels with the use of other, more coercive, open remedies. I also suggest that the way in which the use of the DOI has been delineated supports the specialization model of interaction from Chapter 2.

4.B. The Architecture of the HRA

This section examines the legal provisions underpinning review of legislation pursuant to the HRA. It begins with one possible reading of the scheme (a 'clear statement rule plus' reading), which serves as a contrast to how the UK courts have, through the jurisprudence, constructed the process of reasoning where there is a human rights challenge to legislation.[2]

4.B.1. 'Convention rights'

The HRA protects 'Convention rights' and this phrase is defined in section 1(1) to refer to the rights provided in a Schedule to the Act. These rights are Articles 2–12 of the ECHR and Articles 1–3 of the First Protocol to the ECHR, which together constitute a classic catalogue of civil and political rights.

The HRA also refers to the jurisprudence of the ECtHR. Section 2(1) provides that a court, when determining a question in connection with a Convention right must take into account, inter alia, 'any judgment, decision, declaration or advisory opinion of the European Court of Human Rights'. The formula 'take into account' is to be distinguished from the way in which courts are obliged to treat the decision of a higher court within the common law system. The Strasbourg court's decisions are given merely persuasive rather than binding authority, and this lesser status was a deliberate feature of the legislation, explored further in Chapter 5.C.

4.B.2. 'So far as possible' and section 4

Section 3 provides the interpretative duty that guides the Act's system of review of legislation. Courts are under a duty to read and give effect to legislation in a way that is compatible with Convention rights, 'so far as it is possible to do so'.

[2] This book does not examine the HRA system for review of executive action: the Act's innovations of weak-form review relate only to *primary* legislation. If the conduct of a public authority is not expressly authorized by primary legislation, the courts can rule that conduct unlawful and award such relief as they consider 'just and appropriate': HRA s 6 and s 8(1). Likewise, subordinate legislation (not passed by Parliament) that is incompatible with human rights can be invalidated, provided that the empowering primary legislation does not prevent the removal of the incompatibility: HRA s 4(4).

Section 4 provides that if a court is satisfied that a legislative provision is *incompatible* with a Convention right, it may make a declaration of that incompatibility.[3]

The rules governing the exercise of the DOI power are structurally related to the interpretative power under the Act. The House of Lords in *Wilson v First County Trust Ltd (No 2)*[4] clarified that section 4 is not engaged unless the court decides that the relevant provision is not Convention compliant, *despite* the interpretative duty in section 3. Hence, the interpretation of legislation in accordance with section 3 is an essential preliminary step to making a DOI.[5]

The provisions governing DOIs signify the anticipated gravity of the remedy.[6] The power to issue a DOI is restricted to higher courts[7] (including the High Court, Court of Appeal, and Supreme Court) and is a discretionary power. A DOI can only be made after the executive has been given a chance to make arguments to the court. (If a court is considering making a declaration, it must give notice to the Crown and a Minister is entitled to be joined as a party to the proceedings.[8]) Additionally, the making of a DOI triggers a 'fast-track' power for repeal or amendment of impugned legislation, at the discretion of the relevant Minister.[9]

4.B.3. 'Clear statement plus'?

An interpretative provision such as section 3 could operate as a 'clear statement rule'. This would protect human rights against legislative erosion unless the law *clearly and unambiguously* limited rights. The justification for such a clear statement requirement is to ensure that lawmakers advert to the fact that legislation affects fundamental rights, as well as ensuring that any decision to encroach into fundamental rights is made in way that is visible, and is made by the legislature rather than the executive.[10] Cass Sunstein, for instance, argues that a clear statement requirement operates on the idea that where fundamental rights are affected by legislation, democratic deliberation is required, and by requiring clear statements of legislative authority for suspect government conduct, courts can promote that deliberation in the legislature.[11]

[3] HRA s 4(2). This also applies to subordinate legislation made in the exercise of a power conferred by primary legislation, where that primary legislation prevents the removal of that incompatibility: s 4 (3)–(4).

[4] [2003] UKHL 40 [14].

[5] *Wilson* (n 4).

[6] This was also emphasized by the White Paper to the Human Rights Bill: GB Home Office, *Rights Brought Home: The Human Rights Bill* (Cm 3782, 1997) [2.9].

[7] HRA s 4(5).

[8] HRA s 5(1)–(2).

[9] HRA s 10, Schedule 2. This aspect of the Act will be considered in detail in Chapter 6.

[10] An assumption here is that clearly worded incursions on rights will be apparent to the legislature as such and receive meaningful attention in the legislative process. Whether this procedural protection is a *meaningful* safeguard on executive power depends on the actual engagement of members of the legislature, and the public, in scrutiny and deliberation.

[11] His example is the Israeli Supreme Court's means of protecting freedom from torture, not by deciding the questions of whether the conduct of the Israeli secret services was ultimately permissible, but rather holding that it was not for the secret services to decide what were and were not legitimate interrogation techniques; explicit authorization from the Knesset for the impugned techniques was required: CR Sunstein, *Designing Democracy: What Constitutions Do* (OUP, Oxford

A clear statement rule is one way of protecting human rights as prioritized norms in a legal system without giving them the status of *inviolable* legal rules.[12] The principle of legality, which protected human rights in the UK prior to the HRA, is effectively such an approach:

> the principle of legality means that Parliament must squarely confront what it is doing and accept the political cost. Fundamental rights cannot be overridden by general or ambiguous words. This is because there is too great a risk that the full implications of their unqualified meaning may have passed unnoticed in the democratic process.[13]

Were the interpretative duty under the HRA to function as a clear statement rule, what purpose then would a DOI serve? We may expect DOIs to capture the types of cases that do involve a clear legislative statement that violates human rights safeguards and would lead to invalidation of a statute under strong-form review. This was directly implied by the introduction of the DOI power *as an alternative* to the power to invalidate statutes.[14]

This could be described as a 'clear statement plus' form of rights protection. On this reading, the DOI is an additional protection for rights, but a type of 'soft power'. It would signal the judicial opinion that the legislature had violated rights. As commentators and judges have observed, such a judicial statement would be expected to have political significance, but only as a statement of a 'non-legal wrong'.[15] The significance of the declaration would be that the relevant legislation violates a norm that is constitutionally important, but ultimately protected only insofar as the legislature decides it will be. On this understanding, the DOI has been referred to as a non-remedy or effectively an admission of being unable to remedy a violation of rights because primary legislation is clear.[16]

On the wording of the HRA, it was open for sections 3 and 4 to operate in this manner. It has been argued that section 3, on its face, could be seen as merely a statutory endorsement of the principle of legality expounded in *Simms*.[17] However, the 'so far as it is possible to do so' formulation left a wide discretion to judges to

2001) 3–4. See also C Sunstein, 'Beyond the Republican Revival' (1988) 97 Yale Law Journal 1539, 1582–5.

[12] Clear statement rules can be employed to protect different types of norms beyond individual rights, such as federal divisions of power. See WN Eskridge and PP Frickey, 'Quasi-Constitutional Law: Clear Statement Rules as Constitutional Lawmaking' (1992) 45 Vanderbilt Law Review 593.

[13] *R v Secretary of State for the Home Department ex parte Simms* [1999] 3 WLR 328, 341 (Lord Hoffman).

[14] *Rights Brought Home* (n 6) [2.10]–[2.11].

[15] D Feldman, 'The Human Rights Act and Constitutional Principles' (1999) 165 Legal Studies 165, 187.

[16] D Feldman, *English Public Law* (1st edn OUP, Oxford 2004) 979.

[17] G Marshall, 'The Lynchpin of Parliamentary Intention: Lost, Stolen or Strained?' [2003] PL 236, 236–7, who further suggests that it was only the assertions of some Ministers in the debates on the Human Rights Bill that suggested it created a new principle of interpretation. See also I Loveland, *Constitutional Law, Administrative Law and Human Rights: A Critical Introduction* (4th edn OUP, Oxford 2006) chapter 21; cf. T Campbell, 'Incorporation through Interpretation' in T Campbell, K Ewing, and A Tomkins (eds), *Sceptical Essays on Human Rights* (OUP, Oxford 2001) 84, 101.

shape the interpretative duty: a range of other readings of section 3 were also possible. In *Ghaidan v Godin-Mendoza*, it was suggested that, while one tenable reading of 'so far as possible' could be that section 3 was confined to resolving ambiguities,[18] it could be taken to imply 'at least, the broadest powers of interpreting legislation that the courts had exercised before 1998'.[19] Prior to the HRA, UK courts were under an obligation to interpret domestic legislation 'so far as possible' in light of the wording and purpose of European Community Directives.[20] In relation to this duty, the House of Lords had found it 'possible' to read words into legislation designed to give effect to the UK's treaty obligations.[21]

Perhaps unsurprisingly, the limits of the section 3 power of correction, and the attendant role of the DOI, proved to be the thorny issue in the early years of the HRA system. By 2004, the approach to these questions became settled as a matter of judicial doctrine; and it became apparent that section 3 was *not* a clear statement rule. Rather, the choice between section 3 and section 4 was a choice between two remedial paths.

4.B.4. A remedial choice

Early on two principles were established in the case law that made clear that section 3 was not merely a clear statement rule but a partial power to correct legislation. The first principle was that section 3 allowed judges to depart from the clear and unambiguous meaning of statutes. The second was the order of inquiry to be followed by courts when a human rights challenge was made to legislation, which separated the choice between sections 3 and 4 from the merits issue of human rights compatibility.

In *R v A (No 2)*,[22] the first case in which the House of Lords employed section 3, the majority judgment stated that the fact that primary legislation clearly stated a limitation on human rights did not of itself mean that courts could only issue a DOI:

> [T]he interpretative obligation under section 3 . . . is a strong one. It applies even when there is no ambiguity in the language in the sense of the language being capable of two different meanings . . . Parliament specifically rejected the legislative model of requiring reasonable interpretation.[23]

The judgment made clear that the duty went beyond ordinary principles of interpretation, sometimes making it necessary to adopt an interpretation that 'linguistically may appear strained'.[24] Section 3 included the power to read down legislative provisions, as well as reading-in, that is, implying words or clauses into a

[18] [2004] UKHL 30 [28].
[19] *Ghaidan* (n 18) [118].
[20] *Marleasing SA v La Comercial Internacional de Alimentacion SA* (Case C-106/89) [1990] ECR I-4135, 4159 [8].
[21] *Litster v Forth Dry Dock & Engineering Co Ltd* [1990] 1 AC 546, 577.
[22] [2001] UKHL 25.
[23] *R v A (No 2)* (n 22) [44].
[24] *R v A (No 2)* (n 22) [44].

statutory provision. Following *R v A*, in the cases of *R v Offen*,[25] *R v Lambert*,[26] and *Ghaidan v Godin-Mendoza*, the House of Lords reaffirmed this principle. This meant that, where legislation was found to infringe rights, and did so in clear and unambiguous terms, courts now had a choice between judicial rectification (through reading down/in) and returning the matter to the legislature. The 'so far as it is possible to do so' clause in section 3 delimited that remedial choice.

Furthermore, the order of inquiry for human rights review of legislation established in *R v A* (and affirmed in later cases)[27] made clear that section 3 operated as a *corrective* technique. The court was to first ascertain whether legislation, *read according to ordinary principles of interpretation*, was incompatible with Convention rights. Only if there was such an incompatibility would the court inquire into whether it could read and give effect to the legislation in a manner compatible with Convention rights. Hence, as a matter of logic, the use of section 3 was a matter beyond ordinary interpretation, only employed once a human rights violation had been found.

The result of this reasoning by the House of Lords in these early cases, which has endured for the life of the HRA, was to divide the work of the court into two phases when faced with a challenge to legislation: the merits decision on the existence of a rights violation, followed by the remedial decision.[28] In this second phase, section 3 is the first resort to address the prima facie rights violation by modifying the impugned legislation through strong interpretative techniques. Where this is not possible, the DOI is the available alternative. The remedial choice between sections 3 and 4 is therefore a choice between an immediate judicial remedy or a (possible) legislative remedy.

The order of inquiry under similar provisions of the Victorian Charter of Human Rights and Responsibilities Act 2006 (VCHRRA) serves as a useful alternative understanding of how the HRA could have developed.[29] The interpretative duty under the VCHRRA is phrased more restrictively than section 3 HRA. It provides that 'so far as it is possible to do so *consistently with their purpose* all statutory provisions must be interpreted in a way that is compatible with human rights'.[30] In *R v Momcilovic*, it was held that this duty is not a special rule of interpretation; rather, it is a directive that requires the court to explore all possible interpretations and adopt the one that least infringes Charter rights.[31] It is only after having chosen an interpretation that the court considers whether even this

[25] [2001] 2 All ER 154. [26] [2002] 2 AC 545.

[27] A Kavanagh, *Constitutional Review under the UK Human Rights Act* (CUP, Cambridge 2009) 23–4.

[28] The section 3 versus section 4 point in HRA cases has come to be commonly dealt with under the heading 'Remedy', supporting this division of merits analysis and remedial analysis (also noted by Kavanagh (n 27) 119).

[29] *R v Momcilovic* [2010] VSCA 50 (Victoria Court of Appeal). The High Court, on appeal, held that the impugned legislative provision was in fact not applicable: *Momcilovic v The Queen* (2011) HCA 34. The majority of judgments of the High Court however appeared to affirm the Court of Appeal's position on the interpretative duty requiring courts to choose the least rights-restricting interpretation available, rather than creating a new interpretative power.

[30] s 32 VCHRRA (emphasis added). [31] *R v Momcilovic* (n 29) [35].

most 'Charter-friendly' interpretation violates a Charter right. Under this reasoning, the interpretative duty is not a corrective device and the courts inquiry is not divided into merits and remedial stages in the same way as under the HRA. If there is a violation of Charter rights, then the only available power is to issue a declaration. The view of the court in *Momcilovic* was that the declaratory remedy was central to the scheme of the Act and the defining feature of 'dialogue' under the VCHRRA.[32]

Under a clear statement rule, we can readily see how the relevant norms are protected in a way that leaves space for the legislature to pass legislation regardless of judicial opinions on what human rights require. Incursions into rights are presumptively to be avoided, but the legislature can limit rights to the extent it chooses clear wording. However, if the choice between section 3 and section 4 is a remedial choice, the role that is left to the legislature depends on how the courts *exercise* this choice.

One possible method that has been suggested (in light of the innovative, non-coercive nature of the DOI) is that courts could correct legislation in cases where there is little reason to doubt that a law violates rights ('easy cases'). But when faced with a 'hard case', where the question of proportionality or the scope of the right in question is not straightforward, the court ought to issue a DOI and allow the legislature to decide what action to take.[33] We can query whether such a distinction between easy cases and hard cases can be maintained in practice. But setting aside these concerns for a moment, we can see how this type of approach is a good conceptual fit with the dual review model of institutional dialogue. The DOI would communicate the court's opinion that the legislation infringed rights, with judges acting safely in the knowledge that the law would only change if the political branches of government, upon their consideration, agreed that a human right was being unjustifiably limited. Alternatively, in keeping with the specialization model of dialogue, the remedial choice between section 3 correction and a DOI could also be made on the basis of the courts' evaluation of which institution is better placed to remedy the human rights problem in the first instance. This, as I will argue below, is how the HRA has developed doctrinally.

4.C. The Limits of Section 3 HRA

Even under strong-form systems of review where courts can invalidate primary legislation, judicial correction of legislation can be controversial.[34] 'Reading-in' legislative provisions in particular attracts the criticism that courts are overstepping the judicial role by legislating, rather than interpreting and applying the law. There

[32] *R v Momcilovic* (n 29) [95].

[33] This approach is suggested by Alison Young, who draws the relevant distinction as between 'contestable' and 'non-contestable' issues: A Young, *Parliamentary Sovereignty and the Human Rights Act* (Hart, Oxford 2009) 140–1.

[34] For example, the leading Canadian case on Charter remedies, *Schachter v Canada* [1992] 2 SCR 679, where the court accepted that reading-in was a legitimate remedy, but should be employed only in a narrow range of cases.

are several statements in HRA case law stating likewise that the task of courts is to interpret law, not make law, and that this demarcates the choice between reading-in/reading down and a DOI.[35] However, this rudimentary statement of the separation of legislative and judicial power is not an especially useful practical guide. The House of Lords has made clear that section 3 allows departure from the clear and unambiguous meaning of legislation, thereby section 3 is a power to modify legislation to at least some extent.

Existing academic commentary clarifies that the relevant distinction between sections 3 and 4 is not a matter of deciding whether a human rights problem can be fixed by interpretation or would require judges to 'legislate', but whether it can better be addressed through the piecemeal tools of judicial amendment, or the more comprehensive tools available to legislators.[36] The question is not whether the usage of section 3 constitutes judicial amendment of legislation, but whether the extent of judicial amendment is inappropriate or ill-advised.[37]

This provides a helpful way of understanding how the courts have approached the choice to issue a DOI. Below I begin with the 2004 case of *Ghaidan v Godin-Mendoza*, which is the leading statement on the limits to the section 3 remedy. The exceptions that the Law Lords set forth to the operation of section 3 provide the prima facie criteria for making a DOI. These criteria reflected the way in which courts had developed their new powers in major cases prior to *Ghaidan*, but have also provided the guiding principles for courts from 2004 onwards.

4.C.1. *Ghaidan v Godin-Mendoza*

The early case of *R v A* established that section 3 was more than a clear statement rule, but beyond this the Law Lords diverged on the scope of the section 3 duty. The majority espoused an expansive view of section 3 as the 'prime remedial measure' in the HRA system of review of legislation. It appeared to give a very restricted role to the DOI, stating that

> [a] declaration of incompatibility is a measure of last resort. It must be avoided unless it is plainly impossible to do so. If a *clear* limitation of convention rights is stated in *terms*, such an impossibility will arise.[38]

If only an express statement could displace the courts' ability to rectify legislation under the HRA, then review under the Act would resemble the position under the Canadian Charter's notwithstanding clause. The legislature would need to employ a statement to the effect that legislation is to operate irrespective of any violation of a Convention right, before the courts would resort to a DOI. The dissenting

[35] For an overview of the judicial statements, see A Kavanagh, 'The Elusive Divide between Interpretation and Legislation under the Human Rights Act 1998' (2004) 24 Oxford Journal of Legal Studies 259.

[36] Kavanagh (n 35) 270–3.

[37] Kavanagh (n 35) 270–3.

[38] *R v A (No 2)* (n 22) [44].

judgment presented a more restrained view of the potential of section 3: one that granted a wider role to DOIs.[39]

The Law Lords in *Ghaidan* recognized that no clear principles had been established as to what was possible under section 3.[40] The leading judgment affirmed the court's earlier jurisprudence on the fact that section 3 allowed courts to read in words that changed the meaning and effect of legislation.[41] However, it set out two limits to this duty:

> First, Parliament cannot have intended that in the discharge of this extended interpretative function the courts should adopt a meaning inconsistent with a fundamental feature of the legislation. Second, Parliament cannot have intended that section 3 should require courts to make decisions for which they are not equipped. There may be several ways of making a provision Convention-compliant, and the choice may involve issues calling for legislative deliberation.[42]

By clearly recognizing limits to the scope of section 3 short of a legislative statement explicitly limiting Convention rights, the court adopted a moderate position between the different views in *R v A*.[43] The two broad limits can be understood as follows. The first concerns the nature and extent of the change made to the legislation itself. The second is concerned with the effects of the legislative change and the court becoming embroiled in making choices that require broader deliberation. However, to better understand the content of each of these limits, we need to look beyond *Ghaidan* to the use of DOIs which informed Lord Nicholls' statement, and the application of these criteria in subsequent cases.

4.C.2. Limit 1: The nature/extent of legislative modification

(a) The 'fundamental feature' test

Ghaidan stands for the proposition that courts should not modify the law to an extent that would frustrate a fundamental feature of the legislative scheme. Different expressions were used in the various judgments to this effect: the meaning adopted must be compatible with the 'underlying thrust' of the legislation being construed;[44] and the implication of words must 'go with the grain of the legislation'.[45] The proper focus of the section 3 duty can therefore be understood to be incidental or interstitial human rights incompatibility, which can be corrected without going to the fundamentals of the legislation and its policy objectives.

The fundamental feature test can be illustrated by the judgment in *Ghaidan* itself. This was an appeal concerning a man's claim to succeed to the tenancy of his deceased homosexual partner. The Court of Appeal found that the Rent Act 1977,

[39] *R v A (No 2)* (n 22) [108]–[109] (Lord Hope).
[40] *Ghaidan* (n 18) [27] (Lord Nicholls).
[41] *Ghaidan* (n 18) [32].
[42] *Ghaidan* (n 18) [33].
[43] P Craig, *Administrative Law* (6th edn Sweet & Maxwell, London 2008) 563.
[44] *Ghaidan* (n 18) [33] (Lord Nicholls).
[45] *Ghaidan* (n 18) [121] (Lord Rodger).

which allowed married and de facto heterosexual partners to succeed to a tenancy as the surviving spouse of the original tenant, discriminated against the survivor of a homosexual partnership in a manner which violated the right to a family life. It then read the Rent Act 1977 to extend the relevant provision to homosexual partners. The landlord appealed to the House of Lords, on grounds that, inter alia, it was not possible to use section 3 in this way.

The leading judgment considered what social policy lay behind the protection of the tenancy of a surviving spouse and concluded it to be that the survivor of a couple who have made their home together 'should be regarded as having a special claim to be treated in much the same way as the original tenant'.[46] It was decided that to extend that protection to the surviving member of a homosexual couple would be in keeping with this social purpose.[47] Notably, the Secretary of State, intervening, did not object to the inclusion of homosexual couples in the provision at issue and in fact argued in favour of section 3 rather than use of a DOI.

The earlier case of *R (Anderson) v Secretary of State for the Home Department* is a helpful contrast.[48] Here, the House of Lords issued a DOI on the grounds that Parliament had deliberately given the Home Secretary sentencing powers that the court had determined to violate the right to have one's sentence determined by an impartial tribunal. The legislation gave the Secretary of State the ultimate decision on the length of imprisonment for mandatory life prisoners, while taking away that discretion in relation to other categories of offenders. Though the language of the *Ghaidan* test was not used, the Secretary of State's continued sentencing role can be understood to have been a fundamental feature of the sentencing regime; apparent from the way in which the sentencing legislation had developed over time.[49] Hence, a DOI was the appropriate remedy.

This guiding rule that section 3 cannot be used when to do so would violate a fundamental feature of the legislative scheme does not eliminate the need for decisions to be made as to what the fundamental features, or cardinal principles, of the legislative scheme *are*.[50] Whether a human rights incompatibility is a fundamental, deliberate part of the legislation, or the product of insufficient attention or oversight, may not be apparent, and may leave space for judges to ascribe a purpose that allows for modification. I return to this in subsection (c).

(b) Where the rights incompatibility is embedded in the scheme of the legislation

A variation on the first limit on section 3 occurs where the human rights incompatibility is not the matter of a specific provision, but is somehow embedded in the scheme of the legislation. The concern here is that correcting the incompatibility

[46] *Ghaidan* (n 18) [13] (Lord Nicholls).

[47] *Ghaidan* (n 18) [19]–[20].

[48] [2002] UKHL 46.

[49] It was understood in this way by Lord Rodger in *Ghaidan* (n 18) [111].

[50] The government's right of intervention provided by s 5 HRA allows Ministers to make arguments on what the fundamental features of the legislative scheme are and what policy purposes it is designed to serve.

would require substantial rewriting of the statute. Even though correcting the incompatibility may not undermine the policy of the scheme, the extent of the change required nevertheless goes beyond the tools of judicial rectification.

A good example is the DOI issued in *International Transport Roth GmBH v Secretary of State for the Home Department*.[51] The Immigration and Asylum Act 1999 introduced a system of penalties for carriers who unknowingly transported clandestine entrants to the UK. The scheme was a harsh one, implemented in the vigorous pursuit of immigration control. The burden of establishing blamelessness lay on the carrier, and there was no possibility of variation in the penalty or any mitigating circumstances, even where the drivers themselves alerted the authorities. For non-UK residents, vehicles were detained pending any decision on liability, with compensation available only in very limited circumstances. Lord Simon Brown, writing for the majority in the Court of Appeal, recognized that the harshness of the scheme was designed to encourage vigilance on the part of carriers travelling to the UK,[52] but the scheme, taken as whole, was 'not merely harsh but truly unfair'.[53] Examining the possibility of correction through section 3, Lord Simon Brown concluded that it was 'impossible to recreate [the] scheme through any interpretative process . . . We cannot create a wholly different scheme . . . so as to provide for an acceptable alternative means of immigration control. That must be for Parliament.'[54]

(c) The gravity of a declaration of incompatibility

Throughout the cases, and much of the commentary, the focus on the limits of section 3 has been a concern with how far is too far: at what point should the courts hold back and leave choices as to whether and what types of legislative changes are needed to the executive and legislature? Cast in this way, it can be seen as an act of institutional humility to employ a DOI and allow the legislature to remedy the fault, if it so chooses. In fact, in *International Transport Roth*, Lord Simon Brown specifically stated that the court would fail to accord appropriate deference to Parliament were it to attempt to make the scheme of carrier penalties human rights compliant.[55]

Yet, at the same time, the logic of issuing a DOI because correcting the human rights incompatibility would strike at the fundamentals of the legislation suggests that the very policy or purpose of the legislative scheme is implicated in the human rights violation. A decision that legislation needs to effectively be rewritten because the rights incompatibility is embedded within the legislation may similarly come across as a strong criticism of the legislation. For example, the decision in *International Transport Roth* that it would be impossible for the court to correct the

[51] [2002] EWCA Civ 158.

[52] *International Transport Roth* (n 51) [25].

[53] *International Transport Roth* (n 51) [26], [31].

[54] *International Transport Roth* (n 51) [66]. The first instance judge had attempted to correct the scheme using section 3: at [12].

[55] *International Transport Roth* (n 51) [66].

incompatibility went alongside a condemnation of the legislative scheme as requiring individuals to pay too high a price for the policy goal of fortifying immigration control; stating 'the troubling features of the regime are all inter-linked: to achieve fairness would require a radically different approach'.[56]

The first instance[57] and House of Lords[58] decisions in *MB* illustrate how a DOI may seem the more confrontational route, and higher courts may sometimes understand section 3 to be a more cooperative approach. This case concerned a challenge to the system of non-derogating control orders under the Prevention of Terrorism Act 2005 (PTA) on the grounds that the legislative scheme infringed the right to a fair trial. At first instance, Justice Sullivan reached a forceful conclusion to issue a DOI:

> Standing back and looking at the overall picture, there can be only one conclusion. To say that the Act does not give the respondent in this case, against whom a non-derogating control order has been made by the Secretary of State, a fair hearing in the determination of his rights under Article 8 of the Convention would be an understatement. The court would be failing in its duty under the 1998 Act, a duty imposed upon the court by Parliament, if it did not say, loud and clear, that the procedure under the Act whereby the court merely reviews the lawfulness of the Secretary of State's decision to make the order upon the basis of the material available to him at that earlier stage are conspicuously unfair. The thin veneer of legality which is sought to be applied by s 3 of the [Prevention of Terrorism] Act cannot disguise the reality that controlees' rights under the Convention are being determined not by an independent court in compliance with Article 6.1, but by executive decision-making, untrammelled by any prospect of effective judicial supervision.[59]

On appeal, the DOI was overturned. The House of Lords narrowed the scope of the judicial inquiry, deciding that evaluations of unfairness ought to be considered in the limited context of the particular controlled person, rather than across the PTA regime. While there could be cases of control orders made under the PTA where the 'core, irreducible minimum of procedural protection would not be met', in those cases the relevant provisions of the Act were to be read down, so as only to take effect where it was consistent with fairness for them to do so.

Baroness Hale's judgment can be contrasted with the approach taken by Justice Sullivan. Her view was that, albeit with 'strenuous efforts from all, difficult and time-consuming as it will be', the procedures under the PTA could be made to work fairly and compatibly in many cases.[60] To ensure this in all cases, the provisions could be read subject to an implied condition that they would not operate where to do so would be incompatible with the right of the controlled person to a fair trial.[61] She considered it not only a duty upon the court to provide this remedy, but moreover desirable because Parliament must have thought the

56 *International Transport Roth* (n 51) [66].
57 *Re MB* [2006] EWHC 1000 (Admin).
58 *Secretary of State for the Home Department v MB* [2007] UKHL 46.
59 *Re MB* (n 57) [103].
60 *Re MB* (n 57) at [66], [70].
61 *Re MB* (n 57) [72].

legislation was compatible with human rights when it passed the Act, and in 'interpreting the Act compatibly with rights, we are doing our best to make it work'.[62]

Insofar as a DOI impugns the fundamentals of legislation—the very scheme of the legislation—it is understandable that the court may take exercising this power to be a grave step. The use of section 3 may be conceived as the more accommodating, cooperative remedy in certain circumstances. In fact, in a number of cases the government itself has argued for a section 3 interpretation in preference to a DOI.[63] Indeed, it has done so consistently in relation to the control orders regime.[64]

An alternative strategy is for judges to focus on identifying an underlying policy that is charitable to the legislature. An important tradition of statutory interpretation is that courts presume Parliament did not intend to act cruelly or unfairly.[65] As mentioned above, characterization of the legislative process is not a straightforward task. By choosing a more laudable purpose, courts can give themselves more space to interpret legislation compatibly with rights. In making a similar argument, Aileen Kavanagh draws attention to the court's approach in *R v Offen*. Here, a draconian 'two strikes and you're out' automatic life sentence provision was considered to have the purpose of protecting the public from dangerous offenders, and this enabled the court to come up with a restrictive interpretation such that the provisions only applied to dangerous offenders.[66]

4.C.3. Limit 2: remedial decisions for which the court is ill-equipped

By contrast, the second broad limit to the use of section 3 is not based on the extent of the change made to the legislation, but the claimed limits of the courts' capacity to make certain types of remedial choices. A DOI may be employed in preference to judicial correction even if the interpretation required involves a relatively minor change to the legislation in linguistic terms, because of the broader *effects* of the legislative change, or the *type of inquiry* that courts must engage in to decide on a remedy. In *Ghaidan*, this limit was justified on the grounds that remedial choices 'may involve issues calling for legislative deliberation'.[67] This section examines what content has been given by the courts to the general idea that some remedial questions call for legislative deliberation.

Chapter 1 presented legislative remedial capacity as one rationale for open remedies, where compliance with human rights standards requires systematic and/or positive action. I argued that this rationale is logically separate from the idea that there is room for disagreement over whether the existing law and practice

[62] *Re MB* (n 57) [73].

[63] For example, in *R (H) v Mental Health Review Tribunal for the North and East London Region & the Secretary of State for Health* [2001] EWCA Civ 415; *Ghaidan* (n 18); *R (Wright & Ors) v Secretary of State for Health* [2009] UKHL 3; *Secretary of State for the Home Department v MB* (n 58).

[64] Chapter 8.D will address the control orders regime in further detail.

[65] Kavanagh (n 27) 77–8.

[66] Kavanagh (n 27) 75.

[67] *Ghaidan* (n 18) [33].

infringes rights guarantees. Rather, it is based on: first, cooperation in the advancement of rights, such that courts may limit themselves to identifying a violation, and leave the design and implementation of the necessary action to the other branches of government; and second, the desirability of wider deliberation on what type of remedial action is to be taken.

Judicial reliance on this second limit to section 3 (and criterion for a DOI) aligns well with the specialization model of dialogue in Chapter 2. In the cases discussed below, the courts have openly reasoned that a DOI is the more appropriate remedy so that the legislature can decide *how* to respond; not so that the legislature can decide *whether* to respond.

(a) Re S *and* Bellinger

The second limit on section 3 stated in *Ghaidan* was not relevant to the situation in that case. It was included on the basis of two earlier cases in which the House of Lords articulated constraints on the exercise of section 3 based on evaluations of judicial capacity.

The first case was *Re S*,[68] one which challenged the system of care for children removed from parental care. In response to systemic breaches of Article 6 and Article 8 rights by local authorities in relation to care orders, the Court of Appeal created a system of judicial supervision, where no such supervision was provided by the Children Act 1989. The scheme adopted was inspired by suggestions from a conference of experts on how to improve the public care system for children, evidence of which was provided to the court.[69] An appeal was made to the House of Lords on the question of whether a court could introduce such a system of supervision under the provisions of the HRA.

The court held that the introduction of judicial supervision, where the legislature had entrusted the care of children removed from their parents to local authorities rather than courts, defied a fundamental feature of the Act. Additionally, the court found that the limits of section 3 were transgressed by virtue of the 'far-reaching practical repercussions' of the system that the Court of Appeal had created. The House of Lords was openly averse to the use of a remedy that involved ongoing judicial supervision of public bodies. The court held that the additional administrative work and expense could be expected to have a material effect on the allocation of local authorities' scarce resources and thereby impact upon the discharge of responsibilities towards other children.[70] Additionally, the introduction of formal reporting requirements 'would affect the whole manner in which authorities discharge... their parental responsibilities'.[71] According to Lord Nicholls, these were 'practical repercussions which the Court [was] not equipped to evaluate',[72] and it was for the legislature to decide how to amend the Act.[73]

[68] *Re S (Minors) (Care Order: Implementation of Care Plan)* [2002] UKHL 10.
[69] *Re S* (n 68) [31]–[32] (Nicholls LJ).
[70] *Re S* (n 68) [43].
[71] *Re S* (n 68) [43].
[72] *Re S* (n 68) [40].
[73] *Re S* (n 68) [44].

The leading judgment was critical of the Court of Appeal remedy for a further reason, which was that the remedy was designed to be prospective, and to prevent future violations of rights by local authorities. The system imposed obligations on local authorities even in the absence of any finding that the authority was acting unlawfully or proposed to do so.[74] This was held to be beyond the judicial task, for the system went beyond providing a judicial remedy to victims of actual or proposed unlawful conduct by local authorities. This type of preventative action was also seen to be a task for the legislature, not the courts.

The second case was *Bellinger v Bellinger*.[75] This case concerned the interpretation of a provision in the Matrimonial Causes Act 1973 that provided parties to a marriage must be 'respectively male and female'. Mrs Bellinger (a post-operative male to female transsexual) sought legal recognition of her marriage to Mr Bellinger. The court found that the exclusion of transsexuals from the institution of marriage constituted a violation of their Article 8 right to a private and family life, taken in conjunction with the Article 14 non-discrimination protection. Very little was required in linguistic terms to correct this violation. The court need only have expanded the meaning of female to include post-operative transsexuals. The statute did not impede this meaning as it provided no definition of male or female, rather the definition of these terms as being determined by biological features upon birth was provided by the 1971 precedent in *Corbett v Corbett*.[76] The court however did not grant Mrs Bellinger recognition of her marriage, instead issuing a DOI.

The reason that the court advanced for why legislative deliberation was required was that the violation of transsexuals' Convention rights ran further than the instant case: the UK lacked a comprehensive system for the recognition of gender change. Lord Nicholls stated that giving male and female an extended meaning:

> raises issues whose solution calls for extensive enquiry and the widest public consultation and discussion. Questions of social policy and administrative feasibility arise at several points, and their interaction has to be evaluated and balanced. The issues are altogether ill-suited for determination by courts and court procedures. They are pre-eminently a matter for Parliament...[77]

Particular emphasis was placed on the difficulty of determining at which point gender change ought to be legally recognized and whether it ought to be limited to post-operative transsexuals. Lord Nicholls drew attention to the fact that the case concerned one individual and her particular circumstances. The evidence before the court was therefore limited and not 'a proper or indeed a responsible basis on which to change the law'.[78]

In both *Bellinger* and *Re S* we can see similar justifications employed: the need to weigh up policy concerns and administrative concerns, and the impact of changes being wider than the parties to the immediate case. However, the decision in

[74] *Re S* (n 68) [48]–[49] (Lord Nicholls).

[75] *Bellinger v Bellinger* [2003] UKHL 21.

[76] *Corbett v Corbett (otherwise Ashley)* [1971] P 83. This decision had, in any event, been heavily criticized over the years. See ibid [13] (Lord Nicholls).

[77] *Bellinger* (n 75) [37].

[78] *Bellinger* (n 75) [40].

Bellinger has come under criticism for being too concerned with wider legislative changes, rather than deciding the case before the court.[79] The court need not have considered the criteria for recognition of gender in all contexts. Uncertainty about where the line should be drawn—the systemic questions facing recognition of gender change—did not affect the claim of Mrs Bellinger for 'wherever the line marking the transition from one sex to another is to be drawn, Mrs Bellinger [was] on the reassigned gender side of the line'.[80] The court could have decided that the legal status of female for the purposes of marriage extended to include Mrs Bellinger, without setting out any broad ruling on where the line of legal gender change should lie. Such a decision would still have involved judicial restraint, but in the form of a *narrow ruling* rather than an open remedy. Parliament would still have been free to enact comprehensive legislation in response.

We can identify two rationales underpinning the court's decision not to engage in a narrow ruling. The first is a clear reluctance to be the responsible institution for demarcating the line of gender recognition on a case-by-case basis. The judgment stated:

> Today the case before the House concerns Mrs. Bellinger. Tomorrow's case in the High Court will relate to a transsexual person who has been able to undergo a less extensive course of surgery. The following week will be the case of a transsexual person who has undergone hormonal treatment but who, for medical reasons, has not been able to undergo any surgery. Then there will be a transsexual person who is medically able to undergo all or part of the surgery but who does not wish to do so. By what criteria are cases such as these to be decided?[81]

The *Bellinger* decision invited the formulation of comprehensive criteria on when to recognize gender change, devised by the legislature, in clear preference to piecemeal, gradual judicial development.

Second, the court could act on this preference for a clear and comprehensive policy in the knowledge that such a policy would be forthcoming. Legislative reform was in development, in response to a ECtHR decision finding that the absence of any legal recognition for transsexuals violated the ECHR.[82] The judgment of the court explicitly referred to this as an important factor in issuing a DOI.[83] A DOI was the more cooperative approach here because the executive and legislature had begun to take responsibility for remedying this human rights problem. We can speculate as to whether, without this clear expectation of impending legislative change, the court's calculus may have been different and it may have sought to take a more forceful approach. *Bellinger* should be understood

[79] T Hickman, 'Constitutional Dialogue, Constitutional Theories and the Human Rights Act 1998' [2005] PL 306; G Phillipson, 'Deference, Discretion and Democracy in the Human Rights Act Era' 60 Current Legal Problems 40, 65–8; Loveland (n 17) 669–70.

[80] *Bellinger* (n 75) [39].

[81] *Bellinger* (n 75) [40] (Lord Nicholls).

[82] *Goodwin v United Kingdom* (2002) 35 EHRR 18.

[83] '[These questions are] pre-eminently a matter for Parliament, the more especially when the Government, in unequivocal terms, has already announced its intention to introduce comprehensive primary legislation on this difficult and sensitive subject': *Bellinger* (n 75) [37].

as a case where institutional capacity arguments led to a DOI because there were multiple possible routes to a human rights-compatible outcome and the court did not consider itself the appropriate institution to make a choice between them, nor was it *necessary* for the court to do so because legislative action would be forthcoming.

(b) After Ghaidan v Godin-Mendoza

Since *Ghaidan*, two DOIs have been issued on the grounds that the court was ill equipped to remedy the incompatibility. First, the case of *R (Wright and Ors) v Secretary of State for Health*[84] concerned the system of listing care workers deemed unsuitable to work with vulnerable adults. The challenge related to a system of provisional listing, in which the affected care worker was denied any opportunity to make representations before being listed, despite this status preventing their employment in a range of positions. The Court of Appeal attempted to correct the incompatibility of this system with Article 6 by reading-in a provision that gave the worker the opportunity to make representations, except in limited circumstances.

The House of Lords overturned this decision and issued a DOI. The court decided that the system instituted pursuant to the Court of Appeal's decision (which the government had implemented in the intervening period before the appeal) was not sufficient to solve the problem, and concluded that no interpretation under section 3 could solve the problem.[85] The judgment expressly refrained from any suggestions as to *how* the scheme could be made compatible, because the scheme involved a 'delicate balance' between the rights of care workers and the welfare of vulnerable adults, and it was for the legislature to strike that balance in the first instance.[86] Again, it is worth noting that an explicit reason cited in the judgment for not considering what might be done to make the legislation compatible was that the regime was soon to be replaced by new legislation.[87]

Second, in the case of *Smith v Scott*,[88] the Registration Appeal Court (Scotland) faced a similar situation to that in *Bellinger*. Here, the UK's blanket ban on prisoner voting had been held by the ECtHR to violate the Article 3, First Protocol right to vote.[89] The claimant sought interpretation of the Representation of People Act 1983 using section 3 of the Human Rights Act to correct the incompatibility. Specifically, the claimant argued that a clause should be read in that any ban on prisoner voting only applied at the discretion of the sentencing judge.

Here the court, with careful reference to the reasoning in *Ghaidan*, concluded that it was not possible to interpret the legislation to rectify the incompatibility identified, principally because

> there were many possible levels at which the line might be drawn for the enfranchisement or disenfranchisement of convicted prisoners in different categories, and it could be no part of

[84] n 63. [85] *Wright* (n 63) [38].
[86] *Wright* (n 63) [39]. [87] *Wright* (n 63) [39].
[88] [2006] CSIH 9. [89] *Hirst v United Kingdom (No 2)* (2006) 42 EHRR 41.

this court's function to make an uninformed choice among such alternatives . . . Without the benefit of consultation or advice, this court would, in a real sense, be legislating on its own account, especially in view of the wide range of policy alternatives from which a 'possible' solution would require to be selected.[90]

Again, in this case a government response was anticipated insofar as it had stated its intention to change the law and commissioned a public consultation. However, in contrast to *Bellinger*, there were live concerns about the ongoing delays in the government response, despite the looming Scottish election.[91] There were arguably more compelling reasons in this case for a stronger judicial intervention to force the issue to be resolved. Nonetheless, the court refrained from identifying any standards for rectifying this incompatibility. A contributing factor may have been that the court had little evidence or argument before it as a basis for engagement in the question as to what types of restrictions on the right to vote might be appropriate for convicted prisoners.[92]

These later cases again involve courts making DOIs in conditions where a complex scheme needs to be developed, or where choices need to be made between alternative solutions to the human rights problem. Additionally, in both cases, the government made assurances that changes to the law were forthcoming. This suggests the continuing importance of institutional comity such that the courts avoid pre-empting changes to the law through the legislative process by limiting themselves to a DOI.

(c) 'Matters requiring legislative deliberation'

We can now give some specific content to the general idea that remedying a rights violation 'requires legislative deliberation'. Where there are competing concerns of different groups (*Wright*), resource implications of remedial action (*Re S*), or multiple possibilities for a rights-compatible approach (*Bellinger*, *Smith v Scott*), the courts have held that there is need for greater consultation, investigation, and debate than can occur in the immediate proceedings. This is not to say that the second limit to section 3 is a bright-line rule. The following section argues that the choice between section 3 and section 4 remains a contextual inquiry, and these ideas about when legislatures are better placed to devise a remedy are at best guidelines to that inquiry.

Furthermore, in these cases, the stated need for legislative deliberation has related more to a sense of institutional *incapacity* on the part of judges, rather than the positive attributes of the legislative process. Where courts refer to the need for legislative deliberation, they may simply be referring to the ordinary process of legislation, rather than any theoretically grounded concept of a deliberation, and may mean no more than a legislative response designed by the executive and

[90] *Smith v Scott* (n 88) [26]–[27].
[91] *Smith v Scott* (n 88) [39]–[51].
[92] *Smith v Scott* (n 88) [24], [27]. The claimant's argument was based solely on a suggestion made in one concurring judgment in *Hirst*.

formally approved by Parliament. However, stated needs for consultation and full debate in some of the judgments above do suggest a more robust concept of deliberation.

In Part III I consider what type of deliberation has actually followed these decisions; and whether expectations of consultation and debate have been met. Chapter 1 raised the need to take care with arguments based on institutional capacity. It makes little sense for the court to refrain from answering a question on the grounds that it is not well equipped to do so, unless some other institution is better equipped in practice, and able and willing, to make the relevant decision. Statements that certain decisions are 'impossible' for courts to make (such as in *Re S*) need to be viewed critically. In the cases above, the courts have indicated their confidence in a prompt legislative response, even if this confidence has proved misplaced.[93] If the legislature is not willing or able to deliberate on remedial choices promptly or carefully, then the courts, though imperfect, may in practice be the best institution to devise remedial action in the first instance. If necessary, some of the institutional incapacities referred to above could be ameliorated, at least partly. The court can allow amicus submissions, or invite further evidence on a remedy, and thereby increase the information available to make a decision. Furthermore, it should not be assumed that, should a court make a decision granting a concrete remedy, this necessarily discourages legislative deliberation. In Chapter 7 I examine whether it is necessary to make the legislature the *first mover* in devising a remedy, in order to support legislative deliberation.

4.C.4. A contextual inquiry

As I argued in Chapter 1, remedial choices in human rights litigation are an interface between law and politics, often being closely allied to the context of the case and involving an important measure of judicial discretion. Likewise, despite the guiding principles laid forth in *Ghaidan*, the choice between section 3 and section 4 remains a contextual decision in important ways.[94] I have already noted how the first limit to section 3 is a malleable one, leaving room for judges to define what the fundamental purpose of the law is, or how embedded in the legislation human rights violations are. Similarly, courts have taken into account forthcoming legislative action and institutional comity, when ostensibly deciding whether remedial choices have systemic consequences. The existing principles have structured the remedial discretion of the court, but are guidelines rather than bright-line tests.[95] Recognizing this, Lord Bingham has stated that, although the differing expressions used in *Ghaidan* to delineate the scope of section 3 'yield valuable insights . . . none of them should be allowed to supplant the simple test enacted in

[93] In Chapters 6 and 7 I will discuss the legislative responses to *Wright* (n 63) and *Smith v Scott* (n 88), which contrast to the prompt response to *Bellinger* (n 75).

[94] See also Kavanagh (n 27) 47; I Leigh and R Masterman, *Making Rights Real* (Hart, Oxford 2008) 102, 106–10.

[95] Cf. Loveland (n 17) 670 who argues that, in particular, the second limit to *Ghaidan* is not even a helpful guideline and simply displaces rather than resolves the question before the court.

the Act: "so far as is possible to do so"'.[96] This choice between judicial rectification of an incompatible law, and a legislative remedy, remains a multifaceted and discretionary inquiry.

It may also take time for a consistent approach to the choice between sections 3 and 4 to settle. For instance, soon after the House of Lords decision in *Ghaidan* the Court of Appeal issued a DOI in *R (MH) v Secretary of State for Health*.[97] The court noted the dicta in *Ghaidan*, but did not see 'how a process of reading down can be used to add to a statute provisions that it does not contain'.[98] It issued a DOI for the simple reason that the problem with the legislation was that it was missing necessary provisions rather than because any provision positively offended Convention rights; without even considering the possibility of reading-in.[99]

We might also question the practical significance of the *Ghaidan* criteria in subsequent cases. *Smith v Scott* is a notable exception in having considered these criteria closely before issuing a DOI. In relation to all other DOIs made after *Ghaidan* in the study period, the *Ghaidan* principles were not considered in the reasoning of the court. In several cases leading to a DOI, the parties agreed that section 3 was not available.[100] In others, there were simply no submissions on the possibility of using section 3, nor was the matter considered by the court.[101]

This trend suggests one of two things. Either it is obvious in these cases that a DOI is the only appropriate remedy; or reliance on a DOI is such a contextual decision that the arguments of the parties to the case (and their respective interests) have a crucial role to play in the court's willingness to employ a DOI. In fact, with the overwhelming academic focus falling on the *Ghaidan* principles, the matter of whether section 4 can guarantee an effective remedy for the litigant is an aspect of the decision to make a DOI that has been neglected.

4.D. An Effective Remedy for the Litigant

The judicial inquiry under the HRA as to whether remedial action would be better coming from the courts or the legislature bears some important similarities to the rationales for open remedies in stronger systems of judicial review. The choice to issue a DOI resembles, at the level of judicial reasoning, the choice to use the

[96] *Sheldrake v DPP* [2004] UKHL 43 [28].

[97] [2004] EWCA Civ 1609.

[98] *R (MH)* (n 97) [28].

[99] *R (MH)* (n 97) [27]. The declaration was subsequently overturned by the House of Lords, but on the basis that there was no incompatibility in the first place: [2005] UKHL 60.

[100] *R (Morris) v Westminster City Council & Anor* [2005] EWCA Civ 1184; *R (Thompson & JF) v Secretary of State for the Home Department* [2009] EWCA Civ 792; *R (Clift) v Secretary of State for the Home Department* [2006] UKHL 54.

[101] *A & Ors v Secretary of State for the Home Department ('Belmarsh Prisoners')* [2004] UKHL 56; *R (Baiai & Ors) v Secretary of State for the Home Department & Anor* [2006] EWHC 823 (Admin); *R (Nasseri) v Secretary of State for the Home Department* (2009] UKHL 23. However section 3 places a duty on the courts to read and give effect to legislation compatibly with Convention rights, and this duty operates regardless of whether the claimant or the government seeks to enforce it.

coercive forms of legislative remand that we considered in Chapter 1, especially in relation to the second limit in *Ghaidan*. Similar concerns are at play: the range of possible solutions, the desirability of public and legislative deliberation, the need for positive actions that are more easily designed through the legislative process than by judges. However, in relation to the HRA, there is the complicating factor that courts are not making a choice from amongst the full range of constitutional remedies. Since the courts cannot invalidate legislation, where laws (read according to ordinary principles of interpretation) violate human rights, then section 3 and section 4 must cover the remedial field between them. But only one of these two remedies can furnish an immediate effective remedy to the claimant before the court. We should remember that the HRA was not designed to *guarantee* an effective remedy for judicially identified human rights violations. This is the necessary corollary of the Act withholding from judges the power to invalidate legislation.

Nonetheless, given the powerful legal tradition of corrective justice, it would be unsurprising for a court to be mindful of the position of the claimant before it, who has successfully made out her claim of a human rights violation on the merits. It is only by section 3, under the rubric of 'interpretation', that an immediately effective remedy can be provided. This may make courts reluctant to use DOIs in a number of cases, and thereby narrow the use of DOIs to those cases where the legislature is able and willing to remedy the violation of the claimant's rights.

A 2008 study by Rosalind Dixon divided the judicial decisions in the UK employing section 3 and section 4 (in the period between 2000 and 2004) into the categories of criminal and civil law cases versus public/administrative law cases.[102] On this breakdown of cases, the UK courts have overwhelmingly relied on section 3 in civil and criminal law cases (in seven out of nine cases decided under section 3) and used DOIs largely in public law cases (in nine out of ten cases where a DOI was issued, and upheld on appeal). If we expand Dixon's system of classification to include post-2004 DOIs, every DOI from 2004 to 2010 related to a public or administrative law case.[103]

The explanation Dixon offers for this imbalance is that, in relation to civil law claims and criminal law proceedings, the litigant before the court would not benefit from prospective legislative change. Rather,

> constitutional commitments such as those relating to protection of property and the rule of law, will often mean that parliament is either legally or practically prevented from retrospectively altering the rights and liabilities of parties in a particular case.[104]

By contrast, public law rights are more open to legislative change. For example, the litigant in *Bellinger* would be able to benefit from future laws recognizing her as a

[102] R Dixon, 'A Minimalist Charter of Rights for Australia: The UK or Canada as a Model?' (2009) 37 Federal Law Review 335.

[103] The category of public/administrative law cases, following Dixon, includes criminal sentencing cases and detention not pursuant to the criminal process (so includes each of the counter-terrorism law cases).

[104] Dixon (n 102) 344.

woman, whereas the litigant in *Ghaidan* would not have benefited from a future change in the law on succession to tenancies for same-sex partners. Dixon suggests that the knowledge that the litigant could not benefit from a DOI underlies judicial willingness to stretch legislative language and even ignore the legislative intention behind provisions.[105]

If this remedial dimension has been a consideration for judges in the way that Dixon suggests, then they have not stated it explicitly, as a principled component of the application of the HRA provisions. However, as observed above, and confirmed by other studies,[106] where the court is confident that Parliament will in fact amend the law to correct the human rights violation, this has been stated openly as a factor supporting recourse to a DOI.[107] This would suggest that the concern about remedial effectiveness has on occasions gone beyond consideration of whether the legislature would be *able* to provide a remedy to the litigant before the court (as Dixon argues), to consideration of whether the legislature is *willing* to provide such a remedy.

My purpose in this chapter is not a normative analysis of how the courts should or should not use their review powers under the HRA.[108] Rather, I am concerned with how courts have in practice used their new powers. The above analysis suggests that there are competing demands on courts under the HRA. On the one hand, the HRA is designed such that DOIs provide Parliament with a *choice* as to whether to act. On the other hand, traditional notions of corrective justice encourage judges to ensure an effective remedy to the successful litigant before them. If the courts try to ensure that they use their remedial powers in a way that does not deny an effective remedy to the litigant, this weighs against the dual review model of dialogue. It skews the use of DOIs towards situations where the courts already believe, or are assured, that Parliament will provide a remedy.

4.E. Conclusion

Early in this chapter I drew attention to different ways in which the choice between section 3 and section 4 could operate. The type of analysis that the UK courts have undertaken in relation to human rights challenges to legislation has not been based on a clear statement rule. Rather, the choice between section 3 and section 4 is a choice between two different remedial routes, once the court has found that legislation, plainly read, is incompatible with rights. The criteria in *Ghaidan*

[105] Dixon (n 102) 347.

[106] Kavanagh (n 27) 133–42; Dixon (n 102); Leigh and Masterman (n 94) 92.

[107] In the following chapter, I will identify another significant trend amongst the case law, which is that a number of DOIs cover situations where the UK has already made international commitments to change the law in question.

[108] There is debate over whether courts should make expansive use of the s 3 power to ensure that the litigant receives an effective remedy. Dixon argues that this extends the interpretative duty too far, while Kavanagh argues that a concern for the litigant in making the choice between sections 3 and 4 is entirely defensible: Kavanagh (n 27) 119–21, 130–1.

guide this remedial choice, however the remedial decision remains discretionary and contextual. Significantly, it is not only the language of the statute that matters; questions of what the fundamentals of the legislation are, whether the human rights violation is embedded or incidental, whether it has a systemic quality and whether remedial choices are better made by the legislature are all considerations openly at play. Less openly, whether the litigant will benefit from the DOI may also be a consideration.

One factor that has not, on the judicial reasoning, been relevant to the choice between section 3 and section 4 is whether the case before the court is a hard case or an easy case, or whether a case is publicly controversial. The order of inquiry before the courts separates the merits question of whether the law in question infringes rights from the question of what the court can do about it. In this merits phase, the court has applied separate doctrines of restraint (or deference) to the government and/or legislature's view of human rights compatibility.[109] What this means is that despite courts having the option to use a non-binding declaration, they may still defer to the government's evaluation, for instance, that a particular measure is necessary and proportionate to meet a particular social goal, rather than scrutinizing these arguments fully. This is because the two stages have been oriented to different inquiries: deference at the merits stage involves an evaluation by the courts that the government or legislature are better able to decide whether legislation is compatible with rights; while at the remedial stage, the choice is whether remedial action would be better coming from the legislature than the courts. A good example is the case of *R (Pearson) v Secretary of State for the Home Department.*[110] This was the original domestic challenge to the denial of voting rights to prisoners, under the HRA. The court did not scrutinize the reasons for the voting ban, holding that the proportionality of the measures was a matter on which it should defer to Parliament's judgment. The fact that the court could have simply issued a DOI, not compelling any change in the law, was not relevant to this reasoning.

The models of institutional interaction in Chapter 2.E are not models of judicial behaviour, but of the role of the legislature relative to the courts. Nonetheless, judges may use their power to issue a DOI in a way that supports a particular model of interaction. It can be suggested that the logic of judicial reasoning in relation to DOIs is a closer fit to the specialization model than the dual review model, leading to DOIs being made on the basis that, all things considered, it is better to let the legislature devise remedial action, rather than because the DOI is a mere opinion that the other branches of government may not wish to follow. The types of factors that the courts consider in making their remedial choice are similar to the rationales

[109] The doctrine of deference under the HRA has received extensive academic attention. See especially J Jowell, 'Judicial Deference: Servility, Civility or Institutional Capacity?' [2003] PL 592; F Klug, 'Judicial Deference under the Human Rights Act' (2003) 2 EHRLR 125; M Hunt, 'Sovereignty's Blight: Why Contemporary Public Law Needs the Concept of Due Deference' in N Bamforth and P Leyland (eds), *Public Law in a Multi-Layered Constitution* (Hart, Oxford 2003).

[110] A good example of this is the original challenge to the prisoner voting ban in the UK (*R (Pearson) v Secretary of State for the Home Department* [2001] EWHC Admin 239, discussed in Chapter 7.D.

for coercive legislative remand discussed in Chapter 1. This is especially the case in relation to the second limit to section 3. One exception however is the House of Lords' decision in *Belmarsh Prisoners*. Here, several Law Lords emphasized that the DOI left Parliament a choice as to whether to change the law; that its import was 'political not legal'.[111] Chapter 8 considers the response to this decision, which is exceptional for several reasons.

That judicial reasoning under the HRA has supported dialogue-as-specialization becomes clearer on comparison with the approaches that the courts have *not* adopted. The 'clear statement rule plus' approach is a way in which courts may more actively support the dual review model of interaction, by leaving greater space for the legislature to advance its own position on what human rights required.[112] Of course, under the HRA, the UK legislature remains free to decide whether or not to change the law when a DOI is issued, irrespective of what reasoning UK courts employ to get to this remedy. However, the courts' reasoning does have practical significance. If courts employ DOIs more readily in circumstances where the government makes assurances to bring new legislation then it should not cause any surprise when these DOIs meet with legislative responses. This particular factor in the remedial calculus may skew the pattern of compliance with DOIs. In Chapters 5 and 6 I consider some further ways in which the nature of cases leading to DOIs helps explain a steady pattern of reply legislation.

[111] *Belmarsh Prisoners* (n 101) [142] (Lord Scott). Lord Hoffman stated that '[t]he declaration of the court enables Parliament to choose with full knowledge that the law does not accord with our constitutional traditions': [90]. Baroness Hale made clear that the declaration did not invalidate any law or action and that Parliament and the government could choose whether to respond, at [220].

[112] Indeed the *Belmarsh Prisoners* judgment (n 101) is the one example of the judges' depiction of a DOI fitting the understanding of a DOI under the 'clear statement plus' approach (on which see 4.B.3).

5

Judicial Restraint and Activism Considered

5.A. Introduction

Open remedies, when employed as a matter of judicial discretion, are an exercise in judicial restraint of a particular variety. When a DOI impugns the very policy or the 'fundamentals' of legislation, as discussed in the previous chapter, it may not appear especially restrained in terms of judicial criticism of the law. Nonetheless, the DOI, by design, involves judges limiting themselves to simply stating that legislation is incompatible with human rights and taking no further action, nor legally directing the legislature to act.

It has been suggested that weaker remedial powers may allow for stronger rights, that is more robust standards of what human rights principles require.[1] Under the DOI mechanism it can be argued that judges do not need to be minimalist, or deferential, in reviewing legislation:[2] after all, why be restrained when Parliament has the right to disagree? Yet, on the other hand, judges may be reluctant to step outside their traditional role and employ a seeming political tool of persuasion. Furthermore, the fact that DOIs are not coercive invites the courts to act carefully, even strategically, if they do not want the DOI to become an ignored and insignificant statement.[3] It is therefore an open question whether, with their weaker remedial powers, courts applying the HRA will be more robust, or activist, in their determinations of whether legislation is human rights compatible.

Chapter 4 observed that the structure of the HRA inquiry in relation to legislation separates the merits question of whether there has been a violation of rights from the remedial question of whether to issue a DOI. This means that the fact that a case is a 'hard case' on the merits, or a particularly unpopular or controversial case, is not a relevant reason to issue the open remedy instead of the corrective remedy *openly* in the jurisprudence. This makes it difficult to evaluate in any global sense whether the innovative DOI mechanism has supported judicial activism, on the basis of the case law. It is also difficult to establish the counterfactual of how UK

[1] M Tushnet, *Weak Courts, Strong Rights* (Princeton University Press, Princeton 2008) 242–52.

[2] For example, F Klug, 'Judicial Deference under the Human Rights Act' (2003) 2 EHRLR 125, 132–3.

[3] M Tushnet, 'New Forms of Judicial Review and the Persistence of Rights- and Democracy-Based Worries' (2003) 38 Wake Forest Law Review 813, 829–30, observes that courts are not insensitive to the political response to their actions and may be restrained in certain ways, to preserve their power in other ways.

courts *would* behave with stronger powers, against which to compare how they have used DOIs.[4]

There are however two specific areas in which we can examine whether judges have been activist in the defence of human rights, or whether they have been restrained in the use of their already weakened powers. First, since the DOI is a statement directed at legislative action and does not provide an immediately effective remedy to the claimant, it could support broad evaluations of human rights compatibility of legislative provisions rather than narrow rulings (a form of restraint); as a tool of expository justice rather than victim-centred, corrective justice. In 5.B I examine whether DOIs have been limited to concrete and specific violations of individual rights, or whether they have been used as a broader device to draw attention to legislative schemes regardless of whether the claimant has made out a rights violation in her particular case. I conclude that, as a matter of judicial doctrine, broad rulings have not been curtailed, but the practice has been mixed and choice to make a narrow or broad ruling has been largely a discretionary one.

Second, 5.C turns to the approach that courts have taken to the jurisprudence of the ECtHR. In Chapter 3.D I considered one possible understanding of the DOI as an alert of non-compliance with international law, rather than an instrument of municipal dialogue over what human rights require. At a doctrinal level, the courts have presented their conclusions on the HRA's requirements as being closely allied to what the Strasbourg court would decide. Judicial restraint on this aspect of the Act has implications for the role left for the political branches; limiting the scope of any municipal dialogue over DOIs.

The subject matter of the previous chapter, the criteria for a DOI, has benefited from considerable academic attention because of interest amongst UK public lawyers in the limits of section 3 of the HRA. The issues in this chapter relate more specifically to the potential of the DOI itself and have received far less attention. The findings in 5.C in particular also assist in explaining the pattern of institutional interaction over DOIs, which is the subject of Chapter 6.

5.B. Expository Justice

5.B.1. A remedy for victims?

There is a difference between a judicial finding that a person's fundamental human right has been violated by public action, and a finding that legislation is insufficient to respect or protect a fundamental right and hence may lead to a breach of that right in certain circumstances. It is the former that gives rise, in international human rights law if not domestic law, to the right to an effective remedy. The latter is nonetheless a useful function that constitutional review of legislation can

[4] One method could be comparison against judicial review in a system with stronger powers. However, this would then require clear methods by which to control for the range of other factors that may explain differences in judicial willingness to find particular laws to violate human rights.

perform, whereby courts examine how legislation has operated in practice, and identify problems or inadequacies that may lead to breaches of fundamental rights.

Minimalism in relation to constitutional adjudication, a concept developed in the US, is an approach to constitutional review that suggests courts should decide only what is necessary to resolve the case before them.[5] Judicial rulings ought to be narrow and should only override legislation to the extent necessary to resolve the controversy before the court and do justice between the parties, rather than deciding deeper issues of what rights mean or broader issues of what rights require in circumstances beyond those immediately before the court.[6]

DOIs could be understood as a mechanism supporting the opposite approach. By creating this remedy, the HRA invites courts to make an evaluation of legislation even though this will have no effect on the rights and liabilities of the parties before the court. The courts are precluded from the narrow task of doing justice between the parties, in the sense of preventing or otherwise remedying the wrong done to the victim before the court, but are authorized to send a message to the legislature that the legislation offends human rights principles. Understood in this way, DOIs enlist courts in a cross-institutional exercise of ensuring not only that past human rights violations are identified, but that legislative provisions which adversely affect rights are justified by the executive and future breaches are prevented.

But courts may choose not to play this broader function. DOIs may also be narrow rulings, if courts only hold legislation incompatible where there has been a violation of the rights of the victim before the court. In the early case of *Re S*,[7] the court adopted this type of narrow approach and resisted calls to issue a DOI where a legislative scheme provided insufficient safeguards to prevent regular breaches of human rights. The majority stated that 'ordinarily the court will only grant [a DOI] to a person who is a victim of an actual or proposed breach of a Convention right'.[8] Even though the court recognized that the legislation in question lacked effective machinery for the protection of rights,[9] it did not make a DOI because it did not consider that the litigant bringing the case had suffered a violation of her human rights. Lord Mackay's judgment even urged the government and Parliament to give immediate attention to problems with the system, but declined to use the official route to do so.[10]

[5] The original concept of judicial minimalism is credited to Alexander Bickel: AM Bickel, *The Least Dangerous Branch: The Supreme Court at the Bar of Politics* (2nd edn Yale University Press, New Haven 1986). The concept was revived by Cass Sunstein: C Sunstein, 'Foreword: Leaving Things Undecided' (1996) 110 Harvard Law Review 4; C Sunstein, *One Case at a Time: Judicial Minimalism on the Supreme Court* (Harvard University Press, Cambridge MA 2001). For a retrospective of the ensuing scholarship, and the different types of justifications for judicial minimalism, see C Sunstein, 'Beyond Judicial Minimalism' (2008) 43 Tulsa Law Review 825.

[6] Sunstein, *One Case at a Time* (n 5) 10–11.

[7] See 4.C.2.

[8] *Re S (Minors) (Care Order: Implementation of Care Plan)* [2002] UKHL 10 [88] (Lord Nicholls).

[9] *Re S* (n 8) [86].

[10] *Re S* (n 8) [112]. Lord Mackay also made a thinly veiled recommendation for one reform that he believed was necessary.

This statement in *Re S* that DOIs are a form of relief for the victim of a human rights violation raises the obvious question of why they should be limited in this way. Certainly, victims may seek and gain some benefit from a DOI, in the form of future legal reform from Parliament. However, prospective legal reform at large is not a personal benefit to the claimant, who will remain subject to the impugned law unless and until it is changed, and even then may not personally benefit from the legislative changes.[11] The DOI serves a public interest in having a judicial opinion on the compatibility of legislation. The fact that it does not resolve the victim's grievance directly indicates that the device is concerned with more than the subjective entitlements of the individual before the court. As one commentator put it when the HRA was introduced, '[the DOI] procedure cannot readily be accommodated within the dispute resolution model of the judicial role: it renders the . . . proceedings clearly more expository in nature'.[12]

Nor does the wording of section 4 HRA limit courts to issuing declarations only when there has been a concrete violation of the rights of the victim before the court. Section 4 provides that, in any proceedings in which a court determines whether a provision of legislation is compatible with a Convention right,[13] if the court is satisfied that the provision is incompatible with a Convention right, it may make a DOI.[14] The HRA does not even limit standing to seek a DOI. The standing provision in section 7(1) HRA only relates to challenges to unlawful acts of public authorities under section 6(1). Where the claimant seeks a DOI, the relevant standing test has been the general public law test of sufficient interest, rather than actual or proposed victimhood.[15]

5.B.2. Judicial willingness to exercise the discretionary power

In a number of later cases, the higher courts have departed from the narrow position in *Re S* and recognized that DOIs serve a broader function. In *Wright*,[16] the House of Lords considered a challenge to a scheme of listing care workers as unsuitable to work with vulnerable adults. The unanimous judgment of the court (resulting in a DOI) considered the argument that a DOI could not be made against the scheme of the Act, because that scheme would not always engage a human right. Its conclusion was markedly different from *Re S*:

> While the Strasbourg court has the luxury of looking back at the particular circumstances of a concrete case, and deciding whether there has been a breach of article 6 in that case, our

[11] The Court of Appeal in *R (Thompson & JF) v Secretary of State for the Home Department* [2009] EWCA Civ 792 recognized this reality: see text accompanying n 20.

[12] J Miles, 'Standing under the Human Rights Act 1998: Theories of Rights Enforcement and the Nature of Public Law Adjudication' (2000) 59 Cambridge Law Journal 133, 164.

[13] s 4(1) (primary legislation); s 4(3) (secondary legislation).

[14] s 4(2) (primary legislation); s 4(4) (secondary legislation where primary legislation prevents the removal of the incompatibility).

[15] J Beatson et al, *Human Rights: Judicial Protection in the United Kingdom* (Sweet & Maxwell, London 2008) 514. *R (Rusbridger & Anor) v Attorney General* [2003] UKHL 38, [21], [53]–[57].

[16] See 4.C.2(b).

national law has to devise a scheme which will be generally applicable before the particular impact of the decision is known. As Dyson LJ put it in the Court of Appeal, 'the question whether article 6 is engaged should not be decided by examining on a case by case basis the actual effect of provisional listing on an individual worker'. The Secretary of State has therefore accepted that the Court of Appeal's order was appropriate in the light of the challenge to the whole scheme, because it is designed to ensure that breaches do not occur.[17]

This statement clearly supports the idea that DOIs may be employed to draw attention to problematic legislation regardless of whether the legislation has produced a violation in the immediate case. It also highlights the important distinction between the function of individual complaints to the international tribunal at Strasbourg and the function of a national court.

The Court of Appeal in the later case of *R (on the application of F, Angus Aubrey Thompson)*[18] took a similar approach to the House of Lords in *Wright*. Counsel for the Secretary of State argued that the court ought not grant a DOI to the claimants because they had not produced evidence that *their* article 8 rights had been breached, and that proportionality assessments ought to be made on the facts of individual cases, rather than reviewing the legislation 'in the abstract'.[19] But the court did not consider itself to be prevented from granting a DOI for this reason, stating:

It is important to both claimants as well as to the Secretary of State and the public at large to know whether the scheme is incompatible with Article 8 of the Convention on the grounds that there is no right to review notification requirements that are imposed for an indefinite period. If the scheme is incompatible then section 82 will no doubt be amended. Whether in that event either claimant would be able at any time to seek a review would depend on the terms of the amendment. The claimants have a real interest in seeking to have this important issue decided. We do not consider that we are precluded . . . from deciding it.[20]

Similarly, the benefit of judicial guidance was referred to by the first instance judge and the Court of Appeal in the case of *R (on the application of Baiai and Ors)*,[21] where a number of cases were being brought under the legislative provisions aimed at curbing 'sham' marriages. Here the Court of Appeal recognized that it was *principally* concerned with the general scheme, though it must also consider the particular situation of the applicants.[22] This is in keeping with the function of the highest courts: by the time a case reaches a senior court its significance usually extends beyond the parties to the litigation.

Since *Re S*, the courts have generally been willing to employ their power to make a DOI once an incompatibility has been identified, despite a range of government

[17] *R (Wright & Ors) v Secretary of State for Health* [2009] UKHL 3 [22] (Baroness Hale).

[18] *Thompson* (n 11). This DOI was upheld by the House of Lords in *R (Thompson & JF) v Secretary of State for the Home Department* [2010] UKSC 17.

[19] See *Thompson* (n 11) [32].

[20] *Thompson* (n 11) [32].

[21] *R (Baiai & Ors) v Secretary of State for the Home Department & Anor* [2006] EWHC 823 (Admin) [30]; *R (Baiai & Ors) v Secretary of State for the Home Department* [2007] EWCA Civ 478 [9].

[22] *Baiai* (Court of Appeal) (n 21) [9].

arguments as to why the court should not exercise its discretion to do so. Courts have rejected arguments that they ought not issue a DOI because it would serve no useful purpose to the litigant. For example, the court in *Bellinger* rejected the argument that it ought not issue a DOI because the matter was already subject to an ECtHR ruling and therefore the remedial order provisions of the Act (triggered by a DOI or ECtHR decision) were already available to the government. Dismissing the idea that it would encourage 'needless litigation', Lord Hobhouse suggested that the DOI would add weight to the existing case for legal reform,[23] and Lord Nicholls expressly referred to the desirability of a national court formally recording that the present state of the law was incompatible with human rights.[24] Courts have even made DOIs in some cases where the legislation had already been repealed.[25] In these cases the legislation had been applied to the litigants, hence the DOI served as a formal recognition of the violation of their rights.

Further, in the case of *Morris v Westminster City Council*,[26] the Court of Appeal rejected the argument that a DOI should not be issued if the public authority in question had other powers that it could use to prevent any infringement of the claimant's rights. The legislation at issue limited access to public housing for those British nationals whose dependants were under immigration control, but the housing authority had other powers that could have been used to ensure that the claimant received housing. The court recognized that even if the claimant herself might have benefited from other powers, other people denied housing might not have been able to access alternative provisions and would face the full brunt of the legislative incompatibility.[27] In Lord Sedley's view, the 'incompatibility remain [ed] an incompatibility whatever other forms of recourse become available' and there was no good reason to withhold a DOI. In fact, the leading judgment remarked on the peculiarity of the government's resistance to a DOI even once it had lost its argument that the legislation was human rights compatible. It suggested that the language of section 4 conferred 'a jurisdiction which the court was expected to exercise' once it had identified an incompatibility.[28]

5.B.3. Judicial reluctance in relation to DOIs

The examples in 4.B.2 suggest that the court will ordinarily issue a DOI once an incompatibility has been identified because the DOI serves the useful expository function of recording the court's decision that the legislation is incompatible with human rights. The suggestion the DOIs are a remedy only for victims of human rights violations has been set aside in a number of cases. Indeed, it would be ironic

23 *Bellinger v Bellinger* [2003] UKHL 21 [78]–[79].

24 *Bellinger* (n 23) [55].

25 *R (Hooper & Ors) v Secretary of State for Work and Pensions* [2003] EWCA Civ 875; *R (Wilkinson) v Inland Revenue Commissioners* [2003] EWCA Civ 814; *R (Clift) v Secretary of State for the Home Department* [2006] UKHL 54.

26 [2005] EWCA Civ 1184.

27 *Morris* (n 26) [54].

28 *Morris* (n 26) [54].

if that line of reasoning were followed, given the fact that DOIs are clearly not a remedy oriented to corrective justice for the victim, but a remedy oriented to general and prospective legal reform.

Yet, there have been limits to judicial willingness to use DOIs. There are three cases in which the courts have demonstrated reluctance in relation to the political function of the DOI in prompting legislative reform. Two such cases, *R (Nasseri) v Secretary of State for the Home Department*,[29] and *Rusbridger v Attorney-General*[30] indicate the reluctance of courts to be involved in moves for legislative reform. In the third case, *R (on the application of Chester) v Secretary of State for Justice*,[31] the first instance judge and the Court of Appeal exercised their discretion not to issue a DOI because it would be a repeat DOI, and this was considered inappropriate sanctioning of the legislature.

In *Nasseri*, the Court of Appeal overturned a DOI in relation to a 'deeming provision' in the Asylum and Immigration (Treatment of Claimants) Act 2004.[32] This provision created an irrefutable presumption that return of an asylum seeker to certain countries listed in the legislation would not violate the UK's obligation not to return a person to the likelihood of torture or inhuman or degrading treatment (*non-refoulement*).[33] The DOI had been issued because the legislation precluded the Home Secretary from considering the law and practice governing *refoulement* in Greece. The Court of Appeal judgment recognized that, in the event that return of a person to a listed country did violate the obligation of *non-refoulement* (for instance, because that country would then return the person to likely torture) the legislation protected the rights-violating actions of the Home Secretary from challenge under section 6 HRA. The incompatibility would result from the legislation itself because it prevented the Home Secretary from considering the merits of any individual case. The legislation also gave the Home Secretary no discretion to remove countries from the list of countries deemed to be safe: this could only occur through amendment of the primary legislation.[34]

The Court of Appeal examined the evidence concerning Greek law and practice on *refoulement* for itself. Determining that the claimant's right would not be infringed were he returned there, and therefore the legislation was not operating in a manner incompatible with Convention rights *in the immediate case*, the court went on to state:

> [T]he list system renders the United Kingdom's compliance with article 3 of the [Convention] fragile. In the absence of individual examinations of the merits of individual cases by those responsible for specific executive and judicial decisions in those cases, the whole weight of compliance falls on the measures and systems in place for monitoring law and

[29] *R (Nasseri) v Secretary of State for the Home Department* [2008] EWCA Civ 464.

[30] *Rusbridger* (n 15).

[31] *R (Chester) v Secretary of State for Justice & Anor* [2009] EWHC 2923 (Admin), *Chester v Secretary of State for Justice* [2010] EWCA Civ 1439.

[32] Paragraph 3(2), Schedule 3.

[33] The particular *non-refoulement* obligation at issue existed under Article 3 ECHR: *Chahal v United Kingdom* (1996) 23 EHRR 413.

[34] Paragraph 12, Schedule 3.

practice in the listed states, and does so in circumstances where government has no discretion to take a state of the list, but must seek main legislation.[35]

Upholding the decision, the House of Lords noted that this statement from the Court of Appeal was only a comment on the practical reality that the system created a risk of incompatibility, and that unless the Secretary of State chose to keep a close eye on what was going on in listed countries, and invited Parliament to remove countries from the list, the deeming provision might 'produce the wrong results', that is, initiate ultimate *refoulement* in violation of Article 3 ECHR.[36] Parliament had been warned by the JCHR and the Select Committee on Constitutional Affairs that the system did not adequately protect against violations of Article 3, but, in the court's words, 'Parliament must have decided that the administrative convenience of having the list in primary legislation, to avoid administrative law challenges... outweighed the risk that there might be cases where a court found that a listed country was in fact unsafe and issued a declaration of incompatibility.'[37]

We can contrast the decision in *Nasseri* to the statements in *Wright*, where it was clearly stated that national law ought to properly protect against breaches of human rights, and a DOI can alert Parliament where the law does not do so adequately. The reluctance to issue a DOI in *Nasseri* to that effect is puzzling. Given the benefits of a better process in avoiding future violations, it seems excessively restrained for the courts not to use even the non-disruptive remedy at their disposal to formally draw attention to the inadequacies of the regime for Parliament to consider. It also seems unnecessary for the House of Lords to go one step further and suggest that it was entirely legitimate for the legislation to avoid the administrative inconvenience of sufficiently protecting against *refoulement* to torture. Two respected parliamentary committees had criticized the deeming provision during its passage as dangerous on human rights grounds, but the government refused to support amendments. Notwithstanding their recognition that the provisions created a risk of *refoulement*, the House of Lords advanced the formalist view that Parliament as a whole had chosen to take this risk and refused to add any political weight to the ongoing argument that the provisions were dangerous and undesirable. In fact, removals of asylum seekers to Greece were eventually suspended, for the same reasons as were advanced in argument in *Nasseri*, in September 2010, in light of challenges to removals to Greece at the ECtHR and before the ECJ.[38]

[35] *Nasseri* (Court of Appeal) (n 29) [42] (Lord Laws).

[36] *R (Nasseri) v Secretary of State for the Home Department* (2009] UKHL 23 [22] (Lord Hoffman).

[37] *Nasseri* (House of Lords) (n 36) [22].

[38] The suspension occurred after the legislation was challenged under the EU Charter of Fundamental Rights, which was referred by the Court of Appeal to the European Court of Justice (ECJ). While this decision was pending, the ECtHR awarded a judgment against Belgium, finding that the complainant's removal to Greece from Belgium violated Articles 3 and 13: *MSS v Belgium and Greece* Application No 30696/09 (21 January 2011). The ECJ likewise held, in December 2011, that a member state could not return an asylum seeker to a country where systemic deficiencies in procedures and living conditions led to a real risk of inhuman and degrading treatment: *NS & Others v Secretary of State for the Home Department* (C-411/10).

The case of *Rusbridger* goes further and illustrates open judicial hostility to attempts to use DOIs to draw the courts into an expository role. This case concerned the criminal offence of advocating the abolition of the monarchy.[39] This offence had not been prosecuted since 1883. The claimants, intending to publish a series of articles advocating republicanism, sought assurances from the Attorney-General that he would either decline to apply section 3 because it had fallen into desuetude, or that he would not do so because such a prosecution would violate the right to freedom of expression, or that he would seek a declaration that the offence was to be interpreted in a manner in accordance with section 3. The Attorney-General declined to make any such assurances. The articles were published and no prosecution was issued but the claimants sought judicial review of the Attorney-General's decision as well as a declaration as to how the offence was to be read and given effect or, in the alternative, a DOI.

Here the matter was not a legislative scheme that gave rise to risks of human rights violations, but a legislative provision that, in its ordinary interpretation, clearly violated freedom of expression. Lord Steyn recognized that were the law applied, a human rights violation would exist on the merits and the question would be one of choosing between sections 3 and 4.[40] But he held that the litigation was alarmist and unnecessary and that the courts ought not to be bothered with it, because it ought to have been clear to the claimants that the offence would not survive scrutiny under the HRA. The remaining Law Lords were even more forceful in their dismissal of the application. Lord Hutton, for instance, argued that 'sections 3 and 4 of the Human Rights Act are not intended to be an instrument by which the courts can chivvy Parliament into spring-cleaning the statute book'.[41]

The Law Commission had recommended the offence for repeal in 1977, and it had never received the attention of Parliament.[42] Yet, Lord Rodger's reluctance to use a DOI to draw attention to this oversight was plain:

> The claimants are, of course, free to use their influence in a campaign to try and change that political judgment [not to repeal the offence]. But it would be wrong in principle for the courts to allow the claimants to go on with proceedings where the only favourable outcome of any practical use to them would be a declaration of incompatibility that they could use to further any such political campaign.[43]

The third case, *Chester*,[44] indicates the potential scope for DOIs to put pressure on the government and legislature to act, should the courts wish to use them in this manner. This case involved a further challenge to the ban on prisoner voting.

39 s 3 Treason Felony Act 1848.

40 'Any suggestion that a total legislative ban on republican discourse in print could be compatible with article 10 would stretch judicial gullibility to breaking point. It, therefore, appears inevitable that any resultant incompatibility would have to be read down under the strong interpretative obligation under section 3(1)': *Rusbridger* (n 15) [8] (Lord Steyn).

41 *Rusbridger* (n 15) [36]; see also [61] (Lord Walker), [43] (Lord Scott).

42 *Rusbridger* (n 15) [58].

43 *Rusbridger* (n 15) [58].

44 *Chester* (n 31).

Chapter 4 discussed the case of *Smith v Scott*,[45] where a DOI was made with respect to the blanket ban preventing all prisoners in the UK from voting. I noted that one reason for this DOI, on a matter already subject to a ECtHR ruling, was significant delays in the government's timetable for a response and the risk that legislative change would not occur in time for the imminent Scottish election. Two years later, in *Chester*, a second challenge was made to the ban, given continued delays from the government. The judge declined to make a repeat declaration, on the grounds that no additional vindication of the claim was necessary and for the courts to continue to issue DOIs on the same grounds, to actively pressure the government, would be 'offensive to constitutional principles'.[46] This decision was affirmed by the Court of Appeal, which held that it was not for the courts to sanction the government for its delay in responding to a DOI, nor for its failure to give effect to an ECtHR judgment: that sanction should occur at the political level.[47] So, while the courts have not considered it inappropriate to make a DOI even in cases where the Minister accepts the need for legislative change and is acting towards that change, *Chester* indicates that repeated DOIs would cross a line of institutional respect. The HRA preserves the ability of the legislature to do nothing, and this provides a clear justification for courts to refrain from repeat DOIs, at least in the short term.

A complicating factor in *Chester* was that the government had clearly stated, in launching the second stage of its consultation on a response, that certain categories of prisoners would not get voting rights under any new legislation. The claimant fell in one of those categories, that is, post-tariff life prisoners. He did not seek a declaration identical to that in *Smith v Scott*, rather he sought a declaration that his exclusion from the franchise—as a prisoner who had completed the minimum terms of his sentence—was incompatible with the right to vote.[48] This scenario illustrates how DOIs could be used in an active, advisory way, to provide judicial opinions on the parameters of necessary remedial action (in the court's view) by clarifying the scope of the infringement. Again, given the non-coercive nature of DOIs, this advice could be considered by the government and legislature but would not have to be followed. However, the court in *Chester* considered that such use of a DOI would 'over-judicialize' the issue and would be inappropriate given that there were multiple legal solutions available.[49] The court was clearly aware that the matter was politically controversial, and made clear its position that the choice of remedy should remain a political responsibility.[50] Interestingly however, the court did indicate openness to the potential utility of this advisory function as the constitutional relationship between the branches evolved over time.[51]

[45] See Chapter 4.C.3.
[46] *Chester* (High Court) (n 31) [34].
[47] *Chester* (Court of Appeal) (n 31) [27].
[48] *Chester* (High Court) (n 31) [20].
[49] *Chester* (Court of Appeal) (n 31) [28]. See also *Chester* (High Court) (n 31) [52].
[50] *Chester* (Court of Appeal) (n 31) [32].
[51] *Chester* (Court of Appeal) (n 31) [30]–[31].

5.B.4. Conclusion

The designers of the HRA created a novel device, which gave courts the power to make rulings that the political branches did not have to follow. It is not surprising that the courts would be wary in receiving this type of power. On the one hand, they could decline to use it except in situations where they feel it to be absolutely necessary, and thereby avoid the risks of DOIs becoming widely used and devalued. On the other hand, they could use it freely to exert influence over the state of the law, safe in the knowledge that they were only contributing to a political debate, rather than determining the necessary outcome.

We have seen above, in the particular context of narrow versus broad rulings, the courts have trodden a path between these possibilities. They have recognized the guidance-providing, expository function of DOIs, and have not limited the DOI doctrinally, but have also been wary in contributing to certain ongoing debates on immigration practice, archaic offences, and prisoner voting.

5.C. The Strasbourg Dimension

I argued in Chapter 3.D that the contemporary notion of universal and fundamental human rights is a pluralist one. Human rights function at a number of levels and are applied and interpreted by a variety of institutions, including non-judicial institutions. International human rights law does not dictate the level of protection and promotion of human rights in a national context beyond providing a basic minimum and a framework for principled development.

This is the case even with the ECtHR, which is best understood not as a supreme arbiter of human rights protection in Europe, but as a supervisory court which plays an important but ultimately subsidiary or supporting role. However, it is possible for national institutions in Europe to be minimalist in their protection of human rights, seeking only to pre-empt and avoid adverse Strasbourg rulings. Under this kind of minimum compliance approach to human rights protection, the implementation of human rights would be a *predictive* exercise in determining what the ECtHR would decide. If this is the attitude taken to human rights, this limits the space for deliberation by national institutions on what human rights mean.

This section examines how the UK courts have approached the relationship between municipal human rights law and Strasbourg jurisprudence, with the focus on what this has meant for the use of DOIs between 2000 and 2010. I first present the dominant doctrinal approach taken by UK courts to the section 2(1) requirement to take Strasbourg jurisprudence into account, and then look to how this approach has been justified. Section 5.C.2 considers the role of Strasbourg jurisprudence specifically in those decisions leading to a DOI and, lastly, I explore why judges may take an approach which if not in deed, then at least in word, sticks tightly to Strasbourg jurisprudence as the authority for interpretations of what human rights require. One effect of this approach is to enhance the authoritativeness of

DOIs in the political process and increase the likelihood of a positive legislative response; however, this strategy has its own repercussions.

5.C.1. 'No more, but certainly no less'

The HRA does not require UK courts to follow Strasbourg jurisprudence. Rather, the formulation of the duty under section 2(1) preserves the ability of British judges to depart from the decisions and the reasoning of Strasbourg institutions. This was deliberate: a Conservative amendment that would have required judges to follow ECtHR decisions was rejected in the passage of the Act.[52] The Lord Chancellor expressly stated that such a duty would be inappropriate because UK courts must be free 'to give a lead to Europe as well as be led'.[53]

Instead, section 2(1) gives Strasbourg jurisprudence the status of persuasive authority in the evaluation of what Convention rights require. This duty could be discharged simply by the court considering any Strasbourg jurisprudence put before it.[54] Hence, the provision grants a wide ambit of discretion for judges to negotiate the relationship between domestic and international human rights law. This has been characterized as giving UK courts an opportunity—but not a mandate—to make a greater contribution to international human rights law.[55]

The House of Lords addressed the status of Strasbourg jurisprudence early in the life of the HRA. In *R (Alconbury Developments Ltd) v Secretary of State for the Environment*, Lord Slynn stated that the court should follow any clear and constant jurisprudence of the ECtHR, 'in the absence of special circumstances'.[56] This approach evidently restricted the discretion in section 2(1) itself; however, the requirement that Strasbourg jurisprudence be 'clear and constant' and the possibility of exceptions in special circumstances left some room for independent decision-making by UK courts.

In *Anderson*, Lord Bingham affirmed this principle, stating that there must be good reason to depart from principles laid down in a 'carefully considered judgment of the Court sitting as a Grand Chamber'.[57] He emphasized that if courts were to

[52] Hansard HL vol 583 col 513 (18 November 1997).

[53] The three specific reasons stated were that the Convention itself, not the decisions of Strasbourg bodies, was the ultimate source of the law; the UK was only strictly bound, as a matter of international law, to those decisions to which it was a party; and that cases before the courts may involve factors specific to the UK and it is important that UK courts have the necessary discretion to be able to aid the development of human rights law: Lord Irvine of Lairg, HL Debates vol 583 col 514, 18 November 1997. The sentiment was in tune with Ronald Dworkin's position that the ECHR rights should form the basis for a British Bill of Rights, because in the hands of British judges the Convention might be adapted to provide for more generous protection, 'using the rich and special traditions of the British common law'. R Dworkin, *A Bill of Rights for Britain* (Chatto and Windus, London 1990) 22.

[54] R Masterman, 'Taking the Strasbourg Jurisprudence into Account: Developing a "Municipal Law of Human Rights" under the Human Rights Act 1998' (2005) 54 ICLQ 907, 909.

[55] J Lewis, 'The European Ceiling on Human Rights' [2007] PL 720, 725. See also N Krisch, 'The Open Architecture of European Human Rights Law' (2008) 71 Modern Law Review 183, 202–3.

[56] [2001] UKHL 23 [26].

[57] *R (Anderson) v Secretary of State for the Home Department* [2002] UKHL 46 [18]. However this statement was made in response to an argument by the Secretary of State seeking to avoid the effects of the latest decision of the ECtHR.

find legislation to be compatible with human rights where Strasbourg jurisprudence indicated that it was incompatible (that is, if UK courts went below the Strasbourg standard of human rights protection), it would be open to the litigant to later argue before the ECtHR that the domestic interpretation was out of line with the ECHR's requirements.[58]

Over time, the dominant approach of the House of Lords has further tightened the link between judicial decision-making under the HRA and Strasbourg jurisprudence. Instead of emphasizing the Strasbourg jurisprudence as providing a floor of rights protection, the court expounded a theory of a uniform European law of human rights. In the 2004 case of *R (on the application of Ullah) v Special Adjudicator*,[59] Lord Bingham stated:

> It is of course open to member states to provide for rights more generous than those guaranteed by the Convention, but such provision should not be the product of interpretation of the Convention by national courts, since the meaning of the Convention should be uniform throughout the states party to it. The duty of national courts is to keep pace with the Strasbourg jurisprudence as it evolves: no more, but certainly no less.[60]

This can be referred to as the 'mirror principle'.[61] Though the rights created under the HRA and the rights arising under the ECHR are two separate legal creations,[62] and the extent of the rights under the HRA depends on the interpretation given by UK courts to the Act,[63] this interpretation is to 'mirror' the treaty obligations of the UK in respect of the corresponding articles of the Convention.[64] The House of Lords have built on section 2(1) HRA in a way that curtails the discretion in the text and more closely resembles a precedential system.[65] Even in situations where the state of the Strasbourg jurisprudence may suggest a need for further clarity or progressive development, the House of Lords has stated 'it is for the Strasbourg court, not for us, to decide whether its case law is out of touch with modern conditions and to determine what further extensions, if any, are needed to the rights guaranteed by the Convention'.[66]

How have the courts justified this approach to Strasbourg jurisprudence? One justification that has been offered is that the purpose of the HRA was solely to avoid

[58] *Anderson* (House of Lords) (n 57) [18].

[59] *R (Ullah) v Special Adjudicator* [2004] UKHL 26.

[60] *Ullah* (n 59) [20]. For a similar statement, specifically regarding remedies under the Act, see *R (Greenfield) v Secretary of State for the Home Department* [2005] UKHL 14 [19].

[61] JCHR, *Twenty-Ninth Report 2007–08: A Bill of Rights for the UK?* (2008) HL-165, HC-150 [56]; Lewis (n 55) 726–7.

[62] *Re McKerr* [2004] UKHL 12 [26] (Lord Nicholls), who emphasizes this distinction, and states that 'these two sets of rights now exist side by side'. See also [62] (Lord Hoffman).

[63] *Re McKerr* (n 62) [26]. Lord Nicholls's dictum in *Re McKerr* was quoted and affirmed by Bingham LJ in *R (Al-Skeini & Ors) v Secretary of State for Defence* [2007] UKHL 26, [10].

[64] *R (Quark Fishing Ltd) v Secretary of State for Foreign and Commonwealth Affairs* [2005] UKHL 57 [34] (Lord Nicholls). Affirmed in *Al-Skeini* (n 63).

[65] R Masterman, 'Section 2(1) of the Human Rights Act: Binding Domestic Courts to Strasbourg?' [2004] PL 725; M Amos, 'Problems with the Human Rights Act 1998 and How to Remedy Them: Is a Bill of Rights the Answer?' (2009) 72 Modern Law Review 883, 897.

[66] *N v Secretary of State for the Home Department* [2005] UKHL 31 [25] (Lord Hope).

the United Kingdom being in breach of its international obligations and unable to provide, in domestic law, remedies that would be available before the ECtHR.[67] On this argument, there is a tension between the non-binding status of Strasbourg jurisprudence under the HRA and the purpose of the Act,[68] and one way to resolve this tension is to elevate the requirement to 'take into account' Strasbourg jurisprudence to a more demanding duty. However, it should be noted that any such tension is only one-way. If UK courts are less generous to a human rights complainant, then the unsuccessful litigant might seek a remedy at Strasbourg. However, if the UK courts make a decision that is more generous to the complainant than the Strasbourg jurisprudence, there is no direct avenue for the UK government to challenge that decision at the international level. In any event, this would be unnecessary. If Parliament is dissatisfied with the national court's decision, then the appropriate response is for it to legislate as it sees fit, exercising its power under the HRA to override a judicial decision. Hence, the courts need not limit the protection of human rights to the Strasbourg minimum.

A second justification proposed for why the UK courts should seek to do no more, as well as no less, than the ECtHR is that the Act protects 'Convention rights' and their meaning can only be authoritatively expounded by the Convention bodies. On this argument, the uniform and 'true' meaning of the ECHR is what the ECtHR says it is and a reading that departs from the Strasbourg jurisprudence is 'mistaken'.[69] This was emphasized by Lord Buxton in *Anderson*, who stated that 'where an international court has the specific task of interpreting an international instrument it brings to that task a range of knowledge and principle that a national court cannot aspire to'.[70]

This view that only the ECtHR can reach the 'correct' view of what Convention rights require can also be seen in the warning given by Lord Brown in *Al-Skeini* that not only should UK courts stick closely to the Strasbourg position, they should err on the side more favourable to the government:

> There seems to me, indeed, a greater danger in the national court construing the Convention too generously in favour of an applicant than in construing it too narrowly. In the former event the mistake will necessarily stand: the member state cannot itself go to Strasbourg to have it corrected; in the latter event, however, where Convention rights have been denied by too narrow a construction, the aggrieved individual can have the decision corrected in Strasbourg.[71]

This second justification strongly suggests that the function of a DOI is to alert to non-compliance with international law, rather than initiate dialogue over municipal human rights standards. This connection was confirmed by Baroness Hale in

[67] *Quark Fishing* (n 64) [34] (Lord Nicholls).

[68] See *Anderson* (House of Lords) (n 57) [18]. Paul Craig also identifies this tension in the non-binding status of Strasbourg jurisprudence: P Craig, *Administrative Law* (6th edn Sweet & Maxwell, London 2008) 553–4.

[69] *Al-Skeini* (n 63) [8] (Lord Bingham).

[70] *R (Anderson) v Secretary of State for the Home Department* [2001] EWCA Civ 1698 [91].

[71] *Al-Skeini* (n 63) [106].

R (Animal Defenders International) v Secretary of State for Culture, Media and Sport,[72] who stated her belief that when Parliament gave the courts their powers under the HRA:

> it was not giving us the power to leap ahead of Strasbourg in our interpretation of the Convention rights. Nor do I believe it was expecting us to lag behind. The purpose . . . of a declaration of incompatibility is to warn Government and Parliament that, in our view, the United Kingdom is in breach of its international obligations.[73]

The courts have come under criticism for unduly limiting the HRA, and failing to fully explore its potential as a national human rights instrument.[74] However, *even* if we are to understand the HRA as principally a vehicle for the implementation of international law obligations, the mirror principle remains open to criticism. First, it misunderstands the function of the Strasbourg system. There is no imperative that there be a *uniform* approach to human rights throughout the member States; the only imperative is that States do not drop below an irreducible minimum, as ultimately determined by the ECtHR.[75] International lawyer Colin Warbick points out that the ECtHR protects a minimum catalogue of human rights to a minimum standard, and in doing so must deal with human rights violations elsewhere in Europe of an entirely different order to the UK, such as those faced by Kurds in Turkey or in Chechnya.[76]

Appreciating the ECtHR as providing this type of supra-national minimum standard supports an alternative approach for UK courts to take, one in which they are open to develop human rights protections further than the settled ECtHR case law and adapt that case law as appropriate to the national context and legal system.[77] Whereas the account of a uniform European law of human rights elevates

[72] [2008] UKHL 15.

[73] *Animal Defenders* (n 72) [53]. The separate opinion of Lord Scott in the same case took a different view: that there was a tension in the HRA between the role of DOIs in drawing attention to an incompatibility between the legislation under review and domestic human rights protections versus an incompatibility between the legislation and the international obligations of the United Kingdom. He considered that the problem did not arise in the immediate case, but a divergence was possible and in that event it would need to be decided which was the primary purpose of s 4 HRA (see [46]). The majority opinion (Lord Bingham) expressly disagreed with this approach and affirmed the mirror principle (at [37]).

[74] See Masterman (n 54); R Masterman, 'Aspiration or Foundation? The Status of Strasbourg Jurisprudence and the "Convention Rights" in Domestic Law' in H Fenwick, R Masterman, and G Phillipson (eds), *Judicial Reasoning under the Human Rights Act* (CUP, Cambridge 2007); E Wicks, 'Taking Account of Strasbourg?' (2005) 11 European Public Law 405; Lewis (n 55); cf. C Warbick, 'The European Convention on Human Rights and the Human Rights Act: A View from the Outside' in H Fenwick, R Masterman, and G Phillipson (eds), *Judicial Reasoning under the Human Rights Act* (CUP, Cambridge 2007) 25–6, who argues that the HRA was not introduced in a manner appropriate to a national bill of rights and should be understood as a statute implementing international law.

[75] S Grosz, J Beatson, and P Duffy, *Human Rights: The 1998 Act and the European Convention* (1st edn Sweet & Maxwell, London 2000) 20.

[76] Warbick (n 74) 29–30.

[77] Klug and Wildbore refer to these two approaches as the 'dynamic approach' and the 'municipal approach' respectively, in contrast to the mirror principle approach. See F Klug and H Wildbore, 'Follow or Lead? The Human Rights Act and the European Court of Human Rights' [2010] EHRLR 621.

the Strasbourg court to a hierarchical position of superiority, this alternative approach would be better fitted to the ECtHR's own understanding of its role as a subsidiary form of human rights protection. In the case of *Handyside v United Kingdom*, which established the concept of the margin of appreciation, the ECtHR stated:

> [The] machinery of protection established by the Convention is subsidiary to the national systems safeguarding human rights. The Convention leaves to each contracting state, in the first place, the task of securing the rights and freedoms it enshrines... By reason of their direct and continuous contact with the vital forces in their countries, *State authorities are in principle in a better position than the international judge to give an opinion on the exact content of these requirements as well as on 'necessity' of a restriction or 'penalty' intended to meet them.*[78]

Hence, the primary role in elaborating the precise content of human rights, and the extent of acceptable limitations on rights, is played by national institutions—national *institutions* not solely national *legislatures* or *executives*—and this is what grounds the ECtHR's margin of appreciation doctrine. This doctrine is a tool by which the court, as an international court, accommodates national difference,[79] as well as changing societal norms over time.

The mirror principle approach, evinced by the statements above, has been that, if protection of rights is to be taken further than the Strasbourg court has provided, this is the task of the legislature not the UK courts. But this is neither stated in the text of the Convention nor the pronouncements of the ECtHR.[80] The notion that any greater protection cannot be provided by the courts is a *choice* to interpret national institutions to mean the executive and Parliament and not the courts. This choice may be based on ideas of what is constitutionally appropriate in the UK, or it may be independently justified for some other reason, but it is certainly not a rule that is provided by European human rights law. In fact, national courts in several European States assert the power to decide on the limits of the authority of the ECtHR.[81] Nico Krisch has drawn attention to the fact that 'British courts have come to refer to the Convention and to ECtHR judgments with a frequency and diligence hardly matched anywhere else in Europe'.[82]

At a practical level, various commentators have raised concerns that Strasbourg decisions are not suitable to being followed as the binding decisions of a higher court. The decisions of the ECtHR are often highly fact specific and not reasoned

[78] *Handyside v United Kingdom* (1976) 1 EHRR 737 [46] [emphasis added]. We can note the disjunction between this statement and Lord Buxton's statement in *Anderson* (text accompanying n 70), which is ironic given that in that case, the Court of Appeal relied on Strasbourg cases in which the court has misunderstood the law of England and Wales on life sentences.

[79] This doctrine has in fact been criticized for accommodating too much and failing to effectively protect human rights: Krisch (n 55) 207–8; J Brauch, 'The Margin of Appreciation and the Jurisprudence of the European Court of Human Rights' (2004) 11 Columbia Journal of European Law 113, 125.

[80] This argument is also made by Leigh and Masterman, who stress that 'in the eyes of the Strasbourg institutions... no distinction is made between the respective competences of the member States' arms of government': I Leigh and R Masterman, *Making Rights Real* (Hart, Oxford 2008) 70.

[81] Krisch (n 55) 183–4, 189–97.

[82] Krisch (n 55) 202.

in the analytical style of the common law.[83] The court's jurisprudence is often poorly theorized and the reasoning is short,[84] with some judgments essentially declaring the court's conclusions.[85] The application of the margin of appreciation in many cases means that there is not close scrutiny by the court as to the proportionality of limitations on rights, and in certain areas—particularly freedom of expression and freedom of religion—this has meant that States have sometimes been able to limit rights in quite severe ways.[86] In some cases, the Strasbourg court has misunderstood domestic law in reaching its decision.[87] Additionally, just as occurs in a precedential legal system, there will inevitably be questions upon which Strasbourg jurisprudence provides no guidance simply because the factual or legal situation before the national court has not been considered.

In fact, UK courts have sometimes diverged from the formal mirror principle, and exercised independent judgment in elaborating the requirements of Convention rights in specific circumstances, either because the margin of appreciation has applied, or because Strasbourg case law provided little or no guidance, or because the ECtHR has misunderstood national law. In some Court of Appeal and lower court decisions, judges have looked more broadly to the principles underpinning the Convention and rejected an 'over-rigid' approach to Strasbourg case law.[88] Even the House of Lords (and later the Supreme Court) indicated some important limits on the mirror principle towards the end of the study period. For example, in *Re P & Ors*,[89] Lord Hoffman stated that the reasons for following Strasbourg do not apply where the ECtHR has 'deliberately declined to lay down an interpretation for all member States, as it does when it says that the question is within the margin of appreciation'.[90] This judgment properly recognized the room for national courts, as a national institution, to decide for themselves, within the margin of appreciation.[91] In *R v Horncastle and Ors*, the Supreme Court stated that, in rare occasions where the ECtHR failed to sufficiently appreciate or accommodate the

[83] The court's decisions have in fact been referred to as 'Delphic in character': A Smith, 'The Human Rights Act: The Constitutional Context' in CCPL, *The Human Rights Act and the Criminal Justice and Regulatory Process* (Oxford, Hart Publishing 1999) 6.

[84] H Fenwick, R Masterman, and G Phillipson, 'The Human Rights Act in Contemporary Context' in H Fenwick, R Masterman, and G Phillipson (eds), *Judicial Reasoning under the Human Rights Act* (CUP, Cambridge 2007) 6.

[85] Masterman, 'Aspiration or Foundation? The Status of Strasbourg Jurisprudence and the "Convention Rights" in Domestic Law' (n 74) 66.

[86] Fenwick et al (n 84) 6.

[87] See *Anderson* (Court of Appeal) (n 70); *R v Horncastle & Ors* [2009] UKSC 14.

[88] See Masterman, 'Aspiration or Foundation?' (n 74) 69.

[89] *In Re P & Ors* [2008] UKHL 38. See also J Lewis, 'In Re P and Others: An Exception to the "No More, Certainly No Less" Rule' [2009] PL 43.

[90] *Re P & Ors* (n 89) [36]. Lord Hope also stated that Strasbourg jurisprudence ought not be treated as a 'straightjacket', at [50]. However, the judgment still characterized the question before it as predicting what the Strasbourg court would do if faced with the issue before the court. The case concerned the ineligibility of unmarried couples to adopt in Northern Ireland. There was no Strasbourg decision on this type of discrimination; however, on the basis of the court's jurisprudence on discrimination against homosexual couples in this context, Lord Hoffman concluded that it was 'not at all unlikely' that if the issue were to go to Strasbourg, the court would hold that this was unlawful discrimination, at [27].

[91] *Re P & Ors* (n 89) [31].

UK's domestic practices, it would decline to follow the Strasbourg decision, and thereby invite the ECtHR to reconsider its decision.[92] It did so in that case, on the question of whether the UK's approach to the admission of hearsay evidence sufficiently protected the defendant's right to a fair trial. The Supreme Court, looking to UK and comparative jurisprudence, suggested that the right to a fair trial should include a more flexible rule which considered whether the whole of the proceedings were insufficient to guard against a violation of Article 6. When the matter returned to the ECtHR in *Al-Khawaja & Tahery v United Kingdom*,[93] the court followed the Supreme Court's suggestion of a more flexible rule, as well as agreeing that, applying that rule, the safeguards in the UK legislation were sufficient if applied correctly.[94] Likewise in the case of *Animal Defenders*, the House of Lords upheld the UK ban on political advertising against a freedom of speech challenge, adeptly managing to distinguish a Strasbourg case that was very close to the matter being decided, with two judges placing particular emphasis on the fact that ECtHR rulings are closely focused on the facts and should not be easily transposed.[95] At the time of writing, the Grand Chamber of the ECtHR was considering its decision.

The above examples indicate that domestic courts can enter into a dialogue with the ECtHR, and seek to persuade that court of a particular understanding or application of human rights principles, even if the Strasbourg court has the final word in the cases that come before it, as a matter of international law. That being said, the mirror principle remains good law, and continues to be employed and affirmed.[96]

5.C.2. Strasbourg and declarations of incompatibility

The doctrinal position on section 2 HRA applies to all review pursuant to the Act: statute as well as executive action and the common law. In light of the practical difficulties of applying Strasbourg jurisprudence as clear and binding rules, as well as judicial movements away from the strict mirror principle on specific grounds (which can also be seen as willingness over time to limit the scope of the principle itself), it is useful to look beyond the formal position elucidated by the House of Lords in cases such as *Ullah* to what *actually* happened in the subset of cases resulting in DOIs. This section considers whether, in those cases which have led to a DOI, the courts have simply applied Strasbourg jurisprudence, or whether they have sometimes made evaluations of rights compatibility based on a broader, or more independent, judgment.

Where the courts have issued a DOI based on the exercise of predicting what the ECtHR would conclude (or where a declaration relates to a matter that has already

92 *Horncastle* (n 87) [11].

93 *Al-Khawaja & Tahery v United Kingdom* [GC] Application Nos 20766/05, 2228/06 (15 December 2011).

94 *Al-Khawaja* (n 93) [146], [151].

95 (n 72) [42] (Lord Scott) and [52] (Baroness Hale).

96 *Manchester City Council v Pinnock* [2010] UKSC 45, *Re McCaughey* [2011] UKSC 20.

been decided by Strasbourg), their use of the remedy supports an understanding of that DOI as an alert of non-compliance (or continuing non-compliance) with international law. The message conveyed by the DOI is that a change in domestic law and practice is necessary to avoid an adverse decision at Strasbourg. However, if the courts have not relied heavily on Strasbourg jurisprudence, then the DOI may represent a more independent evaluation that the legislation infringes human rights—a statement that legislation is improper and unacceptable in light of fundamental human rights principles rather than a statement that legislation violates a readily ascertainable international standard.

This difference sets the stage for different types of institutional interaction. If the contribution that courts make, using the DOI mechanism, is only to draw attention to violations of the minimum pan-European standards required by the ECtHR, then there may be little space for legislative reconsideration of whether it agrees that the legislation is incompatible with human rights. Certainly, political actors may disagree with the judicial evaluation of the risk of an adverse Strasbourg ruling. But we can expect a national court's prediction of an international court's decision, based on its analysis of the jurisprudence, to be especially weighty.[97] Where DOIs are used in this manner, the courts' behaviour supports the specialization type of institutional dialogue; one where courts take the role of applying legal rules determined from Strasbourg case law, leaving it to the other branches of government to develop a legislative response.

Where judges have instead been engaged in an independent evaluation of the scope of a right and the proportionality of limitations placed on that right, reasoning from general principles or analogical circumstances, there may be more room for alternative visions of the proper scope and limitation of rights. Whether the political branches of government do in fact articulate alternative interpretations remains a separate empirical question, but the possibility at least exists for more than evaluations of risk of adverse Strasbourg rulings. However, we should bear in mind that even these more independent evaluations may be considered to be authoritative predictions if, over time, the practice of the ECtHR indicates that it would affirm the national judicial decision were the matter taken to Strasbourg (a point that will be explored further in the following section).

Examining the eighteen final DOIs (that is, those not overturned on appeal) issued in the study period, ten involved the application of a clear and recent Strasbourg decision which the court has considered to determine the question of compatibility. For example, the first final DOI, in the case of *R(H) v Mental Health Review Tribunal*,[98] was based on the clear incompatibility of a reverse burden of proof in relation to continued detention under the Mental Health Act 1983. The government accepted that if the legislation could not be read differently, a reverse burden of proof was incompatible with the right to a fair trial, as this was the established

[97] It could also be expected that for reasons of comity, considered in 4.C.4, the ECtHR would give significant weight to the conclusions of the national court on human rights compatibility.

[98] *R (H) v Mental Health Review Tribunal for the North and East London Region & the Secretary of State for Health* [2001] EWCA Civ 415.

position of the Strasbourg jurisprudence. Similarly, the DOIs in *McR's Case*, *Anderson*, *R (D)*, *Bellinger*, *Clift*, and *Smith v Scott* were all based on recent Strasbourg decisions which clearly indicated that the legislation under challenge was incompatible with Convention rights.[99] Furthermore, in *R (M) v Secretary of State for Health*, *Hooper*, and *Wilkinson* there had been an admissibility decision concerning the same human rights complaint, which in each case had been followed by a friendly settlement by the UK government. In each case, the court treated this admissibility decision as effectively answering the compatibility question.

In particular, in *Anderson*, the Court of Appeal declined to make a finding of incompatibility in relation to the Home Secretary's sentencing discretion over mandatory life sentences, on the basis of Strasbourg jurisprudence, even though it considered the ECtHR was mistaken in its understanding of mandatory life sentences in UK criminal law.[100] The DOI was issued on appeal, by the House of Lords, only *after* the Strasbourg court had revised its position.[101] Similarly, the challenge to the blanket ban on prisoner voting was rejected by UK courts[102] prior to the Strasbourg ruling in *Hirst v United Kingdom*, and only *after* this decision, did the court in *Smith v Scott* issue a DOI.

In fact, the practice of relying on a clear Strasbourg ruling accounts for every final DOI up to the House of Lords decision in *Belmarsh Prisoners*, with the exception of *International Transport Roth*.[103] As discussed in the previous chapter, in *International Transport Roth* the legislative regime at issue was complex and Lord Simon Brown recognized that ultimately the court needed to undertake a global evaluation of whether the scheme was harsh but fair, or harsh and fundamentally unfair, and in relation to this task:

> Nothing in the Convention itself, or the extensive jurisprudence upon it, dictates, or could ever dictate, precisely when a measure such as this is unfair—when, that is, the limits of permissible individual sacrifice have been exceeded. All that the Convention really provides are the central principles and touchstones by which such a judgment can be made.[104]

In *Belmarsh Prisoners*, the House of Lords was similarly faced with a legislative challenge that could not be determined by reference to a clear Strasbourg ruling. Lord Bingham's leading judgment relied not only on Strasbourg jurisprudence, but

[99] Not all these cases involved the Minister conceding the incompatibility; in some of these cases the government sought to argue that the Strasbourg decision ought not to be followed, e.g. *Anderson* (House of Lords) (n 57). In other cases, the government conceded the incompatibility but nonetheless resisted a DOI, e.g. *Bellinger* (n 23), *R (M) v Secretary of State for Health* [2003] EWHC 1094 Admin; *Smith v Scott* [2006] CSIH 9.

[100] *Anderson* (Court of Appeal) (n 70) [57]–[59] (Lord Simon Brown).

[101] *Stafford v United Kingdom* (2002) 35 EHRR 1121.

[102] *R (Pearson) v Secretary of State for the Home Department* [2001] EWHC Admin 239.

[103] This excludes the decision in *Blood and Tarbuck* (Sullivan J, 28 February 2003), which was unreported.

[104] *International Transport Roth GmBH v Secretary of State for the Home Department* [2002] EWCA Civ 158 [54].

also made wide reference to comparative jurisprudence from the US and Canada, other international instruments (the ICCPR and the Convention on the Elimination of Racial Discrimination), as well as non-judicial sources such as reports of parliamentary committees and the Council of Europe. While none of these materials were binding on the court, Lord Bingham noted that they were useful since there was no Strasbourg authority on the specific point at hand.[105] Lord Hoffman's separate judgment dealt with the absence of clear Strasbourg authority by turning instead to a national account of constitutional values.[106]

For the period after *Belmarsh Prisoners*, most DOIs were made in circumstances where the incompatibility was not apparent from any straightforward application of Strasbourg case law. The separate House of Lords judgments in *R (Baiai) v Secretary of State for the Home Department* illustrate the different ways in which judges may respond to an absence of a clear Strasbourg case. *Baiai* concerned the requirement that people subject to immigration control obtain certification before being able to marry. Even though there was no Strasbourg case law on this point, Lord Bingham's judgment relied solely on Strasbourg jurisprudence, from which he attempted to deduce the scope and nature of the right to marry.[107] By contrast, the concurring judgment of Baroness Hale did not refer to any Strasbourg cases, but instead began with the matter of principle at stake in the case, citing the importance of the right to marry in international and comparative constitutional law, before elaborating on how the certification scheme was arbitrary and unjust.[108]

In *Morris*, the Court of Appeal took account of Strasbourg jurisprudence, but observed that, in relation to immigration control, the ECtHR has not generally scrutinized the actions of national authorities.[109] The majority hence needed to undertake its own proportionality analysis of the housing legislation at issue.[110] In *Wright*, the House of Lords was in a similar position to the Court of Appeal in *Roth*. There was no clear Strasbourg authority on how to resolve the matter before the court. While the general principles regarding the determination of civil rights by administrative tribunals were well known, the difficult question was how these principles applied to the fairness of the particular regime being challenged.[111] The court made its evaluation with no further assistance from Strasbourg than very general statements. In the case of *Thompson*, the Court of Appeal also embarked on

[105] *A & Ors v Secretary of State for the Home Department ('Belmarsh Prisoners')* [2004] UKHL 56 [63].

[106] For a detailed discussion of this judgment and its focus on a local narrative of common law liberty, see T Poole, 'Harnessing the Power of the Past? Lord Hoffmann and the Belmarsh Detainees Case' (2005) 32 Journal of Law and Society 534.

[107] *R (Baiai & Ors) v Secretary of State for the Home Department* [2008] UKHL 53 [14]–[24].

[108] *Baiai* (House of Lords) (n 107) [34]–[44].

[109] *Morris* (n 26) [42] (Lord Sedley).

[110] By contrast, Lord Jonathan Parker, in dissent, reasoned that the wide margin of appreciation at Strasbourg ought to be translated to the discretionary area of judgment that Parliament and the executive ought to be given in relation to immigration measures: *Morris* (n 26) [79]–[81].

[111] *Wright* (n 17) [23].

its own evaluation of the proportionality of the notification requirements for released sex offenders; as there was no authority on whether the current scheme was disproportionate. While earlier Strasbourg decisions had upheld a previous scheme, the Court of Appeal took no guidance from these decisions.[112]

So, overall, the practice has been evenly mixed: in roughly half the cases, DOIs have operated as alerts of situations where legislation violates a minimum standard of human rights as determined with reference to Strasbourg jurisprudence. The main split among the body of DOIs is temporal. While most earlier DOIs were issued in reliance of a clear applicable Strasbourg decision, over time the UK courts have faced situations where they have had to embark on their own evaluation of whether legislation infringes fundamental rights, from 'first principles', drawing on international law, comparative constitutional law, and national constitutional principles. These cases provide situations where the UK courts have made their own contribution to defining the scope and limitation of fundamental rights, and accordingly created some potential for the political branches of government to engage with the court's interpretation.

5.C.3. Comity and limiting creativity

Above it was argued that the main justifications given for the principle that national courts should do no more and no less than the ECtHR are not especially convincing, and hence the question remains as to why UK courts have constrained the discretion that is not only given to them under the HRA, but entirely permissible in international law and a sensible response to the practical realities of Strasbourg jurisprudence.

Nico Krisch has offered an explanatory theory for why the UK courts may choose to stick closely to Strasbourg jurisprudence.[113] He argues that, at the formal level, the legal framework governing national and European human rights protection is a pluralist one. However, in practice these regimes cooperate with each other and it is comity between legal institutions that maintains stability in the European system.[114] In fact, in *Anderson*, where the court was faced with Strasbourg decisions with which it disagreed, the court specifically cited institutional comity as a reason not to depart from Strasbourg, quite apart from the duty in section 2 HRA.[115] In Lord Buxton's view, to say (or imply) that the ECtHR was wrong would be a clear departure from the comity required by membership in an international system such as the ECHR.[116]

A second reason is that the mirror principle reduces the appearance of judicial creativity. The HRA conferred a human rights jurisdiction upon UK courts that was not entirely new, but nonetheless extended beyond what the courts previously had done through interpretative techniques. It also placed the courts under the public

[112] *Thompson* (n 11) [19]–[23]. [113] Krisch (n 55). [114] Krisch (n 55) 197–8.
[115] *Anderson* (Court of Appeal) (n 70) [66] (Lord Simon Brown), [81]–[82] (Lord Buxton).
[116] *Anderson* (Court of Appeal) (n 70) [88]–[89] (Lord Buxton).

spotlight, and it was not long after the introduction of the Act that sections within the popular media, as well as prominent politicians, began to attack decisions made under the HRA.[117] If judges in the UK were ill at ease with their role in interpreting broadly worded substantive norms, one concrete way to contain this new role was to translate it to a task of applying standards developed externally, by an international court. Lord Hope's statement in *N v Secretary of State for the Home Department* typifies this strategy of minimizing the appearance of judicial creativity:

> Our task . . . is to analyse the jurisprudence of the Strasbourg court and, having done so and identified its limits, to apply it to the facts of this case . . . It is not for us to search for a solution . . . which is not to be found in the Strasbourg case law . . . We must take its case law as we find it, not as we would like it to be.[118]

Finally, the fact that DOIs are *not* a coercive form of legislative remand and courts have no direct power to compel a legislative response (let alone a prompt response that genuinely aims to correct the incompatibility) invites courts in the UK to be strategic in their use of the remedy. If the courts are successful in having the DOI understood as an authoritative alert of international legal non-compliance, this impression may have a strong effect *even* in cases where there is no clear Strasbourg decision that determines the question of compatibility. In fact, even where the national judicial decision is not based on the mirror principle, it may be that, over time, UK court decisions are regularly affirmed by the ECtHR, due to comity flowing the other way. This has been the case to date in relation to the *Belmarsh Prisoners* DOI[119] and the *Baiai* DOI.[120] National judicial decisions, particularly if they are carefully reasoned, may benefit from the margin of appreciation principle, such that the Strasbourg court is reluctant to displace them. This may further strengthen the impression that the national DOI foreshadows an ECtHR ruling and further support the specialization model of dialogue, for it indicates that the choice available to the other branches is to either respond to a DOI or else wait for a likely Strasbourg violation.

However, over the study period and beyond, there have been indications of side-effects of this strategy of closely allying the HRA and the ECtHR case law, namely, that it has been used to support the argument that human rights requirements are being imposed on UK law and politics from without, rather than being the matter of national ownership and deliberation. This creates an unhelpful platform for nationalist arguments against following human rights judgments, which serve as a distraction in debates that should be focused on the merits of the decision at hand.[121] Realization of this may play some role in judicial movements away from the mirror principle in select cases, or even recent extra-judicial statements

[117] See Fenwick et al (n 84); F Klug, 'A Bill of Rights: Do We Need One or Do We Already Have One?' LSE Law, Society and Economy Working Papers 2/2007, 14–16. See also 8.B.2.

[118] (n 66) [25].

[119] *A v United Kingdom* (2009) 49 EHRR 29.

[120] *O'Donoghue v United Kingdom* Application No 34848/07 (14 December 2010).

[121] This can be seen most clearly in developments after the study period, considered in Chapter 9.

recognizing the difficulties of following Strasbourg case law strictly and signalling a more flexible approach.[122]

5.D. Conclusion

At the beginning of this chapter I raised the possibility that the use of DOIs could be an opportunity for courts to engage in the independent and sometimes creative exercise of deciding on the scope and limitation of fundamental rights, without having to self-limit due to concern about overstepping their institutional role. Yet, there are still incentives for self-limitation under weak-form review: I have argued that where judicial powers are weakened, judges are invited to be strategic in using these powers.

Generally, the courts have understood that DOIs are concerned with legislative reform rather than victim-centred justice and have avoided the type of judicial minimalism that relies on narrow rulings. The doctrinal position largely acknowledges the expository function of DOIs; however, in some circumstances, the courts have withheld themselves from interfering in particular political debates despite the non-coercive nature of a DOI.

Perhaps more crucially, the doctrinal approach of tying decisions closely to the development of Strasbourg jurisprudence demonstrates clear self-limitation on the part of national judges, at the level of principle, if not in deed. I have suggested above that the mirror principle increases the likelihood of compliance from the other branches of government by limiting the very function that DOIs play. It may also be that the highest courts are wary of breaking new ground with DOIs that may then be affirmed by the ECtHR rulings, translating them into binding international obligations. At the same time, by limiting their own ability to develop human rights principles, the courts did not, in the study period, openly support an approach to human rights in which national courts and legislatures act as partners in building on the international law minimum protection. This is another way in which the judicial use of powers under the HRA supported the specialization model of dialogue: the types of cases that resulted in DOIs tended towards the types of cases where the government and Parliament could be expected to remove the incompatibility, even if this was not universally the case.

Having dedicated attention in Part II to the way in which courts have grappled with the various issues thrown up by open remedies in general, and DOIs in particular, we can now turn directly to the responsive role that the legislature has played. This is the subject of Part III.

[122] See for instance the evidence of Lord Judge and Lord Phillips to the JCHR in 2011: Oral Evidence to the JCHR, 'Human Rights Judgments', 15 November 2011 (HC 873-ii), at Q81. Lord Phillips stated 'Maybe we have had a tendency sometimes to be too strict . . . We really sometimes analyse it with too much detail, as if we were dealing with a decision of the Supreme Court.' Agreeing, Lord Judge stated 'We have not been sufficiently flexible about it. We have not always appreciated—I think we do much more now—that most of the decisions are, in fact, fact-specific decisions. They are not deciding any point of principle. They are saying, "Here are the facts, this is the answer."'

PART III

RESPONSIVE DELIBERATION IN PRACTICE

6

The Pattern of Institutional Dialogue

6.A. Introduction

Part I introduced the variety of open remedies in human rights adjudication and observed that DOIs are the weakest exercise of judicial power by design, enlarging the potential role for the legislature relative to the courts. However, we ought to look beyond the structural or formal characteristics of these remedies, to what type of institutional interaction they have supported in practice. This is the task of Part III.

This chapter analyses the overall pattern of response to DOIs from the commencement of the HRA up to May 2010. It details and explains two main empirical observations. First, over this period, the political branches of government never used the power to refuse to take remedial action. DOIs were authoritative rulings despite their non-binding status and the role played by the political branches of government was crafting legislative reform, not deciding whether to change the law. Second, DOIs received little direct attention in the Houses of Parliament and most reply legislation was drafted by the executive and not given serious consideration in legislative debates. However, from 2006, the JCHR emerged as a site of consistent legislative engagement with DOIs.

This pattern has led some to consider that DOIs in the UK provide evidence that judicial rulings on fundamental rights are simply too powerful for the political branches to advance their own views of what rights require. Certainly, the practice over the first ten years of the HRA does not give us a real-world example of the dual review model that is one aspiration for weak-form review. Rather than forge a new path, DOIs under the HRA have followed a similar path to other, more coercive open remedies in stronger systems of judicial review; what I have called the specialization model of dialogue.

This chapter considers the factors giving rise to this pattern of response and draws attention to some important subtleties of the practical operation of DOIs. First, despite the significant number of DOIs in the early phase of the Act, these DOIs were generally not controversial. Second, the government had pragmatic reasons to pressure departments into making *some* response, and eschewing the route of open refusal to act. Third, in those few cases where DOIs were controversial, there were alternative ways available for the government to resist the DOI and assert its chosen policy, making open refusal to act less necessary. This analysis challenges suggestions that the political branches have been dominated by judges and have not played a significant decision-making role. It advances the argument, made in Part I, that even where open, declaratory remedies are treated as mandating legislative change, rather than provisional opinions on human rights, there is still an important role left to the executive and the legislature.

This chapter also begins to examine whether the structures of the HRA support public justification and accountability in the exercise of this political role, or in fact do little to stem the concentration of executive power. While this chapter is concerned with the overall trends in relation to DOIs, Chapters 7 and 8 delve into a series of specific case studies of responsive deliberation, where reply legislation *did* receive dedicated attention in the Houses of Parliament. These examples provide the opportunity to evaluate the *nature* of legislative deliberation on human rights, where it did occur. I also consider to what extent assertions about the legislature's superior capacity to devise remedial measures are borne out in practice.

6.B. Statistics and Policy

Part II considered how the courts have approached DOIs predominantly from a doctrinal perspective. Part III examines how the executive and legislature addressed these DOIs. But first, it is useful to look at some statistics about the body of DOIs issued from 2000 to 2010, as well as one important aspect of DOIs external to domestic politics.

6.B.1. The body of DOIs

Over the first ten years of the Act, from October 2000 to May 2010, UK courts issued twenty-six DOIs. Eight declarations were overturned on appeal, leaving eighteen final DOIs (that is, where appeal options were exhausted or the Minister chose not to appeal the decision). In four of these cases, the offending legislation had been repealed or amended by the time a declaration was made, leaving fourteen occasions which engaged the executive and legislature's discretion to act upon a declaration to repeal or amend a law that continued to be valid and in force.

The most significant feature of the operation of DOIs throughout this period was that the UK government remained committed to addressing the incompatibility identified by the court in relation to each final DOI.[1] In all cases where the government proposed remedial action, Parliament passed the measures, and only in one case did parliamentary review significantly delay remedial action.[2]

[1] Despite government commitment to address all final DOIs, at the dissolution of Parliament on 12 April 2010, remedial action on two final DOIs remained outstanding (*R (Baiai & Ors) v Secretary of State for the Home Department* [2008] UKHL 53 and *Smith v Scott* [2006] CSIH 9). The one remaining DOI subject to appeal was upheld by the UK Supreme Court on 21 April 2010: *R (Thompson & JF) v Secretary of State for the Home Department* [2010] UKSC 17. The *Baiai* and *Thompson* DOIs were addressed by the Coalition government in 2011, though at the time of writing a response to the DOI in *Smith v Scott* remains outstanding. For discussion of these developments, see the epilogue (Chapter 9).

[2] Discussed in 6.C.2.

This simple statistic has been seized upon by some commentators to suggest that the judiciary have played the overpowering role in any dialogue over DOIs. For instance, one evaluation in 2008 stated that:

> the governmental responses to those declarations of incompatibility issued under the Act have uniformly endorsed and implemented the judicial readings of compatibility put forward. If this is a dialogue, it is one in which the judicial voice is being heard the loudest.[3]

The authors concluded that '[the] pressing issue for those who are sceptical of judicial power under the HRA [is] the failure of the elected branches to challenge, or otherwise refuse to endorse, a judicial reading of incompatibility.'[4]

This chapter questions this appraisal of the operation of DOIs, arguing that it fails to appreciate the subtle ways in which the courts and the government used their powers. But before moving on to consider the institutional dynamics over the study period, certain basic features of the body of DOIs should be understood.

6.B.2. The nature of issues giving rise to DOIs

Appendix I provides an overview of the DOIs issued in the first ten years of the HRA. We can note three features of the types of cases being sent back to the legislature over this period. First, the composition of cases supports the general claim that courts, granted a human rights jurisdiction, are able to draw attention to the claims of those who are otherwise neglected in the political process. Almost all of the cases leading to a declaration concerned a marginalized or unpopular minority group:

- Two declarations related to the mentally ill
- Four declarations related to restrictions imposed under immigration law
- Three declarations related to criminal sentencing and one related to prisoners' rights
- Two declarations related to sexual offences (and one decision related to the situation of those listed as unsuitable to work with vulnerable people)
- One related to counter-terrorism
- One related to the legal recognition of transsexuals.

This feature of DOIs suggests that they have drawn attention to human rights issues that might otherwise be neglected because of the lack of influence that the affected groups have in the political process. In Chapter 2, when considering accounts of dialogue that envisage courts and legislatures playing specialized functions, I introduced the concepts of 'blind spots' and 'burdens of inertia'.[5] Legislative blind spots occur where the law has an especially harsh effect in certain circumstances or on particular people whose interests are not subject to careful

[3] I Leigh and R Masterman, *Making Rights Real* (Hart, Oxford 2008) 118.
[4] Leigh and Masterman (n 3) 119.
[5] See discussion at 2.B.3(b).

attention in majoritarian processes. The fact that many DOIs concerned unpopular minorities suggests that many of these cases were blind spots, for example *Bellinger* and *Smith v Scott*.[6] 'Burdens of inertia' occur where legislation ought to be amended in light of contemporary understandings of human rights, but there is no particular impetus for reform and hence legislative amendment does not get sufficient priority amongst other political business. As we will see in 6.D, this was the type of issue raised in cases such *R (H) v MHRT* and *R (M)*.

Neither blind spots nor burdens of inertia are situations in which a court is upsetting a careful and deliberate decision on the specification of a right or its justified limitation. Here DOIs play a useful checking function, complementary to the legislative process, because once these claims are put on the legislative agenda there may be little principled support for maintaining the status quo. Political actors might readily see the injustice, or disproportionate nature, of the way in which the law operates in relation to certain people. This is an even stronger possibility after a significant passage of time or a change in government or the composition of Parliament. In 6.D I argue that this type of interaction best describes the early phase of the HRA.

The concentration of rights covered by DOIs indicates a second aspect of the institutional division of labour, which is that courts have restrained themselves to certain rights, and in particular to questions of procedure and non-discriminatory treatment. Virtually all of the declarations related to Article 5 (right to liberty), Article 6 (right to a fair trial), Article 8 (right to a family and private life) and, in some cases, Article 14 taken in conjunction with one of these rights (non-discrimination in the enjoyment of Convention rights).[7] Notably, no declarations have been made in relation to freedom of thought, conscience, and belief, nor freedom of expression, nor freedom of association (Articles 9, 10, and 11).[8]

The high concentration of Article 5 and Article 6 cases may be explained by a sense of expertise amongst UK courts, newly entrusted with a responsibility to protect human rights, when faced with questions raising rule of law concerns. Another factor that may explain the concentration of DOIs is that Articles 5, 6, and 12 do not contain limitation clauses that allow for such restrictions as are necessary in a democratic society, unlike Articles 8–11 of the Convention.[9] Hence, they do

[6] Discussed in detail in Chapter 7.B and 7.D respectively.

[7] Beyond this, two declarations related to Article 12 (right to marry) read together with Article 14: *Bellinger v Bellinger* [2003] UKHL 21 and *Baiai* (n 1); one declaration concerned Article 6 as well as Article 1, First Protocol to ECHR (right to property): *International Transport Roth GmbH v Secretary of State for the Home Department* [2002] EWCA Civ 158; and one declaration concerned Article 3 First Protocol to ECHR (right to vote): *Smith v Scott* (n 1).

[8] Although DOIs have been sought in relation to these rights, for example *R (Rusbridger & Anor) v Attorney General* [2203] UKHL 38; *Connolly v Director of Public Prosecutions* [2007] EWHC 237 (Admin); *R (Animal Defenders International) v Secretary of State for Culture, Media and Sport* [2008] UKHL 15; *Ghai v Newcastle City Council* [2010] EWCA Civ 59.

[9] There are more restricted limitations available on these rights, for instance, the Article 6 right to a fair trial may be subject to limitations that are 'strictly necessary' to protect other vital interests such as the safety of witnesses and national security: *Rowe v United Kingdom* [GC] (2000) 30 EHRR 1 [61].

not require the court to engage in proportionality review of the pursuit of policy. Neither of these factors explains the prevalence of DOIs upholding the Article 8 right to a private and family life, which comprised almost one-third of final DOIs. However, over half of these decisions either involved a procedural matter, or a non-discrimination concern.[10]

The third notable feature is that ten of the eighteen final DOIs were issued in circumstances where the ECHR case law clearly supported the finding of incompatibility, and in a number of these cases, the impugned legislation itself had been subject to adverse judgment against the UK at Strasbourg and implementation of that judgment was pending.[11] I argued in Chapter 5 that the dominant doctrinal approach to the HRA supports an understanding of the DOI as a municipal alert of non-compliance with international law, and indeed, in many cases, the DOI was not even a *prediction* of what Strasbourg would decide but an affirmation of what Strasbourg had *already* decided. However, this feature is not universal, and in relation to most of the DOIs from 2004 onwards the UK courts had to engage in a more independent evaluation of whether the law infringed human rights, without relying on a Strasbourg judgment to answer the question of compatibility.[12]

Given the types of cases being transmitted to the political branches of government under the DOI mechanism, we should not automatically assume that these DOIs would give rise to reasonable disagreement. Rather any appraisal of the potency of judicial viewpoints over the political branches of government needs to focus more carefully on institutional interaction over DOIs, on a case-by-case basis. In 6.D, I argue that the dominant dynamic in the study period was that DOIs were not controversial. Further, in 6.E, I argue that even in those cases where DOIs were controversial, it is too simplistic to say that the political branches merely endorsed the judicial viewpoint, and were 'doing the will of the courts', as some commentators have claimed.[13]

6.B.3. The government policy on responding to DOIs

At an operational level within the UK government, responsibility for dealing with DOIs was not centralized within a single government department or Ministry. Rather, litigating HRA cases and responding to a DOI was the task of the department responsible for the relevant policy area. Despite this decentralized responsibility, the Human Rights Unit (HRU) in the Ministry of Justice gradually

[10] *R (M) v Secretary of State for Health* [2003] EWHC 1094 Admin and *R (Thompson & JF) v Secretary of State for the Home Department* [2009] EWCA Civ 792 both concerned procedural rights to challenge administrative determinations. See also *R (Morris) v Westminster City Council & Anor* [2005] EWCA Civ 1184 and *R (Gabaj) v First Secretary of State* (Administrative Court 28 March 2006, unreported), both of which concerned discrimination in the provision of housing.

[11] For details see at 5.C.2.

[12] E.g. *Morris* (n 10); *Baiai* (n 1); *R (Wright & Ors) v Secretary of State for Health* [2009] UKHL 3; *Thompson* (n 1).

[13] Leigh and Masterman (n 3) 118–19.

assumed a coordinating role in relation to DOIs, as well as the role of reporting these declarations to the JCHR.[14] Over the study period, the HRU took on the role of an internal government adviser and watchdog in relation to DOIs, though the character of any response lay within the competence of the affected government department.

The HRU was also responsible for persuading the ECtHR, in litigation before that court, that DOIs constituted an effective remedy in the UK.[15] I noted in Chapter 3 the suggestion that the UK government will be under pressure to respond to each DOI because the domestic court's decision will likely be upheld in Strasbourg, if a dissatisfied litigant pursues an ECHR complaint. However, the treatment of DOIs in ECHR admissibility proceedings furnishes a more immediate, pragmatic reason for the executive to adopt and implement a general policy of responding to DOIs. In order for a complaint to be admissible to the ECtHR, the applicant must have exhausted domestic remedies.[16] However, the applicant is only required to exhaust those remedies which provide effective and sufficient redress. The fact that the HRA provides limited entitlement to remedies in relation to human rights infringements in primary legislation has therefore given rise to the question before the ECtHR of whether applicants making a complaint against the United Kingdom must first have resort to an HRA claim in the domestic courts *before* making a complaint at Strasbourg.[17]

One policy aim of the HRA was precisely that claims would be litigated first (and hopefully in many cases only) in domestic courts rather than going to the Strasbourg court, thereby stemming the tide of complaints against the UK at Strasbourg, and reducing the cost and delays in human rights enforcement.[18] Yet, in the 2002 admissibility decision in *Hobbs v United Kingdom*,[19] the ECtHR held that the DOI conferred only a power, not a duty, to amend the offending legislation by order, and hence was not sufficiently 'effective' to provide redress to an applicant. This opened the possibility of litigants making claims against primary legislation directly to the ECtHR.

The UK government persisted in later admissibility proceedings before the ECtHR to argue that DOIs were in fact an effective remedy in practice, at least in situations where the applicant was in a position to benefit from a future change in the law.[20] In 2007, the UK government argued again that a declaration was

[14] Oral evidence of Human Rights Minister, Michael Wills, and the Head of the Human Rights Division of the Ministry of Justice, Edward Adams to the JCHR, 2 December 2009, London <http://www.publications.parliament.uk/pa/jt200910/jtselect/jtrights/uc112-i/uc11202.htm> accessed 8 July 2010. Responsibility for implementation of the HRA was originally given to the Lord Chancellor's Office, then to the Department of Constitutional Affairs in 2002, which then became part of the new Ministry of Justice in 2005.

[15] Interview with Rob Linham, Head of Litigation in the Ministry of Justice, 22 February 2010, London.

[16] Article 35(1) ECHR.

[17] This issue only arises where the breach relates to primary legislation. In relation to the acts of a public body or subordinate legislation, the UK courts can provide an effective remedy.

[18] GB Home Office, *Rights Brought Home: The Human Rights Bill* (Cm 3782, 1997) [1.18].

[19] Application No 63684/00 (18 June 2002).

[20] *B and L v United Kingdom* Application No 36536/04 (29 June 2004); *Upton v United Kingdom* Application No 29800/04 (11 April 2006).

sufficiently certain and effective for Article 35 purposes but this time it cited in support of its contention its record in relation to the fifteen final DOIs that had been made by UK courts.[21] It emphasized that in no case had it refused to address a DOI: the practical reality was that a declaration was highly likely to lead to legislative amendment.

The Chamber did not accept this argument, but did state that 'at some future date evidence of a long-standing and established practice of ministers giving effect to the courts' declarations of incompatibility might be sufficient to persuade the Court of the effectiveness of the procedure'.[22] On appeal, the Grand Chamber agreed that it would be 'premature' to find that the DOI was an effective remedy,[23] but also agreed that, some time in the future, the practice of giving effect to DOIs could be 'so certain as to indicate that section 4 of the HRA is to be interpreted as imposing a binding obligation'.[24]

The decision in *Burden* indicated support at least for the UK's argument that it was the function of a remedy in practice, rather than its formal legal status alone, that determined its effectiveness. However, by striving to convince Strasbourg to refuse complaints against the UK unless and until the UK courts determine the question of compatibility for themselves, the government placed itself in a position of needing to demonstrate an established practice of giving effect to DOIs. Hence, it became the standing government policy to address all DOIs, that is, not to exercise the discretion not to respond.[25] The HRU became responsible both for defending claims in Strasbourg and impressing the need to respond to a DOI on other government departments. According to the Head of the HRU:

> It is our job to make sure that we keep the pressure on, to keep asking them, 'What are you doing? How far have you got? What is the next stage? Anything we can do to help?' And to keep supporting them and also to an extent holding them to account to make sure that they do respond in a timely way to adverse judgments.[26]

It is notable that the UK government has only relied on its record of responding *in some fashion* to DOIs. This leaves significant latitude as to (a) the nature of response, (b) the time taken to repeal or amend the impugned legislation, and (c) whether the litigants receive any concrete remedy in their case (the argument in *Burden* was limited to a litigant benefiting from a *future* change in the law; rather than any retrospective remedy that may be provided).

In the actual operation of the HRA, practical matters such as which department is responsible for making decisions, and whether there is any centralized supervision, should not be underestimated. The fact that the HRU, responsible for litigating claims at Strasbourg, placed internal pressure on other government departments to take some action after a DOI is a further factor explaining the

21 *Burden v United Kingdom* (2008) 47 EHRR 38 (Grand Chamber) [24].

22 *Burden & Burden v United Kingdom* (2007) 44 EHRR 51 [39].

23 *Burden* (Grand Chamber) (n 21) [41].

24 *Burden* (Grand Chamber) (n 21) [43].

25 Adams (n 14) Q66.

26 Adams (n 14) Q66.

trend that no DOI has met with open refusal. This can be contrasted to the more general incentive to avoid an adverse ECtHR ruling. As we will see in 6.E.2 and 7.D, this prospect may not necessarily weigh heavily on a government department if a DOI condemns a firmly held policy, given that the censure of an adverse decision at Strasbourg may be far from immediate, and even in the event of such a ruling, the department may still have considerable time and discretion in changing policy.

6.C. The Legislature's Role after Declarations of Incompatibility

6.C.1. The institutions of the UK legislature

Before analysing the legislature's treatment of DOIs in the UK, the institutions that exist for deliberation on legislation within the UK Parliament should be introduced. This parliament comprises a lower chamber of elected, constituency representatives (the House of Commons) and an upper unelected chamber with a mix of hereditary members and appointed members (the House of Lords). Either House can introduce legislation, and each House will debate the legislation and be able to make amendments to it. However, the elected House is more powerful in two respects. First, the leaders of the executive (generally referred to as the government) are drawn principally, though not exclusively, from the House of Commons; chosen by whichever political party has a Commons majority. It is the government that determines the legislative agenda, and the legislature's role in relation to legislation is ordinarily review of and assent to measures designed by the executive.[27] Second, the House of Commons has the ability to enact legislation despite the disagreement of the House of Lords, though the procedure to do so is a time-consuming one.[28]

In addition to the ordinary legislative avenues for deliberation, Parliament decided in 1998 to establish a joint parliamentary committee of both houses responsible for human rights (the JCHR). The new Committee's terms of reference were to consider 'matters relating to human rights in the UK (but excluding consideration of individual cases)' as well as proposals for remedial orders, draft remedial orders, and remedial orders made under s 10 HRA.

6.C.2. The low profile of DOIs

It might be assumed that DOIs would by their nature enjoy a high profile amongst Members of Parliament. After all, DOIs involve judges passing censure on legislation on the grounds that it infringes fundamental rights and freedoms, within a legal system where judges were not previously able to pass judgment on legislation in this way. Yet, parliamentary debates in both Houses demonstrate very little

[27] As discussed in Chapter 2.F.

[28] Parliament Acts 1911 and 1949. There are also political conventions governing the relationship between the two houses, in particular, convention specifies that the House of Lords will not block legislative proposals which comprise part of a successful political party's election platform.

discussion of DOIs, and, in most cases, little deliberation on reply legislation. Over the first decade of the HRA, the parliamentary JCHR emerged as the only vehicle for consistent parliamentary engagement in human rights issues. However, its monitoring role in relation to DOIs was only established in practice later in the study period.

There have been exceptions to the trend of minimal legislative engagement. Some debate occurred over legislative replies to *Anderson*, *Morris* and *Gabaj*, and *R (M)* considered in this chapter. Furthermore, in relation to three DOIs, a Bill was introduced into Parliament specifically designed to address the identified human rights infringement (as opposed to amendments merely being included in bills which primarily served other purposes). The legislative debates in these instances provide the chance to analyse in depth the nature of legislative deliberation that has occurred in the aftermath of a judicial declaration, and these debates are the focus of Chapters 7 and 8.

6.C.3. The development of follow-up procedures

We know already that the HRA was an innovative bill of rights and the DOI mechanism was one of several original provisions. But the HRA did not expressly provide for what was to happen *after* a DOI was made, in order to bring the matter to Parliament's attention.

The Act did provide for the executive to be notified in the course of proceedings that may result in a DOI.[29] However, it did not provide any mandatory duties, not even procedural requirements, upon the making of a DOI. This may have been an oversight in design or is perhaps explained by the assumption that such a court decision would naturally enjoy a high public profile. This can be contrasted with the other forms of legislative remand discussed in Chapter 1, where the court gives the legislature a window of time in which to implement a remedy, after which a judicial remedy will be provided. It can also be contrasted with the procedure that follows a decision by the ECtHR, where States are required to report on their implementation of court judgments to the Committee of Ministers, who are responsible under Article 46 ECHR for supervising the execution of ECtHR judgments.

It could be argued that the absence of any follow-up mechanisms is consistent with the non-binding, purely expository character of DOIs. Yet, later incarnations of the HRA model in Australia and New Zealand have seen the introduction of specific duties on the executive in the aftermath of a DOI in order to better support the legislature's responsive role. The Australian Capital Territory Human Rights Act 2004 provides that the Attorney-General must present a copy of the DOI to the Legislative Assembly within six sitting days. The Attorney-General must then prepare a written response and present it to the Legislative Assembly within six months.[30] Similarly, the VCHRRA provides that a copy of any declaration of inconsistent interpretation must be given to the Attorney-General, who must prepare a written response and lay before Parliament both this response and a copy of the declaration.[31] While both Acts preserve the ability of the legislature to

[29] ss 5(1)–(2) HRA.
[30] s 33 Human Rights Act (Australian Capital Territory).
[31] s 37 VCHRRA.

decide whether and how to respond to a declaration, both Acts impose at least a procedural duty on the executive to draw Parliament's attention to the declaration.[32]

The absence of any follow-up duty in relation to DOIs, combined with decentralized departmental responsibility for addressing court decisions, contributed to the problem of poor information concerning DOIs and the political responses to them. In a 2006 JCHR inquiry, several major NGOs noted their difficulties in accessing the political process for the implementation of judgments.[33] One NGO commented, in relation to the process of implementation of domestic and Strasbourg decisions:

> [Our] experience of the process is that it is somewhat opaque. It is even difficult for us (who follow the process closely) to know exactly when and how to intervene in the oversight process. We have no guidance and/or information about what the government is doing to facilitate the implementation of these judgments.[34]

Despite the absence of any mandatory provisions for action, a centralized structure of reporting to Parliament did gradually develop, as the JCHR assumed a monitoring role in relation to court judgments.[35] However, before examining these practices, we ought to examine the mechanisms that the HRA *does* provide for responding to a DOI: the remedial order provisions.

6.C.4. Remedial orders

The HRA provides a special avenue for remedial legislation following a judicial DOI: if there are 'compelling reasons', a government Minister may make legislative amendments by executive order as necessary to remove the incompatibility. Schedule 2 provides two possible procedures to enact a remedial order. Under the non-urgent procedure a draft order is laid before Parliament, along with an explanation of the judicial decision and reasons for the order, and must be approved by an affirmative resolution of each House before being made. Under the urgent procedure, an order may be made before being put to Parliament, but must be approved by Parliament within 120 days of being made, else it ceases to have effect.

The original remedial order procedure in the Human Rights Bill was more wide-ranging. It was envisaged as the ordinary route of response and gave broader powers to the relevant Minister to make legislative amendments.[36] The rationale was that the legislative timetable would generally not allow for an immediate legislative response to a DOI, leaving affected persons in limbo, and remedial orders were

[32] There is also a reporting requirement under s 92K Human Rights Act 1993 (New Zealand).

[33] JCHR, *Sixteenth Report 2006–07: Monitoring the Government's Response to Court Judgments Finding Breaches of Human Rights* HL Paper 128, HC 728 (18 June 2007) [154].

[34] (n 33) Evidence 22 (Letter dated 14 March 2007 from the Committee on the Administration of Justice).

[35] See 6.F.

[36] Cl 10 Human Rights Bill 1998.

designed to prevent this.[37] The Home Secretary argued that a government that was committed to protecting human rights would want to respond quickly.[38]

However, this proposed expedited remedial route brought to the fore the tension underpinning DOIs between providing a prompt remedy to successful litigants and preserving a role for Parliament to deliberate whether and how to respond to a declaration. From the vantage point of traditional fundamental rights discourse, the wronged individual deserved to enjoy their rights as recognized by the court and an immediate response was warranted to restore rights that had been denied. This was the government's stated position.[39] Although the Act would not allow *courts* to grant a more concrete remedy than a declaration where primary legislation infringed rights, the power to make fast and wide-ranging amendments would allow the *executive* to not only remedy the violation of the litigant's rights, but effectively act to fix the situation of all similarly affected persons.

Yet, from the vantage point of creating a role for Parliament in deciding whether to repeal or amend legislation following a declaration, the original provisions were problematic. The procedure involved an even lower level of parliamentary consideration than legislation would ordinarily receive. Instead of anticipating a legislative remedy, it anticipated an executive remedy as a routine response; the correlative feature of giving a wide-ranging, fast-track power to a government Minister was to reduce the powers of the legislature itself.

The remedial provisions under the Bill therefore attracted significant concern in the parliamentary debates and were criticized as undermining the claimed policy underpinning the Bill: to give Parliament a key role in the system of fundamental rights protection.[40] Amendments were made that constrained the Minister's powers to situations where there were 'compelling reasons' for a remedial order, as well as expanding the possibility for parliamentary oversight in non-urgent cases. When the JCHR was formed, it was entrusted with a scrutiny role over proposals for remedial orders, draft remedial orders, and remedial orders. This ensured that, where remedial orders were used, they would receive dedicated parliamentary scrutiny. The JCHR subsequently argued that the remedial procedure (even the urgent one) reconciled the tension between immediacy and deliberation, because it had been designed to allow for *both* urgent action and effective parliamentary scrutiny by requiring retrospective authorization.[41]

Despite this reconciliation, remedial orders were of marginal practical significance from 2001 to 2010. The response to the first DOI made under the HRA[42] illustrates the type of response that the government anticipated when the Human Rights Bill was introduced. The government promptly issued a remedial order,

[37] Hansard HC vol 314 col 1138 (24 June 1998).

[38] Hansard HC vol 314 col 1137 (24 June 1998).

[39] Hansard HC vol 314 col 1137 (24 June 1998).

[40] On this see KD Ewing, 'The Human Rights Act and Parliamentary Democracy' (1999) 62 Modern Law Review 79, 93.

[41] JCHR, *Sixth report 2001–2002* HL Paper 57, HC 472 (17 December 2001).

[42] *R (H) v Mental Health Review Tribunal for the North and East London Region & the Secretary of State for Health* [2001] EWCA Civ 415.

dealing precisely with the identified violation, and declared that a system of ex gratia compensation would be instituted for past victims.[43] Yet this proved to be an exceptional outcome. In relation to no other DOI over the study period was the remedial order power used.[44] The tension between providing a speedy remedy to victims and taking the time to introduce primary legislation, with at least the potential for full legislative debate, was resolved, in practice, in favour of primary legislation.

Nevertheless, in the early phase of the HRA detailed in the following section, the responses to DOIs remained reasonably prompt without recourse to the remedial order procedure. From 2005, the response time to DOIs began to stretch, with two legislative replies taking more than three years and two further replies having been delayed by three and four years respectively with no amendments made by the end of the study period.[45]

In view of these delays, from 2007 onwards, the JCHR called on the government to make greater use of remedial orders.[46] The Ministry of Justice suggested that their limited use was due to the complexity of matters raised by these DOIs and the need for the full legislative procedure.[47] Below I argue that these claims may be disingenuous since the relevant delay occurred in presenting any statement or measures to Parliament at all, rather than because time was allowed for parliamentary consideration. In fact, we see in 6.E that the response to *Morris*, after many years' delay, was introduced as a last minute amendment to a Bill before Parliament.[48]

An alternative explanation for section 10's fall into disuse is simply that the *will* amongst the executive to address problems identified by the courts waned. As we will see in the remainder of this chapter, initial levels of responsiveness dropped away over the study period as DOIs were increasingly perceived to be addressing not outdated legislative provisions, or interstitial human rights problems, but attacking the policies of the incumbent government.

6.D. A Quick and Willing Response: 2000–2004

From 2000 to 2004, government departments were willing to act promptly in putting reply legislation to Parliament, and we see that very little parliamentary attention was directed towards these legislative reforms. In this section I suggest two reasons for this early pattern of inter-branch cooperation. First, the bulk of these early cases were non-controversial, and demonstrate the courts playing the valuable checking role in relation to legislation described in 6.B. The second reason is

[43] Mental Health Act 1983 (Remedial) Order 2001 (SI 2001 No 3712).

[44] However, the remedial order procedure was revived after the study period, in the early phase of the Coalition government. For discussion, see Chapter 9.A.

[45] See Appendix I.

[46] JCHR (n 33) [118]–[119].

[47] Ministry of Justice, *Responding to Human Rights Judgments* (Cm 7524, 2009) 33.

[48] See 6.E.1.

the *method* of legislative response: remedial action commonly occurred by way of a late amendment inserted into an already complex bill. Experience shows two main concerns with this method of response: that it may function to dampen parliamentary consideration even where deliberation would otherwise be warranted, and that it may unnecessarily hold up uncontroversial remedial action.

6.D.1. The checking function of judicial review of legislation

The range of DOIs analysed in this chapter is comprehensive; concerned with patterns across the *full range* of declarations. This is valuable because an exclusive focus on 'exciting' cases—human rights decisions that give rise to contestation and disagreement—tends to support the assumption that matters of human rights do *always* give rise to such political controversy. In practice, many human rights cases are 'quiet' cases, where legislation is modified with little controversy over matters of principle. Their existence is also important and should be accounted for in our understanding of human rights protections. In fact, 'quiet' cases comprise the bulk of the early DOIs in the UK.

The first final DOI, in *R (H) v MHRT*, is a good example of a 'quiet case'. The Mental Health Act 1983 required a detained person to prove that their mental illness no longer justified their detention in order to secure release, imposing a reverse burden of proof that clearly violated the right to liberty under Article 5 on the basis of established ECHR principles. The government accepted that a reverse burden of proof was a violation of the right to liberty, but argued that the law could be read down to avoid this. The Court of Appeal decided that such an interpretation would strain the language of the provision too much and issued a DOI.[49]

The Minister did not appeal since she considered that the judgment made no error of law and was in line with government policy intentions.[50] The government published a draft remedial order within four months of the court decision. The order received a limited amount of media attention for being the first use of the remedial order power.[51] The JCHR initiated a public consultation on the order, which yielded few responses; something the committee considered to be 'probably an indication of the relatively uncontroversial nature of the proposal'.[52] The Committee argued that the circumstances justified use of the urgent remedial procedure because the law affected the liberty of the individual. The Minister accepted this and replaced the remedial order with an urgent one.[53]

The order itself attracted little interest in Parliament. The Minister for Health justified the order as part of a commitment to compliance with the ECHR and the

[49] *R (H) v MHRT* (n 42) [34].

[50] Letter from Jacqui Smith, Minister of State Department of Health to the JCHR, 15 October 2001 <http://www.publications.parliament.uk/pa/jt200102/jtselect/jtrights/57/57ap07.htm>.

[51] 24 July 2001 *Daily Telegraph* <http://www.telegraph.co.uk/news/uknews/1335047/Brief-encounters.html> accessed 14 February 2010.

[52] JCHR (n 41) [5].

[53] Ninth Standing Committee on Delegated Legislation (11 April 2002) <http://www.publications.parliament.uk/pa/cm200102/cmstand/deleg9/st020411/20411s01.htm>.

HRA in the area of mental health.[54] Of the two main opposition parties, the Liberal Democrats welcomed the order.[55] The impugned legislation had been introduced by the Conservatives, but they too supported the order. One Conservative MP was concerned to defend those who introduced the impugned laws: arguing that the world was a different place in 1983 and 'no blame should attach to those who considered the 1983 legislation'.[56] At the same time it was agreed that the provisions of the Act were wrong, 'in the modern world'.[57]

This episode demonstrates how the DOI mechanism can operate in a cooperative and uncontroversial way, with members of the executive and legislature accepting the court's decision (and the necessary censure involved) and acting promptly to see the legislative problem corrected. It is also an example of the burden of inertia, where legislation has not been changed even though it can now be seen to be an impermissible restriction of rights.

Further examples of this cooperative dynamic include the second final DOI in *McR's Case*.[58] This DOI related to the offence of attempted buggery in Northern Ireland, clearly incompatible with Article 8 ECHR. The repeal of the offence, along with equivalent offences in England and Wales, was included as an amendment to the Sexual Offences Bill 2003 and excited no legislative debate or controversy. Here, the court identified a human rights problem that had been overlooked in previous reforms of sexual offences legislation, up to and including the 2003 reforms. Likewise, the DOI in *R (D) v Secretary of State for the Home Department*[59] concerned the Home Secretary's sentencing discretion over discretionary life prisoners also subject to Mental Health Act detention. The sentencing discretion over discretionary life prisoners had been removed; however, this subset of prisoners was caught in the interface of two regimes of detention. Here too the declaration was uncontested, and no appeal was made by the Minister after the first instance decision. A response came within a year of the court decision and the amendment attracted no debate.[60]

In the period from the commencement of the Act in October 2000, until the end of 2003, there were ten final DOIs. Most of these declarations followed a similar pattern. In two cases, the legislation at issue was repealed before the DOI was issued.[61] In all but one of the remaining eight DOIs, legislative responses were prompt.[62] In five of these eight cases, the legislative amendment which addressed

[54] n 53, Smith, col 3. [55] n 53, Gidley, cols 7–8.
[56] n 53, Heald, col 6. [57] n 53, Heald, col 6.
[58] *McR's Application for Judicial Review* [2002] NIQB 58.
[59] [2002] EWHC 2805.
[60] Hansard HL vol 653 cols 918–19 (14 October 2003); s 295 Criminal Justice Act 2003. See Explanatory Note to the Criminal Justice Act [642].
[61] *R (Hooper & Ors) v Secretary of State for Work and Pensions* [2003] EWCA Civ 875 and *R (Wilkinson) v Inland Revenue Commissioners* [2003] EWCA Civ 814.
[62] Six DOIs were met with a legislative response within a year; with the DOI in *McR's Case* receiving a response in less than two years. The one case of delay, *R (M)* is discussed in 6.D.2. Here too the legislative change was not controversial.

the DOI was not subject to any debate.[63] Further indication that many of these early declarations were relatively uncontroversial was that, in these eight cases, no appeal was made from the initial DOI to a higher court.[64] By contrast, in relation to the eleven DOIs from 2004 until 2010, eight were appealed all the way to the House of Lords/Supreme Court.

In these cases, rather than judicial voices overpowering political opinions, quick compliance and lack of debate can be explained by the fact that there was no disagreement over the need for, and nature of, legislative change. In relation to these 'quiet cases', which identify problems with legislation that have been overlooked by the legislature, judges perform an additional check on legislation (on a case-by-case basis) and the benefits of this function do not come with any clear disadvantages.[65] Prompt and consistent legislative responses removing identified problems are wholly a positive development.

6.D.2. The method of legislative reform: some concerns

Where DOIs relate to human rights problems that are uncontroversial and easily corrected, there may not be a great need for, or interest in, legislative deliberation. However, the *method* of legislative reform suggests a second reason for minimal parliamentary consideration of remedial action. In several cases, a prompt response was secured by including a late amendment to an existing large and complex bill before Parliament.[66] By proceeding in this way, the government did not support deliberation, in terms of providing notice of proposals and adequate time for review. One concern with this method is that the executive may have significant discretion in crafting remedial action, and an absence of legislative review means that it is not held to account for the choices it makes. A second concern is that this strategy can lead to uncontested remedial action being delayed by problems elsewhere in the proposed legislation.

An example of the first concern is the response to the decision in *Roth*. This DOI related to the scheme penalizing owners and drivers of vehicles who brought clandestine entrants into the UK (the carrier liability regime). In Chapter 4 I noted that this case involved an overall evaluation of the fairness of the legislative scheme. The problematic features were so woven together that the court decided that the scheme needed to be rewritten to provide for basic fairness.[67]

[63] The three exceptions were the responses to *R (Anderson) v Secretary of State for the Home Department* [2002] UKHL 46 (discussed in 6.E), *Bellinger* (n 7), and *Blood and Tarbuck v Secretary of State for Health* (Sullivan J) unreported, 28 February 2003 (both discussed in Chapter 7).

[64] In *Anderson* (n 63) and *Bellinger* (n 7) the DOI was made by the House of Lords, so no appeal was available in any event.

[65] Mark Tushnet, a judicial review sceptic, refers to this as the 'sober second thought' effect and describes it as a real benefit of both weak- and strong-form review: M Tushnet, 'New Forms of Judicial Review and the Persistence of Rights- and Democracy-Based Worries' (2003) 38 Wake Forest Law Review 813, 830.

[66] *McR's Case* (n 58), *Roth* (n 7), *Anderson* (n 63); *R (D)* (n 59); *R (M)* (n 10); *Morris* (n 10); *Gabaj* (n 10).

[67] See 4.C.2.

The government introduced amendments to the regime during the passage of the Nationality, Immigration and Asylum Act 2002.[68] These reforms were directly informed by comments in the Court of Appeal judgment on various aspects of the regime and provided for greater procedural safeguards and varied penalties,[69] but *at the same time* expanded the carrier liability regime, including more onerous penalties.

There was very little parliamentary consideration of the new aspects of the carrier liability regime introduced to meet the concern in *Roth*. The amendments were introduced late in the legislative process in the House of Commons with a cursory explanation that they 'address[ed] the non-binding concern of the Court in *Roth*'[70] and were passed with no discussion in the Commons as the consequence of a guillotine (a motion bringing debate to an end) that prevented any debate on the carrier liability amendments. Some MPs took issue with the guillotine. One MP noted that these provisions were not debated at all, despite the fact that they raised substantial issues and had been the subject of judicial decisions.[71] A second MP noted that a number of bodies had worked hard to ensure that their views were put to parliamentary debate and their views would not be heard.[72] There was scarcely any more attention paid to the measures in the House of Lords.[73]

There were far more pressing matters that commanded the efforts of those MPs and peers engaged in review of the Bill, which was passed on a rapid timetable. In the Commons, scrutiny was focused on concerns with a new authority to carry system that enlisted carriers in immigration control. In the Lords, while several peers did engage in human rights-based scrutiny of the Bill, they also had problematic new immigration and asylum restrictions to contend with, including the withdrawal of social security assistance from asylum seekers.[74] The debates reflect far deeper human rights concerns than addressing the DOI in *Roth*.

The DOI in *Roth* itself was fairly imprecise in identifying specifically what made the scheme incompatible, and left considerable latitude to legislators as to how the law ought to be changed. The fact that the provisions introduced in response to this declaration neither received any legislative attention, nor came before the courts again, demonstrates how the executive was not required to publicly justify its remedial choices, which included amendments that made the scheme harsher. This example also illustrates how the executive can use the method of legislative response to avoid detailed scrutiny of remedial measures.

[68] Section 125 and Schedule 8 Nationality, Immigration and Asylum Act 2002.

[69] Explanatory Note to the Nationality Immigration and Asylum Bill 2002 [300]–[325].

[70] Winterton, Hansard HC vol 386 col 927 (12 June 2002).

[71] Hughes, Hansard HC vol 386 cols 928–9 (12 June 2002). He also commented that when the time for debate was being allocated, Members did not have sight of the new schedules and clauses.

[72] n 71, Malins, col 929.

[73] Lord Berkeley, advocating the interests of freighting companies, stated his pleasure that something was being done in response to calls from the transport industry: Hansard HL vol 636 col 1131 (24 June 2004).

[74] Provisions that were later challenged for violating the Article 3 prohibition on inhuman and degrading treatment: *R v Secretary of State for the Home Department (ex parte Limbuela)* [2005] UKHL 66.

An example of the second concern—that remedial action may be unnecessarily delayed because it is inserted into larger reforms—is the response to *R (M)*.[75] Here provisions in the Mental Health Act 1983 were held to violate Article 8, because of the absence of any mechanism for a patient subject to the Act's regime to challenge the appointment of their nearest relative. This was a significant failing given that the nearest relative was an important safeguard for those certified and detained under the Mental Health Act, yet the appointment of the nearest relative was automatic and could be a family member with whom the patient had an estranged or even abusive relationship.

The incompatibility was admitted by the government in the legal proceedings. The UK government had entered a settlement at the ECtHR in 2000 on the exact issue of the inability of the applicant to change their nearest relative. Yet, the incompatibility was not rectified until 2007, four years after the DOI. This was not because of any desire to retain the existing law: the regime was clearly problematic and no justification was offered by the government in court nor in Parliament for the impugned law. The reason for the delay was the inclusion of this relatively minor legislative change together with an overhaul of the entire field of mental health legislation, including replacing the 'nearest relative' position with a less powerful substitute. The proposed changes raised strong concerns in Parliament.[76] Opposition was so widespread that the Bill failed in 2002 and again in 2004, and ultimately, a far less ambitious Mental Health Act was passed in 2007.

The eventual legislative response to the DOI, which was to add patients to the list of people able to displace the nearest relative, was subject to some review and challenge in both the House of Lords and House of Commons.[77] Select parliamentarians questioned the government as to why mental health patients should be distinguished from all others in their inability to nominate their nearest relative or carer in the first place, rather than have an initial choice imposed on them. In fact, one peer suggested that this continuing discrimination in the new provisions raised questions as to whether the legislative response was compatible with human rights.[78]

However, the need to change the law to allow for the nearest relative to be replaced was itself uncontroversial, and even the legislative review given to whether this change went far enough was a small fraction of the review given to the overall Bill from 2002 to 2007. This uncontroversial remedy was unnecessarily held up by its inclusion in large-scale reform. The practical consequence of this delay was that for many years after the human rights infringement had been identified by the court, patients subject to the mental health regime continued to have no means to change their nearest relative. In 2007, the JCHR stated its disappointment with the

[75] *R (M)* (n 10).

[76] See the conclusions of the Joint Committee on the Draft Mental Health Bill 2004–5: *Report on the Draft Mental Health Bill 2004* HL Paper 79, HC 95 (23 March 2005) [398]–[399], 91.

[77] Hansard HL vol 688 cols 666–73 (17 January 2007), Hansard HC vol 461 cols 1094–110.

[78] Lord Patel, Hansard HL vol 688 cols 667–8 (17 January 2007).

government's method of responding, stating its view that the incompatibility ought to have been remedied by an urgent remedial order.[79]

By giving the government such discretion over when and how to propose changes to the law, the HRA allows for extended delays even in situations where laws are clearly disproportionate to any legitimate goal and the need for reform is generally agreed upon. Such delays are significant for the victims of human rights violations. The government also dominates the legislative agenda and may fail to initiate or support legislative deliberation on the response to a DOI. While the early phase of the study period was dominated by cases where the DOI was uncontroversial, there was a marked shift from 2004 onwards. The discretion left to the executive over the nature and timing of any legislative response assumed an even greater significance in this later period.

6.E. The Space for Political Decision-Making

So far this chapter has identified two reasons why the political branches did not use their power to refuse to respond to a DOI from 2000 to 2010. The first was the government policy of responding to all DOIs in some way, in the interests of establishing DOIs as an effective remedy before the ECtHR. The second was that the dominant dynamic over the early phase of the Act was one in which DOIs were uncontroversial and were not seen to endanger the pursuit of policy.

In this section, I suggest a third reason why the government did not refuse to address any of the DOIs made. Since the DOI mechanism is so permissive, it allows for more passive methods to resist judicial findings that are controversial, rather than open defiance. Two such methods, which have tended to be employed together, are: first, to delay making a response; and second, to make minor adjustments to the impugned law and argue that the law now meets human rights standards. Both are seen in the response to *Morris* and *Gabaj* (discussed in 6.E.1). It is also possible to pursue the policy animating the impugned law, but through a *new* means unaddressed by the immediate judicial decision on human rights. This is seen in the response to *Anderson* (discussed in 6.E.2). The availability of each of these strategies reduces the need for outright disagreement with the judicial decision and open refusal to act, even in situations where the government is unhappy with a DOI.

Importantly, these concrete examples support the argument that even though the UK government did not refuse to repeal or amend affected legislation after each DOI in the study period, this does not mean that there were not meaningful decisions for the political branches of government to make. We see that considerable discretionary space exists in designing legislative and policy responses to judicially identified human rights violations, opening up important questions for democratic deliberation. The nature of legislative and public deliberation on the

[79] JCHR, *Sixteenth Report 2006–07* (n 33) [124].

appropriate legislative response, if it occurs at all, is a separate matter. In 6.E.3 I explore the implications of the space that exists for political decision-making in crafting reply legislation.

6.E.1. Reasserting policy: the response to *Morris* and *Gabaj*

The DOIs in *Morris* and *Gabaj* in 2005 concerned discrimination in entitlement to social housing. By contrast to the bulk of declarations in the early phase of the HRA, these were controversial DOIs, where the government did not openly accept that the judicial decision was correct nor that legislative change was required. Rather, the responsible Minister's initial response was that she needed to decide whether or not to amend the impugned provisions, since the decisions 'raised important policy issues [necessitating] further consideration and consultation with other government departments'.[80]

The law at issue concerned the social housing entitlement of British nationals. Entitlement to housing was based on the existence of a priority need, including the need to care for dependants such as children, and sick or elderly relatives. Yet, the law required authorities to be blind to a priority need of a British national where his or her dependant was subject to immigration control, that is, required leave to remain in the UK. The government's justification was a policy of preventing migration by non-nationals for the purpose of obtaining social housing ('benefits tourism'). The Court of Appeal held that the legislation was clearly disproportionate to this goal, as British nationals in clear need of housing were being deprived of it, with attendant harsh effects on their ability to enjoy a private and family life.[81]

The government's response demonstrates two ways in which DOIs can be resisted where there is continued support for the impugned law, *other* than open refusal to change the law. The first is delay or prevarication. The Minister's early ambivalence about the DOI was followed by a three-year delay before any remedial action was taken. We know already that the government has control over the legislative agenda, and changes to the law are designed and proposed to the legislature on the executive's timetable. Section 6.C described how, under the HRA, the government is not under any mandatory duties or time limits to report to Parliament. Moreover, any interim changes to policy, or use of remedial order powers under the HRA are similarly a matter of executive discretion. The government Minister responsible for the policy area to which a DOI relates may simply choose not to exercise this discretion and adhere fully to the pre-existing policy.

This was what occurred after *Morris*. The government's reason for delay was that it was a 'difficult and complex' task to strike a balance between the policy objective of ensuring that non-nationals did not have access to social housing, and addressing

[80] Letter from Yvette Cooper MP, Minister for Housing and Planning to the JCHR, 27 June 2006: JCHR, *Twenty-Third Report 2005–06, The Committee's Future Working Practices* HL 239, HC 1575 (24 July 2006) Appendix 4.

[81] *Morris* (n 10) [45]–[48].

the court's decision.[82] The Minister did not openly disagree with the court's decision, but this statement (and the continued application of the law) made clear the government's continued adherence to the policy objective animating the discriminatory treatment. In the three-year period of legislative inaction, no care was taken to devise interim measures and the law subject to the DOI continued to be applied by housing authorities with full effect.[83]

After almost three years of correspondence with the government, by April 2008, the JCHR stated to Parliament its concerns over the extended delay and argued that, if the government intended to allow the law to stand in order to maintain its policy, it ought to at least make that position clear. Indeed, normative justifications for making judicial decisions non-binding presume that, where the legislature does not act to address the DOI, the decision to maintain the legislation will be clearly articulated and reasons given. Delay is a temporary form of resistance but can continue for many years[84] and this strategy does not support a deliberative democratic process because no official decision is stated and no public justification or debate occurs in the legislature. We should also note that the government of the day is also temporary, and may be able to delay action past its term in office.[85]

Eventually, the legislation was amended. Yet, the government continued to resist the judicial finding that discriminating against British nationals with migrant dependants in the allocation of social housing was impermissible. Straightforward repeal of the provision containing the discriminatory exclusion was rejected as a solution because this would not strike 'the right balance—an appropriate balance between our strong policy [of preventing benefits tourism] and the requirements . . . of the ECHR'.[86] Rather the chosen response was to modify the law while retaining the differentiation in the new legislative scheme.[87] Under the new legislation dependants who were subject to immigration control could count towards establishing a priority need for housing, but housing authorities had a far more limited duty in these cases only to arrange an offer of accommodation in the private sector for at least one year. The government insisted on withholding social housing. This approach, in the Minister's words, 'set a fair balance between the interests of UK taxpayers and the rights of migrants who come to the country with no claim on public funds'.[88]

The government's eventual response to a DOI that, by all indicators, it would rather not have responded to, was to adopt the behaviour observed, for instance, in

[82] *Morris* (n 10) [45]–[48]; Letter from Yvette Cooper MP to the JCHR, 27 February 2006: JCHR, *Sixteenth Report 2006–07* (n 33) Appendix 38.

[83] Letter from Vivien Gambling, Chairman of the Housing Law Practitioners Association to the JCHR, 29 June 2006; Letter from Fiona Woolf CBE, President of the Law Society: JCHR, *Sixteenth Report 2006–07* (n 33) Appendix 35–6.

[84] Examples within the study period extend to four or even five years: see Appendix I.

[85] The Labour government delayed its action in this way on prisoner voting, discussed in 6.D. It also delayed, for four years, its response to religious discrimination in marriage laws (*Baiai* (n 1)), which had proved controversial with the Church of England, so this incompatibility was also not remedied by the time Labour left office.

[86] Iain Wright, Under-Secretary, Department of Communities and Local Government, Public Bill Committee Hansard HC col 523 (24 January 2008).

[87] Housing and Regeneration Act 2008, Schedule 15.

[88] Baroness Andrews, Grand Committee, Hansard HL col 524 (23 June 2008).

Canada, as the way that disagreement manifests under the specialization model of dialogue. Rather than use its formal power to defy the court ruling, the executive can pursue its policy through modifying its original legislation, sometimes only marginally, and advancing a new justification as to the proportionality of the balance being struck between public policy and human rights. Canadian commentary has also noted the use of the legislative record to advance the case for why the legislation is compliant with fundamental rights, anticipating any future judicial review of the reply legislation.[89] Similarly, here the relevant Minister put on record a detailed argument in the House of Lords as to why the new measures were a proportionate intrusion into the right to a private and family life.[90]

This brings us to the second question in our analysis: to what extent was there engagement within the legislature in evaluating this delay in action and/or the adjustment of the law? Two observations can be made. First, the JCHR emerged here as a vehicle for holding the executive to account in some way for its inaction and its lack of any statement to Parliament, compensating for the absence of any formal follow-up mechanisms. The Committee's sustained pressure on the government through letters and reports from 2006 to 2008 placed at least some burden of public justification on the government, and drew attention to the uncooperative approach of the relevant department. The Committee also provided an avenue for civil society views to be conveyed to the legislature; drawing attention to the continued enforcement of the housing exclusion by public authorities and the hardship caused.[91] These concerns were picked up in legislative debates in 2008, when a new housing Bill was introduced which did not address the DOI. An amendment was brought in the House of Commons to repeal the housing exclusion, but the government refused to do so.[92] So at least some legislative attention was directed to the delay in responsive action, and the government did, following this, bring its own amendment to address the DOI.

Second, the government's chosen response was subject to some scrutiny and critique in the legislature as to whether the new measures were in fact proportionate restrictions on rights, or impermissible discrimination. Again, in keeping with the pattern identified above, the government's proposed response was introduced as a late amendment in the already large Housing and Regeneration Bill 2007–8, and with no notice given to the JCHR.[93] This dampened consideration of the provisions when they were introduced in the House of Lords, but the government was nonetheless challenged in later debate in the House of Lords on its choice to retain discrimination in its amendment.[94] When the Bill returned to the Commons, MPs too expressed

[89] K Roach, 'Dialogic Judicial Review and its Critics' (2004) 23 Supreme Court Law Review 49, 59–60.

[90] Baroness Andrews, Hansard HL vol 703 cols 816–21 (9 July 2008).

[91] See n 83.

[92] Proposed amendment by Andrew Love, Public Bill Committee, Hansard HC cols 521–3 (24 January 2008).

[93] The JCHR criticized this lack of notice, given its long-standing interest in the matter. See Evidence 24, *Thirty-First Report 2007–08: Monitoring the Government's Response to Human Rights Judgments Annual Report 2008* HL Paper 137, HC 1078 (31 October 2008).

[94] Hansard HL vol 703 cols 815–21 (9 July 2008).

concern as to whether the new amendments in fact addressed the human rights incompatibility as well as concern as to whether an offer of private housing would alleviate the difficulties faced by affected homeless persons or simply create new rights violations.[95] However, the Minister only reiterated the position that this was an appropriate balance because the government sought to maintain its policy of withholding social housing from British nationals with non-national dependants.[96]

The response to the DOIs in *Morris* and *Gabaj* illustrates the space that exists for political decision-making in devising a response to a DOI, even when the government does not choose to refuse to address the DOI. As long as there is a range of specifications of human rights in a particular context, there will be room for the executive to claim to be respecting rights with its amendments, even if there is disagreement as to whether the legislative changes meet the requirements of fundamental rights. Ultimately, the protection accorded to rights, in practice, depends on the choices made in the reply legislation, which in this case did continue to advance the government's original policy and retain discrimination against British nationals with migrant dependants.

That there is a space for legislative decision-making on reply legislation is especially the case where limitations of rights are permitted on a proportionality standard. However, Chapter 8 demonstrates how this may occur even where rights are not formally limited. Alternatively, it may be possible for the government to maintain the policy underpinning impugned law through a different means, one unaffected by the DOI made, or even by the dictates of human rights law. This can be illustrated through the *Anderson* example.

6.E.2. Political control of prison terms and the response to *Anderson*

The DOI in *Anderson* determined that the Home Secretary's discretion to determine the term of imprisonment of mandatory life prisoners was incompatible with the right to a fair trial. In Chapter 5, I raised this DOI as one case in which the finding of incompatibility was justified on the basis of a directly relevant ruling of the ECtHR. The Home Secretary unsuccessfully resisted the finding of incompatibility in the House of Lords, arguing that the relevant ECtHR ruling was mistaken and ought not to be followed.[97]

Once the DOI was made, the Home Secretary made a statement to Parliament stressing the purely hortatory and non-binding character of the declaration, stating that the House of Lords had not ruled that the Home Secretary's sentencing powers in relation to life prisoners were *unlawful* and hence the existing law was unaffected by the court's decision.[98] He continued to assert the policy behind the impugned provisions, arguing that it was fundamental to democracy in the UK that critical decisions in relation to the penalties for the most serious offences be made by

[95] Hansard HC vol 479 cols 611–15 (21 July 2008).
[96] Wright (Parliamentary Under-Secretary for Housing), Hansard HC vol 479 cols 612–13.
[97] *Anderson* (n 63) 871.
[98] Blunkett, Hansard HC cols 100–102W (25 November 2002).

someone accountable to Parliament.[99] The government undertook to devise a response to the DOI while continuing to pursue this policy.

The law was changed by the Criminal Justice Act 2003, which removed the Home Secretary's role in setting minimum terms of imprisonment in relation to murder. Instead, the Act adopted a statutory scheme of minimum sentences for a series of offences, sending 'clear messages about the tariffs that Parliament expects to be imposed'.[100] The Act allowed variation from these minimums, but curtailed judicial discretion by only allowing variations on a set of scheduled principles. These principles could be amended by the Home Secretary at any time.

The erstwhile position in the UK allowed the Home Secretary to respond in a very direct way to public pressure by imposing a minimum term of imprisonment at his or her discretion, regardless of any judicial recommendation.[101] It was this political responsiveness that fell foul of the right to have one's sentence determined by an independent and impartial tribunal. The reply legislation resurrected political control, and limited judicial discretion, albeit in a form untouched by the discussion in *Anderson*, and at a greater distance from the requirements of human rights law. In terms of the substantive outcome for criminal sentencing, the effect of the changes was to significantly increase sentences for murder, as openly acknowledged by the Home Secretary.[102]

Some Members of Parliament recognized the dynamic of passive resistance to having political control over life sentences curtailed. One peer, who criticized the law as imprudent and unjust, aptly captured what the legislation was attempting to do:

> [S]uccessive Home Secretaries have resisted every move to challenge their powers on life sentences and they have been forced to withdraw from decision-making only because the Government have lost a series of cases in the European Court and before our own courts applying the Human Rights Act. Even now, the present Home Secretary is not prepared to let the matter go, but has tabled amendments to the Criminal Justice Bill that set significantly higher starting points for tariffs in murder cases, including whole life tariffs for some types of murder.[103]

There was nothing in the decision in *Anderson* concerning the length of tariffs, or mandatory sentencing. In fact, on the same day, the House of Lords affirmed that the mandatory life sentence did not infringe Convention rights.[104] The government embraced this finding and built its legislative reply on this basis.

Again, in relation to the Canadian Charter, commentators have identified that it will often be possible for the executive/legislature to respond to a finding of human rights violation in a way that meets immediate legal concerns, but raises broader concerns over whether the new measures are a desirable development of the law.

[99] Blunkett, Hansard HC col 100W.

[100] Blunkett, Hansard HC col 101W.

[101] In fact, just prior to the DOI in *Anderson*, the Home Secretary increased the tariff for one high-profile murderer from 28 years to 50 years: C Gale and A James, 'Is Murder "Most Foul"?' (2003) 67 Journal of Criminal Law 131, 135–6.

[102] Hansard HC vol 405 col 869 (20 May 2003).

[103] Lord Dholakia, Hansard HL vol 648 col 886 (21 May 2003).

[104] *R v Lichniak and Pyrah* [2002] UKHL 47.

For instance, judicial findings that certain police powers violated human rights were met with new laws removing the impugned laws but expanding police powers in new areas not addressed by the judgments.[105] Reply legislation may also raise new human rights concerns of a different nature, something I will consider further in Chapter 8 in the context of counter-terrorism legislation.

The legislative reply to *Anderson* was one of the few responses that received attention in both Houses.[106] Examining the treatment of the DOI in the legislative debates, we see that despite the Home Secretary's emphasis on the non-binding quality of the DOI in his initial statement to Parliament, the DOI proved to be a powerful statement by the courts. At no stage in the debates over the legislative response was there contestation over the DOI itself or any suggestion of ignoring it. The sentiment across the government, members of the legislature, and the JCHR was that the Home Secretary was compelled to relinquish his sentencing power because the law required it.[107] As we know, the DOI closely mirrored the position of the ECtHR on the Home Secretary's sentencing powers as a matter of international human rights law, which helps explain this sentiment. At the same time, there were a number of speeches supporting the policy animating the impugned law and arguing that the role of the Home Secretary in determining sentences was proper and desirable, both in the impugned scheme and in the proposed new scheme. The responsible Ministers stated that the government was 'trying to re-establish the role of Parliament and our democratic processes' after the existing scheme had been 'overturned' by the House of Lords, and that Parliament was asserting its 'legitimate role', because by contrast to judges, MPs were directly accountable. The Opposition front bench agreed, describing the change in the law as 'unfortunate' and stating that the public had an entitlement to expect more than just 'judicial input' into sentencing.[108]

This type of response again typifies disagreement under the specialization model of institutional interaction. Disagreement with the judicial decision did not (and given the ECtHR dimension, could not realistically) lead to open refusal to change the law. Still, the government resisted any condemnation of the Home Secretary having sentencing powers, and reaffirmed the desirability of these powers because of his political accountability to Parliament, and hence to the electorate. The legislative reply was constructed to accept the court's ruling but 'achieve the same result' as the previous law.[109]

[105] K Roach, *The Supreme Court on Trial: Judicial Activism or Democratic Dialogue* (Irwin Law, Toronto 2001) 176–9.

[106] The measures were, however, introduced as amendments at the Report phase in the House of Commons, with little notice and little time for review, something that several MPs expressed concerns about. See Hansard HC vol 405 cols 880–900 (20 May 2003).

[107] Even the Home Secretary referred to his powers having been 'overturned' by the House of Lords: Hansard HC vol 405 col 868 (20 May 2003). The Under-Secretary of State stated that the Minister's powers had been removed by the courts: Hansard HC vol 405 Goggins, cols 900–2 (20 May 2003).

[108] Grieve, Hansard HC vol 405 col 884 (20 May 2003).

[109] Blunkett, Hansard HC vol 405 col 869 (20 May 2003).

6.E.3. Implications of the remedial discretion

The fact that there may be a significant space or discretion available to the executive/legislature in devising remedial measures provides a third reason why no DOI met with defiance over the study period. It may be unnecessary for the government to take the sensational route of open disagreement with a judicial decision so long as more passive methods of asserting its chosen policy are available. The DOIs discussed above were potent enough to compel some change to law in the face of dissatisfaction with the court's ruling, but political actors could still identify a different means to pursue the policy behind the incompatible law, in preference to open refusal to act (such as in *Morris*) or because open refusal was not really possible (as in *Anderso*n).

In relation to *Morris*, I argued that where a DOI concerns a right that can be subject to proportionate limitations, this leaves space for the political branches to make minor changes and advance a new justification of what is an appropriate and legitimate way to pursue their chosen policy, even if the judicial decision is treated as an authoritative conclusion that the previous legislation was unacceptable. Where the DOI concerns procedural safeguards on administrative powers or criminal sentencing, the continued pursuit of policy may be even easier, because the incompatibility does not go to the policy itself. Many of the DOIs issued over the study period were these kinds of procedural incompatibilities. That being said, procedural rights are not necessarily uncontroversial. The strength of procedural safeguards in relation to counter-terrorism powers is the clearest example, as we will see in Chapter 8.

We know from Part I that any normative appraisal of this type of operation of a bill of rights—in terms of the relative powers of courts and the political branches of government—will vary according to one's normative standpoint. For sceptics of judicial review, the fact that the government has not been willing or able to openly defy DOIs even where it would prefer to retain existing legislation may indicate that the courts have too much effective power to override political judgment. For a liberal legalist, the removal of legislation identified by the courts to infringe fundamental rights signifies the protection of human rights. The fact that new laws may be undesirable for other reasons, such as the lengthening of criminal sentences after *Anderson*, is not a concern for human rights law but a matter of politics.

From the practical perspective of supporting a deliberative democracy, the concern is how these remedial decisions are made. Legislative replies may raise new issues of human rights compatibility; they may also simply raise new substantive concerns about what is the right direction for law and policy to take. The important question in both these situations is whether these decisions are made through a careful and informed deliberative process. Especially if the legislative response is to *expand* executive powers, it is vital that the government is subject to a burden of justification.

The function of a DOI as a check on legislation relies not only on the government's willingness to enact a response, but on this response gaining attention from an institution that will hold the executive accountable. Legislative changes do not automatically go before a court, nor is the government required to consult with victims or affected parties (unlike remedies that require the parties to agree on a solution and present it to the court for approval). If neither the public nor the legislature require the government to justify its chosen response, then the DOI may do little to stem the concentration of executive power in practice. The fact that DOIs leave such a wide discretion to the government to delay and establish no formal burden of justification to the legislature or the public creates the potential for poor deliberative outcomes after DOIs are made. On the other hand, over the study period, the JCHR came to compensate for the absence of formal follow-up duties. The JCHR played a very limited role in assessing the government's chosen response to *Anderson*, but in relation to later decisions in *Morris* and *Gabaj* took on the role of a watchdog and ensured some pressure on the government to take a stance on the DOI. Section 6.F takes a dedicated look at the evolution of the Committee and its engagement with DOIs.

6.F. The Joint Committee on Human Rights

So far in this chapter, I have sought to explain two observations about the political treatment of DOIs: that the government has never refused to comply with a declaration and that there has generally been little parliamentary attention given to legislative responses in the two Houses of Parliament. This final section turns to the JCHR, which established itself over the study period as the principal site of legislative engagement with DOIs. Chapter 3.C questioned whether, under a statutory bill of rights such as the HRA, legislative rights review could come to be dominated by judicial standards. The manner in which the JCHR's scrutiny function developed over time illustrates some reasons why a compliance-oriented approach to human rights may develop in a legislative committee dedicated to human rights, even under weak-form review. Section 6.F.2 turns specifically to DOIs. Here we see that the JCHR moved to take on two types of role in relation to these remedies: it acted as an interface between judicial decision-making and legislative decision-making, and it also operated to make the responsive process more deliberative by providing a conduit for views from civil society into Parliament.

6.F.1. The role of parliamentary committees and the early operation of the JCHR

The JCHR was an innovation of the HRA beyond attempts in Canada and New Zealand to engage the legislature in evaluations of human rights compatibility. The formation of the Committee was suggested in order to strengthen the capacity of the legislature for independent review of legislation.[110] The use of a select

[110] J Straw and P Boateng, 'Bringing Rights Home' (Labour Party Consultation Paper 1996) 12.

committee, with permanent staff and its own legal adviser, was one way to ensure that legislation received regular attention, outside the government drafting process itself. The Committee has been able to undertake the onerous practical task of sifting through Bills and drawing attention to human rights concerns; a task beyond the time and expertise of the vast number of parliamentarians.[111] Select committees are also armed with powers to seek evidence and can assist Parliament by providing relatively impartial advice and information.[112] The JCHR has questioned the government's conclusions on human rights compatibility and reached its own independent conclusions.[113]

In performing this function of reviewing legislation, the Committee's approach from 2001 to 2005 provides an example of what was described in Chapter 3.C as a *compliance-oriented* form of rights review. In an account of its own working practices in 2005, the JCHR stated its primary role was to alert the Houses of Parliament where they were at risk of legislating in a manner that would later be held by a court to be incompatible with the ECHR.[114] In this role of anticipating judicial decisions, the Committee relied on legal advice and presented its arguments based on legal reasoning. Its formula for reporting its conclusions was framed specifically in terms of the degree of risk that a court would find legislation incompatible (low, significant, or substantial).[115] Lord Lester, a prominent member of the Committee, described the role of the JCHR as one of a legal adviser to Parliament, with a scrutiny role similar to the assessment of a court.[116]

The experience of the JCHR in this period illustrates several reasons why a legislative committee might assimilate a lawyer's approach to assessing human rights implications. First, it could be argued that as a matter of principle, the role of parliamentary committees is only an advisory one, hence they should avoid political matters and concentrate on providing relatively impartial expertise to Parliament. Hence, parliamentary expert Robin Blackburn predicted in 1998 that the JCHR's work would be 'in the nature of a technical exercise, comparing and predicting the compatibility of the law proposed with the prospect of litigation'[117] because broader political questions concerning the desirability of legislation, open to diverse and ideological views, were for the Houses of Parliament, not the Committee, to debate and decide. These sentiments were echoed by David Feldman, the JCHR's first legal adviser, who argued that human rights law as applied by courts provided independent standards against which to scrutinize new laws, relatively unaffected by political considerations.[118]

111 D Feldman, 'Parliamentary Scrutiny of Legislation and Human Rights' [2002] PL 323, 325.

112 P Craig, *Administrative Law* (Sweet & Maxwell, London 1999) 78.

113 A Lester, 'Parliamentary Scrutiny of Legislation under the Human Rights Act 1998' [2002] EHRLR 432, 436–7.

114 JCHR, *Nineteenth Report 2004–5: The Work of the Committee 2001–2005* HL Paper 112, HC 552 (6 April 2005) [44].

115 JCHR (n 114).

116 Hansard HL vol 636 col 1122 (24 June 2002); A Lester, D Pannick, and M Carss-Frisk, *Human Rights Law and Practice* (2nd edn Butterworths, London 2004) 604.

117 R Blackburn, 'A Human Rights Committee for the UK Parliament' [1998] EHRLR 534, 538.

118 Feldman (n 111) 328–30.

These types of understandings of the role of a parliamentary committee can shift over time (and we will see that they did). However, there are also practical reasons for compliance-oriented review, which have had an enduring effect on the Committee. First, Feldman highlights that, in his experience, arguments of a legal nature, based on a specified incompatibility identified by some case law, were more successful in securing government action, because a positive response to advice was often accompanied by a desire to avoid the risk of future incompatibility in the courts.[119] Feldman also identifies the importance of these types of legal arguments as a way of extracting information from government departments where they might not otherwise be forthcoming.[120]

Second, a compliance-oriented approach can also assist in avoiding conflicts on political principles between Committee members and amongst broader groups in Parliament. The JCHR managed to avoid one of the main political hurdles to parliamentary scrutiny, namely, that legislative debate routinely proceeds on party-political lines. Based on a study of the Committee in 2005, Janet Hiebert observed that the JCHR had largely overcome the obstacle of party discipline and had gained the respect of parliamentarians for being motivated by principled, rather than partisan, considerations.[121] In fact, the JCHR almost always produced unanimous and non-partisan reports.[122]

Hence, there may be good reasons for a parliamentary committee to take a compliance-oriented approach to human rights questions; and attempt to treat rights as legal norms independent of political disputes. However, Chapter 3 argued that a legalized approach can limit the deliberative potential of political institutions. Moreover, in the UK, the usefulness of the JCHR acting as a legal adviser was put into question by the government's stated preference for its internal legal advice. In 2006, the Minister for Justice emphasized to the JCHR that the government was 'highly legally tooled up', receiving a number of levels of internal legal advice which in its view could not be trumped by the Committee's opinions.[123]

In 2006, the JCHR commissioned an inquiry into its working practices. In her report, Francesca Klug described the range of views amongst JCHR members about their role.[124] At one end was a perception that the role of the Committee was to highlight the risk of adverse court findings and not to substitute members' views for the legal adviser's view. At the other end, many members were concerned that the Committee was too focused on black letter law and this rendered its advice less

[119] D Feldman, 'The Impact of Human Rights on the UK Legislative Processes' (2004) 25 Statute Law Review 91, 112.

[120] Feldman (n 119). This may nonetheless be a weak discipline on government. In particular, the argument that legislation will be *implemented* in a way that respects rights, even though it may formally confer overbroad powers, has made it easy for government lawyers to certify compatibility. See M Tushnet, 'Non-Judicial Review' in T Campbell, J Goldsworthy, and A Stone (eds), *Protecting Human Rights: Instruments and Institutions* (OUP, Oxford 2003) 224–7.

[121] JL Hiebert, 'Parliamentary Review of Terrorism Measures' (2005) 68 Modern Law Review 676–80.

[122] D Oliver, 'Constitutional Scrutiny of Executive Bills' (2004) 4 Macquarie Law Journal 33.

[123] Oral Evidence, JCHR, *Human Rights Policy* HL Paper 143, HC 830-I (16 January 2006) Q45.

[124] JCHR, *Twenty-Third Report 2005–06* (n 80) Appendix 1 ('Klug Report') [11.5]–[11.6].

relevant to substantive issues, both in terms of parliamentary and public debate. Non-legal members felt that they were left in a passive role compared to the legal adviser and members of the JCHR with a legal background, since legal advice was almost always followed.

Klug's report recommended that, within the structure of human rights principles, questions of social needs and proportionality were matters that parliamentarians were well placed to consider (as well as difficult to predict judicial opinions on). Were the JCHR to consider these questions for itself, Klug argued this would help the Parliament to 'find its own voice' in debates over human rights.[125] This recommendation was adopted by the JCHR, which decided not to simply 'second guess' judicial decisions in future cases.[126] The JCHR decided to seek, and provide to Parliament, more oral and written evidence and attempt to exert greater influence on the legislative agenda. This included actively pursuing human rights principles through law and policy, not simply employing them as limits on action.[127] This was an ambitious new role that the Committee claimed for itself, in effect an attempt to reclaim a greater law-making role for Parliament. In particular, the JCHR decided at this point to assume a greater role in relation to DOIs.

6.F.2. Engagement with DOIs

From 2001 to 2005, the JCHR's treatment of DOIs was in keeping with the general trend of a lack of attention to DOIs within the legislature. Despite the formal role given to the JCHR in scrutinizing remedial orders, it did not, until 2006, extend this responsibility to monitoring DOIs in a timely or systematic fashion. (We already know that only one DOI resulted in a remedial order in this time.)

The Klug Report noted an evolving informal practice of government departments keeping the JCHR informed of responses to declarations.[128] Although the JCHR had traced government responses, it had not scrutinized legislative amendments, nor had it made its own recommendations to Parliament as to whether, and if so how, the government ought to respond.[129] The Report recommended that the JCHR could take a more pro-active role in this regard, to maintain the centrality of Parliament (rather than the executive) to the scheme of the HRA in relation to legislation.

From 2006 to 2010, the JCHR became the principal site for legislative engagement with DOIs. The role that the JCHR came to play, as evidenced by its interaction with the executive and its reporting to Parliament, can be understood as an interface between judicial decision-making and legislative decision-making in

125 Klug Report (n 124) [12.6]–[12.7].
126 JCHR, *Twenty-Third Report 2005–06* (n 80) [77].
127 JCHR, *Twenty-Third Report 2005–06* (n 80) [77].
128 Klug Report (n 124) [10.10].
129 Klug Report (n 124) [10.9].

relation to DOIs. The Committee was a strong advocate of compliance with judicial decisions, both domestic and ECtHR decisions, but also sought to encourage the government to take a more robust approach to addressing judicial decisions. This role became important in holding the government to account as the early pattern of prompt responses to DOIs fell away and government departments showed greater resistance to judicial decisions.

The JCHR issued three monitoring reports to Parliament, in 2007, 2008, and 2010. In the JCHR's 2007 monitoring report, it acknowledged that DOIs were not binding and hence did not mandate a response in the same sense as ECtHR judgments. Accordingly, its main recommendations were procedural. In 6.C, I argued that poor follow-up mechanisms were one likely reason for the lack of parliamentary engagement with DOIs. The JCHR sought to correct this by placing pressure on the HRU to take on a coordinating role and enforce a timetable for reporting adverse judicial decisions to Parliament, as well as justifying the government's chosen response (or lack thereof).[130]

However, the JCHR did not limit itself to arguing for better procedures and more transparency over responses to DOIs. Despite its formal recognition that DOIs were non-binding, it consistently operated as an advocate for the importance of compliance with judicial decisions. In particular, the JCHR relied heavily on the prospect of being held to be in violation of international law as a reason for the government to address all DOIs promptly. By 2010, the JCHR's report concentrated on the difficulties faced by the ECtHR and the need for the UK to reduce the burden on that court by responding promptly and pro-actively to judicial findings that human rights were being violated.[131] In particular, the JCHR stressed the need for the government to do more than the bare minimum required to comply with a judicial decision—be it an ECtHR decision or a domestic DOI—and to ensure that all laws and practices that were affected by adverse rulings were examined closely.[132]

We can therefore understand the JCHR as playing a hybrid role: a legislative institution which acted as a watchdog for compliance with judicial decisions. The Committee's attitude to judicial interpretations of rights was not the approach provided by the dual review model of dialogue. The JCHR did not question whether judicial decisions ought to be complied with, and actively argued that judicial decisions were to be treated as providing the minimum required to protect human rights. Rather, its work better fits the specialization model of dialogue, with the JCHR treating judicial decisions as mandating responsive action, but leaving room for important legislative decisions on *how* law and practice ought to change to address the identified human rights problem, including how wide-ranging legislative reform should be.

[130] The JCHR first recommended the MOJ develop follow-up procedures in 2002, but by 2010, responded to the government's continued inaction by issuing its own suggested guidelines: see *Fifteenth Report of Session 2009–10: Enhancing Parliament's Role in Relation to Human Rights Judgments* HL Paper 85, HC 455 (9 March 2010) 69–76.

[131] *Fifteenth Report of Session 2009–10* (n 130) [1]–[10].

[132] *Fifteenth Report of Session 2009–10* (n 130) [168]–[170].

Within this role, the JCHR engaged in sustained, critical correspondence with government departments over their responses to DOIs, placing a regular burden of justification upon them otherwise not provided by the HRA. This included placing continued pressure on government departments in cases of prolonged delay in relation to prisoner voting and discrimination in social housing (that is, where there was passive resistance to a DOI). The Committee also demanded greater justification from the government in circumstances where it was claimed that the incompatibility had been remedied by later legislation,[133] as well as where prospective legislative measures neglected to provide a remedy for past victims of human rights violations.[134]

The 2010 JCHR monitoring report demonstrates the Committee's recognition, based on its then considerable experience, of the wide discretion left to the government and legislature in devising a response to a DOI, even in situations where it was obliged to respond.[135] The report argued for a greater role for the legislature in these decisions, a need to reinforce parliamentary oversight and involvement in the implementation process, in order to ensure greater democratic input into these important remedial choices and to guard against a minimalist approach from the executive which would only invite further litigation.[136]

Second, the JCHR provided an official avenue for the views of civil society organizations to enter the official legislative process and challenge the government. In this way, the JCHR obtained information about the continued effect of impugned laws, as well as giving formal recognition to the arguments of (typically) human rights advocacy groups by including their views in JCHR reports. In fact, the Committee has displayed signs of being a site of human rights learning for members. For instance, certain prominent members were not enthusiasts for international human rights prior to joining the Committee, but developed their views during their time in the JCHR.[137] In deliberative democracy terms, we can see these methods as ways of making the legislative process more inclusive and providing an enclave for deliberation amongst Committee members.

[133] E.g. the reply legislation to *Morris* discussed at 6.E.1. The JCHR also questioned the government's claim that the incompatibility in *Wright* (n 12) had been addressed by subsequent legislation: see n 130, [139]–[143]. The Committee's concerns were validated by a subsequent DOI in the case of *R (on the application of Royal College of Nursing and others) v Secretary of State for Home Department* (Administrative Court; [2010] EWHC 2761; 10 November 2010) in which the court held that the new scheme was not compatible with human rights.

[134] See the discussion in Chapter 7.C.

[135] JCHR, *Fifteenth Report of Session 2009–10* (n 130) [14]–[15]. The recognition that significant political decisions needed to be made as to how to respond to adverse judicial decisions was shared by the Human Rights Division, at [161].

[136] E.g. where a human rights problem may affect a number of different legal regimes, the JCHR has criticized the government for only correcting the legislation directly subject to the DOI: JCHR, *Fifteenth Report of Session 2009–10* (n 130) [168]–[170].

[137] This was the view of both members of the JCHR interviewed and its legal adviser, with specific reference to the Chair of the JCHR (Andrew Dismore) and the Conservative peer (Earl of Onslow). They cited in support the changing positions of these members on human rights issues before and during their time with the JCHR. Dismore in particular switched from being a strong supporter of 90-day pre-trial detention in 2005 to an opponent of more limited 42-day pre-trial detention in 2008.

In conclusion, the JCHR emerged as a unique institution within the scheme of DOIs. The Committee treated judicial decisions as mandating action, and argued for compliance accordingly. However, the Committee also went beyond merely legal vetting, and pressured government to be pro-active in reforming legislation in light of human rights judgments, and hence was a human rights advocate in a broader sense. Its approach over time towards greater evidence gathering and supporting greater positive action to secure human rights in a more systematic fashion demonstrates ways in which legislatures can play a complementary role to judicial review, over and above the minimum of legal compliance with judicial decisions.

The discussion herein has concerned the approach taken by the JCHR towards DOIs; and this is important because the Committee was the principal site of legislative engagement with DOIs in the study period. In terms of *effective power* however, the JCHR has, as a parliamentary committee, been limited in its ability to secure tangible legislative outcomes or even secure legislative debate.[138] (The Committee did secure debates in the House of Lords of its 2008 and 2010 monitoring reports.) I have noted that DOIs are a particularly limited remedy within the spectrum of legislative remand, because courts are unable to hold the political branches to any time limits for remedial decisions to be made, or to ensure that litigants receive relief in their individual cases. While the JCHR eventually adopted these functions under the HRA, it only had the power to, at most, embarrass the executive. So, while the existence of the Committee secured greater accountability of government departments in terms of requiring greater public justification of government decisions, the JCHR could not compel action. In the following chapters, we will see several examples where the JCHR has been an irritant to the government, but has not been able to secure its recommended action. In the case of prisoner voting, the JCHR's lobbying was ignored in the House of Commons.[139] In relation to control orders, several MPs took the Committee's report seriously, but, as we will see in Chapter 8, the government was uncooperative in relation to legislative deliberation on the control orders Bill.

6.G. Conclusion

In Chapter 2, I introduced two different models of institutional interaction between courts and legislatures (ordinarily the executive acting through the legislature)—dialogue as a specialized division of labour across the two institutions or dialogue as judicial review followed by legislative review of the merits of the judicial conclusion. I argued that both were possible understandings of how open remedies such as DOIs ought to operate, even though many commentators have identified DOIs as designed to support the second model.

[138] MC Tolley, 'Parliamentary Scrutiny of Rights in the United Kingdom: Assessing the Work of the Joint Committee on Human Rights' (2009) 44 Aus J Pol Sci 41, 48–9.

[139] Likewise, in relation to the Gender Recognition Act 2004, the JCHR's concerns about retrospective relief were overlooked in both Houses. See 7.C.1.

The overall operation of DOIs from 2000 to 2010 most resembles the specialization model of interaction. The UK's experience over this period is a clear illustration of how the courts and the legislature can develop a working relationship playing distinct roles under a system of open remedies, with courts identifying that legislation infringes human rights in specific circumstances and the legislature deciding how to revise the general position of the law. In the early phase of the HRA, the vast majority of DOIs were not controversial, so this type of specialized functioning did not involve courts overriding or thwarting the policy objectives of the legislature. Indeed, the nature of cases resulting in DOIs gives support to theories that courts can play a role which is complementary to the legislative process, identifying human rights concerns that may otherwise go unattended to.

But even after this phase, when DOIs became increasingly controversial, this type of interaction—in which the role of the political branches of government was to decide *how* not whether to respond to a DOI—continued. The executive did not choose to express its reservations about, or disagreement with, judicial findings of incompatibility by openly refusing to provide a legislative remedy. I have argued that one explanation is the significant discretion that attaches to the task of devising remedial action, sometimes leaving ample space for the continued pursuit of the policy in question.

In Chapter 3, I raised the importance of examining not only legislative output, but the extent to which DOIs drive the legislature towards reflective, principled deliberation, whether that is deliberation on how the law should change or on whether the judicial conclusion was the correct one. Across the entire body of DOIs, only a few legislative responses generated debate in the Houses of Parliament. The provisions of HRA imposed very little discipline on political institutions in the aftermath of a DOI. When and how to propose changes in the law, or whether to use a remedial order were entirely within the government's discretion, without even procedural burdens of public justification. By giving the political branches such a free hand in deciding whether, when, and how to respond to a DOI, the HRA did little to rein in the government's control of the legislative agenda, even though the JCHR over time secured some accountability for remedial action or lack thereof. We have seen in this chapter some ways in which the design of DOIs under the HRA is too permissive to adequately support legislative deliberation and can leave victims of human rights violations unnecessarily waiting for redress.

The remainder of Part III will consider three exceptions to the pattern of limited legislative engagement, as well as one example of deliberative failure. Unlike most DOIs, corrected by way of an amendment within a Bill directed towards a broader purpose, the remedial action after the declarations in *Bellinger*, *Blood and Tarbuck*, and *Belmarsh Prisoners* was introduced as its own Bill, with dedicated second and third reading debates and committee consideration. Chapters 7 and 8 explore the putative benefits of open remedies in practice: do we see careful deliberation on what human rights require and how to realize those rights through law and policy? Do we see any evidence of superior legislative capacity to make certain remedial choices? Or is parliamentary discourse dominated by judicial understandings of rights and oriented only to legal compliance?

7

Remedial Deliberation in the Legislature

7.A. Introduction

In Chapter 1, I identified several rationales for leaving the task of devising human rights remedies to the legislature in the first instance. One rationale was that, in some circumstances, the legislature is better equipped to make decisions about what action needs to be taken than the court. Another rationale was that open remedies can promote deliberation within the legislature on how to protect rights, by treating the protection of rights as a cooperative enterprise across courts and legislatures. The legislative capacity rationale has been used by courts in justifying the use of different forms of legislative remand. The deliberative rationale is instead a concern for institutional design, if we seek to design a bill of rights for a deliberative democracy.

This chapter examines the responses to *Bellinger* and *Blood and Tarbuck*, both of which are examples of principled deliberation on the requirements of human rights following a DOI. Section 7.B details the response to *Bellinger* as an example of a DOI being followed by a (relatively) reflective deliberative process in the legislature. This also provides an opportunity to look into what remedial strengths the legislature demonstrated in this case.

Section 7.C turns to what disadvantages arise from relying on a legislative remedy, even where the legislature is engaged in independent deliberation. We see that the legislature faces certain difficulties in complementing its concern for the general and the prospective, with concern for the particular and the retrospective situation of the claimant. I argue that the denial of retrospective justice to successful litigants, *even* where there is no principled disagreement over the judicial finding of incompatibility, is a problematic feature of the design of DOIs.

Section 7.D looks at the example of prisoner voting in the UK, which illustrates how the permissiveness of DOIs may actually allow the political branches of government to avoid deliberation. The prolonged failure of deliberation in this case leads us to question the rationale that, by restraining themselves from making remedial choices, courts employing a DOI necessarily support legislative engagement on human rights.

7.B. Exploring the Legislative Capacity Rationale: The Response to *Bellinger*

7.B.1. *Bellinger* and the Gender Recognition Act

The DOI in *Bellinger* concerned the failure of the UK's laws to recognize any change of gender, such that transsexuals remained in their birth gender at law. The choice to employ a DOI was justified on the basis that legislative deliberation was required to choose between different options for the legal recognition of transsexuals.[1] This case was followed by a unique response within the series of DOIs from 2000 to 2010: a careful and deliberate process of legislation, actively involving the JCHR and subject to review and debate in both Houses of Parliament.

This was not a situation where the move for legislative reform was prompted solely or directly by the DOI. The government first announced its intention to legislate to recognize the rights of transsexuals some months before the House of Lords judgment.[2] Nonetheless, a series of judicial decisions did provide the impetus for legislative action. From 1990, the UK government had been warned in a number of ECtHR judgments about its failure to afford any legal recognition to transsexuals, though it was not found to be in violation of the Convention.[3] Consequently, an Interdepartmental Working Group on Transsexual People presented a comprehensive report in 2000 calling for a public consultation to decide between different possible courses of action. In 2001, the Court of Appeal in *Bellinger* expressed dismay that no response had been given to this report and no steps were intended to take the matter forward.[4] While accepting that any change in the definition of sex or gender ought to be left to Parliament, the leading judgment stated clearly in closing:

> We would add however, with the strictures of the European Court on Human Rights well in mind, that there is no doubt that the profoundly unsatisfactory nature of the present position and the plight of transsexuals requires careful consideration.[5]

One year later in *Goodwin v United Kingdom*,[6] the ECtHR decided that the UK's continued failure to introduce any legal recognition for transsexuals created ongoing violations of the right to privacy and the right to marry. The court was influenced by the criticisms made by the Court of Appeal in 2001, citing this as

[1] See 4.C.3.

[2] Ministerial Statement, Lord Chancellor's Department, Hansard HC vol 396 col 36WS (16 December 2002). This was between the Court of Appeal and House of Lords hearings. The House of Lords delivered the DOI: *Bellinger v Bellinger* [2003] UKHL 21.

[3] *Cossey v United Kingdom* (1990) 13 EHHR 622; *X, Y & Z v United Kingdom* (1997) 24 EHRR 143; *Sheffield and Horsham v United Kingdom* (1998) 27 EHRR 163.

[4] *Bellinger v Bellinger* [2001] EWCA Civ 1140 (Court of Appeal) [96]. See also the dissenting judgment of Lord Justice Thorpe LJ, at [151].

[5] *Bellinger* (n 4) [109].

[6] *Goodwin v United Kingdom* (2002) 35 EHRR 18.

evidence that the situation of transsexuals in the UK was no longer sustainable.[7] The DOI in *Bellinger* confirmed this conclusion.

7.B.2. The nature of legislative deliberation

In Chapter 3, we considered two different perspectives on the impact of judicial protection of human rights on the quality of democratic deliberation. We considered the potential beneficial impact of judicial decisions as acting as 'door openers' for marginalized issues, as well as furnishing reasoning on the proper scope of human rights for public and legislative reflection. On the other hand, some theorists and political scientists are sceptical of even weak-form review's ability to improve deliberation because of the fear that political discourse will become dominated by judicial interpretations, leaving little space for alternative articulations of what rights require.

The Gender Recognition Bill debates are an example of a series of judicial decisions effectively drawing attention, and lending a sense of urgency, to a marginalized legislative issue. But they do not support the fears of sceptics; they do not even show judicial reasoning to be overtly important. Despite the importance of both domestic and international judicial decisions in precipitating the legislative reforms, very limited reference was made to judicial decisions in the parliamentary debates themselves. Even though several Members of Parliament referred to the *Bellinger* and *Goodwin* judgments in their speeches as the reason why the legislation was introduced,[8] the government itself made its case for the legislation as a matter of ethical imperative, not simply compliance. The Second Reading speeches in the House of Lords and House of Commons characterized the legislation as reflecting the government's commitment to social inclusion and the continuation of a reformist tradition of addressing the needs of minority groups.[9] It was acknowledged that the Bill was 'influenced' by judgments of the ECtHR and the House of Lords,[10] but the primary reason offered for the necessity of the legislation was to 'provide a long-ignored minority with social justice, legal rights and a place in our evolving democracy'.[11] Even though the government had been pushed to action by judicial decisions, it presented the reforms proudly, as a matter of government policy.

In fact, all members supporting the legislation (a large majority) emphasized the powerful ethical case for both legal recognition of gender change and protection of transsexuals from discrimination and abuse. This was characterized as embodying a

[7] *Goodwin* (n 6) [90]–[91].

[8] Boswell, Hansard HC vol 418 col 64 (23 February 2004); Atkinson, at col 78; Key, at col 81.

[9] Lord Filkin, Hansard HL vol 655 col 1287 (18 December 2003); Lammy, Hansard HC vol 418 col 48 (23 February 2004).

[10] Filkin (n 9) col 1288. Lammy (n 9) cols 51–2, for whom the significance of the House of Lords decision was the confirmation that new legislation would need to be brought for the incompatibility to be corrected, rather than it being corrigible through the common law alone.

[11] Filkin (n 9) col 1291. In a similar vein, Lammy stated that the Bill 'affirm[ed]the values of tolerance, inclusion and social justice that we as a country embody', at col 57.

parliamentary tradition of legislating for the concerns of even small minorities, or even a duty on Parliament to address the needs of minorities who lack any real electoral power.[12] Numerous MPs recounted stories from transsexual constituents who had suffered from both the existing state of the law and social attitudes towards them. These narratives were used to justify the need for the legislation to both rectify a wrong as well as to assist in changing social attitudes.[13] Speeches in support of advancing the human rights of transsexuals came from all major parties.

Despite the dominant tenor of debate as a matter of ethics, the fact that a change to the law was required as a matter of human rights law (and that the domestic cases reflected that obligation) appeared to be foundational to the debate. Several MPs openly recognized the need to comply with the ECtHR judgment, in addition to the ethical case for the legislation.[14] That said, the only reference made to judicial reasoning in the relevant decisions was by an opponent of the law, who was dissatisfied with the quality of the reasoning.[15] The response to him (which even he accepted)[16] only confirmed that the obligation to act was taken for granted: 'the reality is that [the cases] are part of our law and we must follow our law'.[17]

Additionally, this was a careful and reflective legislative process, relative to most legislation passed in the UK. A major practical reason for this was that the executive supported robust legislative review. It did so in three ways: by introducing remedial measures in a Bill dedicated to that purpose, by providing a draft to the JCHR, and providing ample time for parliamentary review in both Houses.

The provision of a draft version of the Bill to the parliamentary JCHR allowed it to engage in pre-legislative review and propose changes prior to the proposal's formal introduction into Parliament. The JCHR also launched a public consultation on the Bill, which drew submissions from a wide range of transsexual people with different experiences and the principal opponents of any recognition of gender change. Many parliamentarians received representations from constituents in advance and referred to these in public debate. Their contributions supported the contextualization of human rights claims: making the choices facing legislators more concrete, and making legislators aware of the need to justify forms of discrimination in the law, should they choose to retain them.

[12] Boswell, Hansard HC, vol 418 col 58 (23 February 2004); Oaten, col 67; Key, col 81.

[13] Boswell, Hansard HC, vol 418 col 58 (23 February 2004); Jones, col 64; Woodward, cols 72–3, 77; Atkinson, col 78; Bayley, col 79. Peers also recounted their experiences with transsexual people in the course of their professions as a former trade union official (Baroness Gibson), as a doctor (Lord Chan), and as a sportsperson (Lord Moynihan).

[14] E.g. one MP stated, 'I welcome the Bill... It is right in its own terms, but it will also have the benefit of making UK law compliant with the ruling of the European Court of Human Rights': Boswell, Hansard HC vol 418 col 79 (23 February 2004). Another stated, 'I suspect that, left to themselves, the Government may have been content to let the issue lie, but the European judgment has compelled them to act. In any event, I personally believe that it is right to do so . . . ': Oaten, col 64. See also Atkinson, col 78; Bayley, col 78; Key, cols 81–2.

[15] Bishop Winchester, Hansard HL vol 655 cols 1297–8 (18 December 2003), criticizing the judicial treatment of medical evidence and the value of marriage.

[16] 'I was not questioning the fact that we were bound by the cases, but the quality of the judgment by which we are bound': Hansard HL vol 655 col 1301 (18 December 2003).

[17] Lord Carlile, Hansard HL vol 655 col 1301 (18 December 2003).

Rather than a failure of deliberation, or a form of review concentrated on legal compliance, the legislative debates in reply to *Bellinger/Goodwin* evidence an independent political deliberation on the protection of rights in devising reply legislation. This deliberation did not result from parliamentarians questioning the judicial decisions finding the existing law incompatible, but rather deliberation on how to negotiate the range of issues that emerged in devising remedial action. This can be illustrated by two prominent questions thrown up by the reply legislation, which related to the scope and balancing of rights to privacy, equality, family life, and conscience.

The first concern was the relationship between the new recognition of gender change and the opposite-sex requirement in relation to marriage laws. The government's position was that marriage must remain an institution for heterosexual couples.[18] The legislation therefore required that, if legal change in gender were to result in a marriage between two men or two women, then no change would be recognized unless that marriage was annulled. While no one in the legislature challenged the government's position on same-sex marriage, there was concern that pursuing the ban on same-sex marriage to the point of forcing existing marriages to end was going too far, and amendments were proposed to preserve this small group of marriages.

It is here we can see the legislature performing the type of reviewing role that did not involve looking to judicial decisions or standards, but at the same time involved a scrutiny of legislation that was different from simple political positioning for or against a policy. MPs made reference to public submissions made to the JCHR to illustrate how the Bill required transsexuals to 'trade one set of rights for another'.[19] It was argued that it was not ethical to force marriages to be annulled, and MPs questioned whether the harm to this small group of people was truly necessary or proportional to the government's policy goal in relation to preserving the opposite-sex nature of marriage.[20] While parliamentarians were not successful in passing an amendment to preserve the status of these marriages, partial concessions were made in terms of preserving accrued rights that would otherwise be lost on annulment.[21]

Another such issue was amendments seeking to weaken the protection of privacy for transsexuals. The Bill presented to Parliament made the disclosure of information concerning gender change an offence, outside enumerated exceptions. A cross-party coalition argued that it was the right of religious organizations to know if a person was transgender in order for members to practise their religious beliefs, where those beliefs denied any recognition of transsexuality. Arguing that a balance needed to be struck between different human rights,[22] they sought a

[18] The government was at the time drafting its civil partnership scheme for same-sex couples.

[19] Woodward, Hansard HC vol 418 cols 75–6 (23 February 2004); Bayley, cols 80–1.

[20] Bercow, Hansard HC vol 418 col 87 (23 February 2004); Bayley cols 80, 88.

[21] The government undertook to prepare statutory guidance on the position of accrued pension rights and other benefits; proposed amendments were accordingly withdrawn: Hansard HC cols 1490–5 (25 May 2004).

[22] This type of argument was widely made across the Report and Third Reading debates by those supporting the amendment and later opposing the legislation. In fact, certain religious bodies

wide-ranging conscience exemption from the Bill's anti-disclosure provisions on the grounds of 'religious sensibilities'.[23] Those opposed to these amendments argued that proposed exemptions would erode the very policy of the laws to ensure transsexual people could keep their status private and, in a broader sense, to protect these people from intolerance and mistreatment.[24] In the end, the government stood by the privacy protections in the new law, but made some moderate concessions, which were proposed by the JCHR, in secondary legislation.[25]

Both of these matters were negotiations over the specification of human rights and their balancing against other policies and even other rights. They were understood by parliamentarians as such, and the fact that the Bill was pulled in two different directions by amendments suggests that it ultimately drew a middle line through parliamentary opinion.[26] On both matters, some changes in the government position did result from legislative review. The deliberation on the Gender Recognition Bill therefore demonstrates even some signs of openness to change—probably the most difficult criterion of deliberation to satisfy in a partisan political environment.

7.B.3. The benefits of legislative remedies

So far this example demonstrates that, in circumstances where the government is supportive of legislative review, the legislature is capable of following up on a finding of human rights infringement with deliberation on remedial action that takes human rights principles seriously, but does not simply amount to an exercise in predicting legality before a future court. This section considers a separate question, namely, what benefit there was in having a legislative rather than a judicial remedy in this case, from the perspective of protecting human rights.

This example suggests three main strengths of legislative remedial action. The first advantage to proceeding by way of legislation was the breadth of the subject matter covered by the measures. The scheme provided not only for changes to marriage laws, but also, for example, the issuance of new birth certificates and privacy protections on the disclosure of information. The parliamentary process provided an avenue for open negotiation of the interface between recognition of

commissioned legal advice (submitted to Parliament) that the legislation violated freedom of religion. This met with a detailed response from the JCHR which considered that the legislation did not raise serious human rights issues in relation to religious freedoms. See JCHR, *Twelfth Report: Legislative Scrutiny of Bills 2003–04* HL 93/HC 603 (12 May 2004), [2.2].

23 Hansard HC vol 421 cols 1445–77 (25 May 2004).

24 Bercow (n 23) col 1450; Younger-Ross (n 23) col 1456.

25 Lammy (n 23) cols 1475–6. The JCHR recommended that some disclosure should be allowed so that clergy could take advantage of their legal rights under the legislation not to officiate the marriage of a transgender person: JCHR (n 22) [2.14]–[2.17]. This was provided in the Gender Recognition (Disclosure of Information) (England, Wales and Northern Ireland) Order 2005.

26 The final Bill was passed with a large majority of 355 Ayes to 46 Noes. One MP noted: 'I can see that there would be substantially more opposition to this legislation if I were to insist on [allowing marriages to continue despite a legal change in gender]. So I look at the situation pragmatically and see what I can accept . . . I have reached the view that the Bill might be about right for where we are': Mountford, Hansard HC vol 418 col 86 (23 February 2004).

gender change and a range of other areas of legal regulation and social organization, and the legislation was able to provide a comprehensive framework to deal with gender change, rather than piecemeal, issue-specific reform.

The second advantage was the expansiveness of the scheme's recognition of gender change. The House of Lords in *Bellinger* observed that a variety of tests could be used to recognize gender change and the choice between them was not determined by the present state of human rights law. In other jurisdictions, where judicial adjustments have been made to the definition of male and female in order to allow for legal gender change in family law, recognition has been limited to post-operative transsexuals.[27]

The Gender Recognition Act (GRA) instead provided a system of certification by a specialized Gender Recognition Panel in which a range of factors could be considered in evaluating gender change. By dispensing with the requirement for surgery, the UK went beyond the system adopted both by reform legislation and judicial decisions in other jurisdictions.[28] This has allowed for recognition of a broader range of transsexuals and dealt with some of the difficulties of basing recognition of gender change on surgery alone.

However, strictly speaking, these are advantages that arise from having *legislation* address the task of recognizing gender change, not necessarily from having the legislature be the *first mover* in devising a remedy. Even if the courts had adjusted the common law definition of male and female to ensure the recognition of the marriage of Mrs Bellinger, Parliament could still have enacted this type of comprehensive legislative reform. Furthermore, had the courts limited their recognition of transsexuals to post-operative cases, Parliament could have replaced this judicial solution with a more inclusive administrative system of gender change. What benefits, if any, can we observe from having the legislature act *first* to craft remedial action?

Any answer to this question is necessarily speculative, but the following possibilities can be suggested. First, by leaving the legislature to devise a remedy to a human rights incompatibility, legislative remand may in some circumstances ultimately generate more expansive or generous legislative reform for affected persons. The *Bellinger*/GRA case illustrates that even if courts are limited to incremental changes in the law, the legislature is not so limited. Courts may be unable or unwilling to go as far as the legislature in changing the law. However, if the court does act to correct the immediate human rights incompatibility through incremental change, the legislature (or perhaps more accurately, members of the executive) may prefer to

[27] *MT v JT* (1976) 355 A. 2d. 204 at 209 (New Jersey, USA); *Attorney-General v Otahuhu Family Court* [1995] 1 NZLR 603 at 614–15 (New Zealand); *Re Kevin and Jennifer v Attorney-General for the Commonwealth* [2001] Fam CA 1074 (Australia).

[28] In fact, commentators have argued that the system has been path-breaking in embracing gender, rather than sex, as regulating the legal claims of transgender people: S Cowan, 'Gender is no Subsitute for Sex: A Comparative Human Rights Analysis of the Legal Regulation of Sexual Identity' (2005) 13 Feminist Legal Studies 67; R Sandland, 'Feminism and the Gender Recognition Act' (2005) 13 Feminist Legal Studies 43; cf AN Sharpe, 'Endless Sex: The Gender Recognition Act 2004 and the Persistence of a Legal Category' (2007) 15 Feminist Legal Studies 57, who makes some qualifications to the claims of Cowan and Sandland.

simply leave matters as the judiciary sets them, in the knowledge that no immediate action is necessary. Hence, legislative remand may in some cases result in law reform that goes further than the minimum required to address a particular victim's plight.

A further benefit which may be connected to the legislative remand device is the sense of ownership of, and enthusiasm for, reform that may result from giving the legislature the responsibility for remedial action. The public debates show that, despite the role of courts in necessitating the changes, parliamentarians did take ownership of legal reform, making their own justifications for legislative action. There was barely any reference to the judicial decisions as foisting these new laws upon them; legislators saw this as their own move towards social inclusion and equality.

There are benefits to having a campaign for social inclusion of a minority come from a representative deliberative forum, and most importantly, a forum directed to answering the question of what is the right thing to do, rather than only what legality dictates. As several parliamentarians recognized, the problems faced by transsexuals were not simply to do with legal recognition, but fundamental problems of social stigma and marginalization. Not only did the changes here emanate from the political process, but by engaging in an open debate and more than a compliance-based justification for the legal reforms, parliamentarians argued the case for why change to the law was just and necessary based on human rights as ethical imperatives.[29] It has been argued, based on experiences with gay rights elsewhere, that allowing the legislature to be responsible for changes made to the law can, in the equality and non-discrimination context, enable more long-lasting acceptance of minority rights.[30]

Thus far, we have described the *Bellinger*/GRA case study as a positive example of cooperative dialogue under the HRA, and one in which the legislature was engaged in deliberation on the specification of human rights principles. Even in this case, however, there was one difficulty with the legislative remedy: the absence of retrospective relief for the litigant herself.

7.C. Difficulties with Legislative Remedies: The Retrospectivity Problem

Chapter 1 introduced one objection to legislative remand, which was that the court neglects the victim before it by failing to ensure an effective remedy for the human rights violation that they have suffered and may continue to suffer. The use of a

[29] This is not to say *all* parliamentarians did so. Particularly in the House of Lords, there was a minority who rejected the need to legally recognize transgender people, including some strongly pejorative descriptions of them. For example, Baroness O'Cathain argued that the condition was 'a delusion, a fantasy' and the law ought not to 'go along with transsexual people in this delusion': Hansard HL vol 655 col 1310 (18 December 2003).

[30] T Jacobi, 'Same-Sex Marriage in Vermont: Implications of Legislative Remand for the Judiciary's Role' (2002) 26 Vermont Law Review 381. See also discussion in Chapter 1.C.2.

DOI does not *necessarily* leave the litigant empty-handed, because their situation may be addressed by future legislation, and in fact, the litigant may sometimes be primarily seeking prospective law reform. However, in many cases litigants are seeking a remedy that addresses past injustice. Litigants may be left without effective redress if the legislature does not, when embarking on new legislation, include retrospective measures.

Limited judicial powers over primary legislation are a core aspect of the HRA's hybrid design. The Act was constructed such that victims do not have any right to an effective remedy if the infringement of their rights is brought about by primary legislation, as opposed to executive action. Hence, if litigants do not receive an effective personal remedy where a DOI has been employed, this is not to say that the HRA is failing at something which it was designed to ensure. Rather, our concern is whether the HRA is a *well-designed* hybrid instrument in the first place.

In this section we will see how the weakness of the DOI mechanism in terms of retrospective justice makes the DOI a blunt instrument to achieve the purpose of giving Parliament the ultimate say on the protection of human rights. Even in situations where there is *no principled disagreement* with the judicial finding of a human rights infringement, the litigant may not receive an effective remedy, because of the general and prospective orientation of the legislative process, and discomfort amongst legislators with laws that have retrospective effect.

7.C.1. Retrospective remedies and the Gender Recognition Bill

In *Bellinger*, the litigant was married to a man for over twenty years but her marriage was void. She sought full legal recognition not simply in the future, but also in relation to the status of her *existing* marriage, which she had successfully argued was denied legal recognition in violation of fundamental rights. Yet, the GRA provided no such recognition for Mrs Bellinger or those in a similar position. Any recognition of acquired gender under the new laws would not take effect until a gender recognition certificate was issued, and the Act expressly provided that this would not have retrospective effect.[31] This was not only a matter of symbolic importance to those affected. By failing to retrospectively validate these marriages, the legislation also failed to correct the practical consequences of those marriages going unrecognized, such as pension benefits, parental rights, and property rights.

Little attention was paid to those people in this situation in either House of Parliament. This was despite it being a prominent concern in the JCHR's review of the draft Bill, based on submissions to the public consultation.[32] A number of submissions to the Committee argued that retrospective recognition was required to provide an effective remedy, and moreover it was demeaning and disrespectful to require existing 'married' couples to go through the gender recognition process, as

[31] GRA 2004 s 9.

[32] JCHR, *Nineteenth Report 2002–03: Draft Gender Recognition Bill* HL Paper 188-I, HC 1276-I. See recommendations 3–5, 34–5.

well as a further wedding ceremony, 'before they could be legally regarded as husband and wife as they should have been before'.[33]

The JCHR noted that the Bill was only designed to operate prospectively and was not a satisfactory remedy for those who had fought their cases before international and domestic courts, as the measures 'would provide nothing by way of just satisfaction for the violation of their rights'.[34] It argued that the government should consider allowing the new laws to have some retrospective effect, or at least that litigants who won their claims to Strasbourg and the House of Lords should be allowed to benefit retrospectively from the measures. The government firmly resisted these recommendations. It argued that it was not legally required to provide a remedy, that it would be administratively inconvenient, and that it would sanction same-sex marriage. The JCHR scrutinized all these reasons and concluded that the government's position was unconvincing,[35] but stated to Parliament that the government had 'set its face against retrospectively validating marriages which were invalid at the time when the parties went through a ceremony of marriage'.[36]

The fourth, and most interesting, reason given to the JCHR was, at the risk of caricaturing the argument, that the legislation should not be applied retrospectively because it would have a retrospective effect.[37] This was in fact the only argument on the matter made by the Minister in the Second Reading debates, who stated: '[the] legislation will not be backdated, because we do not have retrospective legislation'.[38]

It was possible that giving retrospective effect to some of the proposed provisions would have had detrimental consequences for accrued rights and liabilities, in a small number of cases.[39] However, this was not the government's argument. It claimed that retrospective legislation was invidious of itself, regardless of whether its effects on past events were detrimental or beneficial to affected individuals.

7.C.2. The norm against retrospectivity

It is useful at this point to distinguish the way in which retrospectivity is used in the legal, remedial context and in the context of legislative debate and theories of the rule of law. Thus far I have not been referring to retrospectivity in a pejorative sense. I have been referring to beneficial retrospective measures that remedy past wrongs. However, the idea of retrospective (or retroactive)[40] *legislation* implicates a

[33] JCHR (n 32) [36]. [34] JCHR (n 32) [44].

[35] For the government's reasons and the response to them, see JCHR (n 32) [39].

[36] JCHR (n 32) [23]. [37] JCHR (n 32) [39].

[38] Parliamentary Under-Secretary of State for Constitutional Affairs (Christopher Leslie), Hansard HC vol 418 col 104 (23 February 2004).

[39] Retrospectively recognized gender change would have adversely affected female to male transsexuals who had expected to reach retirement age at 60, for instance.

[40] On a definitional note, this section refers to retrospectivity, rather than retroactivity. These two terms are often used interchangeably. For our purposes, we can proceed with the concept of retrospectivity as an umbrella concept. This may on occasion encompass *retroactive* laws that expressly state that the law is to have effect as of a date in the past, as well as legislation which is *not* retroactive, but nonetheless is retrospective in that it alters the legal consequences of events which have occurred in the

deeper rule of law principle that law ought not to be retrospective. Often when the label 'retrospective' is used in relation to legislation, it is being used pejoratively, to describe a feature of bad legislation.

Charles Sampford has recently evaluated the concept of retrospectivity and its relationship to the rule of law. He identifies that the parameters of the principle against retrospectivity are difficult to define but, essentially, retrospective law is that which changes the future legal consequences of past events.[41] Once the definition of retrospectivity is clarified, we see that it is not necessarily a *bad* feature of law, and can in fact be good in some cases. Sampford's research identifies that 'many laws have partially retrospective effects. The issue is not whether those effects are retrospective but *the nature and extent of those effects and the reasonableness of their imposition*.'[42] He observes that the label of 'retrospective' nonetheless carries a stigma in political debate, is employed for rhetorical effect in a wide range of situations, and is not always accompanied by a coherent argument as to why the effects are unreasonable.[43]

Thinking about retrospectivity in the terms suggested by Sampford draws our attention to the differences between laws imposing criminal liability for actions that were legal at the time they were committed (retrospective criminal liability), laws imposing civil liability that have some retrospective effect (say, new taxes on assets acquired in the past), and beneficial remedial legislation that corrects a past wrong (say, recognizing a legal status previously denied). We should not dismiss legislation that remedies a past wrong out of hand, simply for being retrospective in effect (as the government did in relation to the GRA). Instead, the question for legislators should be whether the retrospective effects of proposed legislation are problematic, on balance.

Choudary and Roach, when commenting on reply legislation to Canadian DDIs, suggest that 'the norm against retroactive law-making has been internalized by political actors as an indicator of bad or illegitimate laws',[44] such that legislators do not generally reflect on good versus bad retrospective effects. The norm that legislation is general and prospective is so well established that legislation is drafted with only the future in mind, and serious consideration is simply not given to whether legislation should be framed retrospectively in any way.[45]

past. See EA Driedger, 'Statutes: Retroactive Retrospective Reflections' (1978) 56 Canadian Bar Review 268. For an argument that the two terms can be understood as distinct, see J Waldron, 'Retroactive Law: How Dodgy was Duynhoven?' (2004) 10 Otago Law Review 631; cf. JE Fisch, 'Retroactivity and Legal Change: An Equilibrium Approach' (1996–7) 110 Harvard Law Review 1056, 1069, and MJ Graetz, 'Retroactivity Revisited' (1984–5) 98 Harvard Law Review 1820, 1822, who argue that the distinction is 'analytically incoherent' and 'illusory', respectively.

41 See in C Sampford, *Retrospectivity and the Rule of Law* (OUP, Oxford 2006) 9–37 (defining retrospectivity).

42 Sampford (n 41) 23 (emphasis added).

43 Sampford (n 41) 19.

44 S Choudary and K Roach, 'Putting the Past behind Us: Prospective Judicial and Legislative Constitutional Remedies' (2003) 21 Supreme Court Law Review 205, 241–2.

45 Choudary and Roach (n 44) 242.

Choudary and Roach argue that this creates difficulties for legislative remand, because governments fashioning a legislative reply do not fully apprehend the remedial function of reply legislation and act as though in their normal, prospective, law-making capacity.[46]

The authors make this empirical claim based on 'intuition' rather than any analysis of the legislative process itself.[47] Their intuition is borne out by the legislative debates in *Bellinger*. Neither House of Parliament took an interest in holding the government to account for the failure to provide any retrospective relief for past victims. The contribution of the JCHR however defies expectations that legislative actors do not generally reflect on retrospective justice. The parliamentary committee gave detailed thought to how a remedy could be fashioned for the litigant, though it was not successful in having these concerns picked up in the legislative debates. This is further support for the characterization in the previous chapter of the JCHR as an interface between judicial decisions and legislative decisions. In at least drawing the government's attention to the issue of retrospective relief, the JCHR provided some follow-up on an effective remedy, in circumstances where the courts could not provide any.

So far I have argued that even though there is no universal, principled impediment against legislation having beneficial retrospective effects, a stigma attaches to the idea of retrospective legislation within the legislative process. This creates difficulties for legislative remedies in human rights cases where victims seek retrospective relief. However, these difficulties are not insurmountable. The response to the case of *Blood and Tarbuck* demonstrates that the norm against retrospectivity can be overcome, if there is sufficient political will to provide a remedy for successful claimants.

7.C.3. Willingness to provide retrospective relief: the case of *Blood and Tarbuck*

The DOI in *Blood and Tarbuck* concerned the inability of mothers who had conceived children by artificial insemination after the death of their male partner to have that partner registered as the child's father on a birth certificate. This example suggests that, in limited circumstances, members of the legislature are willing to give retrospective effect to remedial legislation.

Prior to the litigation leading to the DOI, the claimants had lobbied their constituency representatives for a change in the law, and one backbencher had introduced a Private Member's Bill to address the matter. The Bill failed for lack of time and the government did not place the matter on its legislative agenda. The claimants then pursued legal action. The first instance judge held that the state of the law violated the right to a private and family life, which government lawyers conceded.

[46] Choudary and Roach (n 44) 242.
[47] Choudary and Roach (n 44) 241.

In response, a second Private Member's Bill was introduced. Though a much smaller legislative initiative, the nature of the debate was similar to the Gender Recognition Bill. The legislative changes were widely identified by MPs and peers across parties as correcting an injustice, and compliance with the judicial decision was treated as a secondary reason, with the primary justification being that this was 'the right thing to do'.[48] Like the recognition of transsexuals, the DOI here served to 'jump start' legislative action where previous attempts from within Parliament had failed,[49] and this time the measures had active government support.[50]

But, by contrast to other reply legislation, the legislation was clearly understood as having a remedial purpose for the claimants. MPs promoting the Bill emphasized the need for the law to be retrospective as well as prospective in order to benefit those whose predicament motivated the legislation in the first place. The Bill's sponsor stated:

> The Bill is retrospective in so far as it deals not only with future cases but with existing ones. I understand that 30 to 40 children are in the predicament that I have outlined . . . Today we as parliamentarians can help those children. We can help those women . . . I believe we have a once-only opportunity for the House to regain its reputation and correct the matter.[51]

The subsequent deliberation on this Bill illustrates both the stigma that generally attaches to retrospectivity, as well as the fact that the legislature is able, if it is willing, to overlook this and enact measures which have a retrospective remedial effect. Although there was cross-party support for the legislation, speeches from members in both Houses indicated discomfort with the retrospective effect of the legislation, but satisfaction that the Bill had been carefully tailored, and was a limited exception to the principle that law ought not to be retrospective.[52] The

[48] Grayling, Hansard HC vol 403 col 609 (28 March 2003). In the House of Lords Second Reading speech the Bill's sponsor referred to the DOI as 'provid[ing] an additional impetus to change the law. But, fundamentally, the Bill represents the right thing to do, the decent thing to do': Baroness Pitkeathley, Hansard HL vol 650 cols 1150–1.

[49] Several parliamentarians stated that the DOI would not have happened if the government had supported the previous attempt to address the problem: Clarke, Hansard HC vol 403 col 604 (28 March 2003); Chope, cols 605–6; Lord Lester, Hansard HL vol 650 cols 1155–6. In the House of Lords, the Minister accepted this criticism—'that is a fair cop, I am afraid we are at fault': Baroness Andrews, col 1160.

[50] The Minister became involved at Committee phase and, at Third Reading, the Minister's position was that this Bill remedied that incompatibility identified by the judge and that it was 'another good reason' why the Minister was happy that the legislation was ready to pass: Blears, Hansard HC vol 406 col 994 (13 June 2003).

[51] McCabe, Hansard HC vol 403 col 603 (28 March 2003).

[52] There are numerous examples across Second and Third Reading debates in the Commons and the Lords; e.g. the Under-Secretary of State for Health stated, 'It is unusual for the Government to support a Bill that operates retrospectively. We all adhere to the general principle of law in that regard but in these circumstances it is absolutely right that the rights of the children are pivotal to our concern': Blears, Hansard HC vol 403 col 611 (28 March 2003). Closing debate, the Bill's sponsor stated: 'I fully understand the issues that some hon. Members have raised about the Bill's retrospective provisions. That is hardly surprising as legislation is rarely made for retrospective purposes. In this case, however, I believe that it is right . . . ': McCabe, Hansard HC vol 406 col 989 (13 June 2003). In the Lords' Second Reading Speech, Baroness Pitkeathley also noted that it was unusual to make law retrospective, but in this case it was right to do so. See also the statement from Baroness Hayman,

relevant Minister justified the retrospective provisions on the basis of addressing the infringement of Convention rights,[53] evincing a concern for the litigants that was lacking in relation to the response to *Bellinger* and *Goodwin*.

Why was Parliament content to provide a retrospective remedy in this instance? The debates indicate that it was relevant here that the actual victims before the court were uppermost in the minds of legislators. Across the debates there was regular and sometimes detailed[54] reference to the small group of existing mothers and children who were affected by the impugned law, and in particular to the personal struggle of the claimant. This suggests that legislative remedies may also provide for retrospective relief, if the legislature is particularly mindful of, and sympathetic towards, specific people wronged by the law. Moreover, in this case, there was also sympathetic media coverage of the DOI.[55]

But many victims of human rights violations are not sympathetic cases in the public eye. We saw in Chapter 6 the breakdown of the beneficiaries of DOIs: these are often members of unpopular, even vilified, minority groups. In these cases, we may not be able to rely on the enthusiasm of legislators for making an exception to their general discomfort with retrospectivity. Moreover, retrospective justice in this case was relatively costless, the matter of writing a name on a birth certificate. As the cost and administrative difficulty of providing a remedy to past victims increases, we may see a corresponding decline in enthusiasm for providing a retrospective remedy, particularly from government Ministers.

7.C.4. Implications for the DOI mechanism

The conclusion to be drawn from the above analysis is that, in circumstances where an effective remedy for the claimant requires some retrospective measures, the legislative process may be a poor, or at least unreliable, means to provide for such a remedy. In some cases, there may be principled reasons why legislation should not be retrospective in effect. But there is also a problem of built-up practice and norms around the task of legislating that mean that legislators are uncomfortable acting retrospectively unless they are in some way compelled to. In practical terms, this means that successful litigants may be left without an effective remedy even when the political branches of government do act to change the law in response to a DOI.

If we treat the HRA as a 'halfway house' that ensures some human rights protection in the UK without giving judges the power to disrupt legislation, then

Hansard HL vol 650 col 1152 (4 July 2003) that 'unusually for a legislator', she welcomed the retrospective provisions.

[53] Blears (n 52).

[54] Clarke, Hansard HC vol 403 cols 604–5 (28 March 2003); Lord Lester, Hansard HL vol 650 cols 1155–6 (4 July 2003).

[55] BBC, 28 February 2003 <http://news.bbc.co.uk/1/hi/health/2807707.stm>; Independent, 1 March 2003 <http://www.independent.co.uk/news/uk/crime/widow-wins-right-to-name-dead-husband-as-childrens-father-612734.html>; Times, 1 March 2003 <http://www.timesonline.co.uk/tol/news/uk/article1058296.ece>; Guardian, 1 March <http://www.guardian.co.uk/uk/2003/mar/01/claredyer>.

the difficulties of justice for litigants may be considered to be simply a sacrifice within this compromise. However, if we are interested in whether weak-form review is not merely a political compromise but a principled alternative, then this particular variant of weak-form review, where the legislature is the first mover, is a blunt instrument for creating or preserving a role for the legislature. It is a blunt instrument because *even where the legislature does not disagree in principle* with the decision of the court, it is in the position to deny an effective remedy to litigants because of oversight, or a lack of will.

This is not to suggest that retrospective justice is the only, or the most important, objective of human rights remedies. As I discussed in Part I, the strengths of legislative remedies are their ability to provide for systemic responses, design positive state action, and choose between different human rights-compatible remedial options; as well as promote legislative deliberation and institutional cooperation. But the trade-off between these general benefits of legislative remedies and the loss to individual litigants may have consequences for the behaviour of litigants and judges. Litigants may be unwilling to argue for a DOI if they have good reason to believe that, even if the legislature will address the declaration, it will not address their situation. And, as I have considered in 4.D, courts may also refrain from using the DOI if they are concerned that legislative reform will not benefit the victim before the court. Moreover, we ought to be concerned about the injustice of neglecting past victims where there is no institutional disagreement over whether they have suffered a human rights violation.

Is there a way to gain the benefits of legislative remand and cooperative remedies, without losing the ability to provide retrospective justice to litigants? In the context of coercive legislative remand, it has been suggested that courts should take responsibility for this problem, by exempting litigants from the effect of the impugned legislation, while leaving the legislature to deal with legislative change in relation to the general population. This is not possible under the HRA. A higher court can either correct the legislation, or declare it to be incompatible: it is not empowered to exempt the litigant from the effect of the legislation found to be incompatible.

In dealing with the government's refusal to give the Gender Recognition Bill any retrospective effect, the JCHR suggested that new laws provide an exemption for the claimants, allowing them to take advantage of otherwise prospective measures. The Committee cited the judicial practice of the ECJ and USSC of ensuring that litigants get the benefit of a court judgment, even if the judgment only operates prospectively for the general population.[56] The government's response was that it would be discriminatory to create different categories of people, some of whom benefit retrospectively and others who do not.[57] Even if judges are comfortable treating the victim before the court more favourably than the general population, the legislative norm of *generality* may cause considerable reluctance amongst legislators to provide relief to specific victims.

[56] JCHR, *Nineteenth Report 2002–03* (n 32) [44]–[48].

[57] See government correspondence to the JCHR (n 32), Appendix 1C.

Ultimately, the reason for making the DOI mechanism so weak is to ensure that any change to primary legislation can only come from the legislature. Given that the power to disagree is rarely used, we can ask if it is truly necessary to design legislative remand in a way that prioritizes disagreement. An alternative is to give the courts stronger powers, such that they are able to exempt the litigant, subject to the legislature being able to override the courts in the event of disagreement. This way the design of the bill of rights would better fit its ordinary operation rather than exceptional cases of disagreement. Additionally, we should not necessarily assume that stronger judicial powers (for remedial reasons) would compromise the deliberative aspirations of weak-form review. Sometimes, allowing the courts to move first in correcting the law may be no worse for democratic deliberation, something I consider in section 7.D.

7.D. Bringing Parliament Along or Avoiding Deliberation? The Prisoner Voting Saga

This book has previously discussed the DOI issued in *Smith v Scott*, which reiterated within domestic law the decision in *Hirst v United Kingdom*[58] that the UK's blanket prohibition on prisoners voting was a disproportionate interference with the right to vote. The decision in *Hirst* was delivered in 2005, the DOI was made in 2007, but by the end of the study period, at the general election in May 2010, the blanket ban on prisoner voting remained unchanged, and the prison population of the UK was therefore unable to vote.[59]

This is one example of sheer unwillingness, and accompanying delay, on the part of the political branches of government to take remedial action. In the previous chapter, I observed that the DOI mechanism permits delay as a type of passive resistance to a judicial decision. The case of the prisoner voting ban demonstrates the extent to which delay is possible *even* under circumstances where there is a Strasbourg ruling requiring legislative action. Where remedial action is considered to be deeply politically unpopular, political actors may not want to take responsibility for changing the law. A judicial finding of human rights violation may therefore be met with hostile failure to consider remedial action. In these circumstances, the DOI may fail to promote careful reflection on extant forms of treatment deemed by the courts to be unacceptable on human rights grounds, or even principled justification by lawmakers on why the limitation on rights is proportionate to a social need and should stand. This example gives us cause to consider whether legislative deliberation on remedial action may sometimes be better supported by a stronger judicial intervention.

[58] *Hirst v United Kingdom (No 2)* (2006) 42 EHRR 41.

[59] With the exception of remand prisoners, who were not subject to the ban.

7.D.1. The need for legislative deliberation

The disenfranchisement of prisoners in the UK was formalized in statute in 1870 along with the principle of forfeiture ('civil death') whereby prisoners relinquished all their civil and property rights. The ban was retained through a series of electoral law changes, up to and including the Representation of the People Act 1983.

The ECtHR recognized in 1987 that the requirement that State parties hold free and fair elections[60] necessarily includes a right to vote.[61] This right is subject to implied limitations, if imposed in pursuit of a legitimate aim and proportionate to that aim.[62] Soon after the HRA came into force, a challenge to the prisoner voting ban was made.[63] The UK domestic court however declined to scrutinize the proportionality of the blanket ban on prisoner voting, holding that the question of proportionate limitation was a matter on which judges should defer to Parliament.[64]

Four years later, in *Hirst*, the Strasbourg court did interrogate the UK government's arguments in favour of the ban.[65] The government's stated reasons for the ban were that it served the legitimate aims of prevention of crime, punishment of offenders, and incentivizing citizen-like behaviour. The court did not take issue with these aims, but held that a general, automatic restriction on the right to all convicted prisoners in prison, irrespective of their offence, the length of their sentence, or their circumstances, was disproportionate. In response to the invitation to defer to the decisions of the UK legislature and judiciary, the court emphasized that the ban had not been subjected to parliamentary consideration of competing interests or the proportionality of the ban in the modern day penal context, nor had the national courts examined its proportionality.[66] Rather, the state of the law represented adherence to a tradition without careful justification.

Still, the Strasbourg decision demonstrated a type of decisional minimalism. When asked by the UK government to indicate what type of restrictions would be permissible under the Convention, the court declined to give any guidance, stating that it was for the UK to decide how to remedy the human rights infringement.[67] Overall, the *Hirst* judgment indicated that some limitations on the right to vote would be permissible, but at the least, these would need to be carefully considered and justified by national lawmakers.

In *Smith v Scott*, the court declined to use section 3 to correct the law in view of the fact that some limitation on voting rights would fall within the State's margin of appreciation, and this margin was for the legislature to work within,

[60] Art 3 First Protocol ECHR.

[61] *Mathieu-Mohin and Clerfayt v Belgium* [1987] 10 EHRR 1.

[62] *Mathieu-Mohin and Clerfayt* (n 61) [51].

[63] *R (Pearson) v Secretary of State for the Home Department* [2001] EWHC Admin 239.

[64] *Pearson* (n 63) [41].

[65] *Hirst* (n 58) [77]–[82].

[66] *Hirst* (n 58) [79]–[80]. The only consideration given by Parliament was that a parliamentary committee in 1967 recommended retaining the ban.

[67] *Hirst* (n 58) [83]–[84].

not the courts. The use of a DOI was justified by the court on the grounds that legislative deliberation was needed, not to decide whether to remove the ban, but to decide whether, and what type of, restrictions should remain on prisoners' voting rights.[68]

7.D.2. Political resistance and deliberative failure

In the five years after the Strasbourg court in *Hirst* called for legislative consideration of the prisoner voting ban, no remedial measures were put to Parliament, not even a draft or a White Paper stating intended policy. The government's initial response to the decision was to announce a public consultation, with both major political parties opposed to removing the ban.[69]

We know from the GRA example that a public consultation can be a way of allowing views from civil society to enter into the legislative process. If conducted in good faith, a consultation can support positive deliberative outcomes, particularly where legislative change to protect rights is publicly controversial. But there were several problems with the consultation on prisoners' voting rights. First, the consultation from the beginning ruled out one possible option—the full enfranchisement for prisoners—yet invited submissions to be made on retaining the blanket ban, even though this was not a permissible response to *Hirst*. Second, the consultation exercise was divided into two stages, with no good reasons given as to why two consultations (significantly extending the timetable) were necessary,[70] particularly when even the second stage did not provide draft legislation for comment. Third, the government delayed on every stage of the consultation timetable. Initial delays were what prompted the DOI in *Smith v Scott* to prevent the 2007 Scottish election being conducted with the ban in force. Yet delays continued, and by late 2009, when the government closed the second consultation, it admitted that change was unlikely to occur in time for the 2010 general election.[71] Fourth, the government did not publish the submissions to either consultation, despite requests from the JCHR,[72] and did not even make a response to the second stage of the consultation. This led the JCHR to conclude in 2010 that the government had displayed a lack of commitment and a 'disappointing disre-

[68] See 4.C.2.

[69] The Shadow Attorney-General, for instance, stated after *Hirst* that giving convicted criminals the right to vote was 'ludicrous' and 'would bring the law into disrepute and many people will see it as making a mockery of justice': The Guardian, 6 October 2005 <http://www.guardian.co.uk/society/2005/oct/06/prisonsandprobation.uk>. The Lord Chancellor sought to clarify that the decision would not lead to the enfranchisement of all prisoners and was instead a decision asking the UK to look more carefully at its laws: BBC News, 6 October 2005 <http://news.bbc.co.uk/1/hi/uk/4315348.stm>.

[70] The Minister avoided the JCHR's question on this, stating only that the issue was 'complex': see JCHR, *Sixteenth Report 2006–07: Monitoring the Government's Response to Court Judgments Finding Breaches of Human Rights* HL Paper 128, HC 728 (18 June 2007), Appendix 12–13.

[71] Evidence of the Human Rights Minister to the JCHR, 2 December 2009 <http://www.publications.parliament.uk/pa/jt200910/jtselect/jtrights/uc112-i/uc11202.htm>.

[72] Letter from the Chair of the JCHR to Jack Straw 21 July 2009, JCHR, *Fifteenth Report of Session 2009–10 Enhancing Parliament's Role in Relation to Human Rights Judgments* HL Paper 85, HC 455 (9 March 2010) Evidence 23.

gard' for the UK's human rights obligations.[73] Others referred to the consultation more candidly as a 'charade', 'a flawed exercise', and 'a delay tactic'.[74]

When queried on the exceptional delays in responding in this case, government Ministers referred to the need to proceed carefully and slowly because the two major parties were in consensus over the blanket ban,[75] and hence the government needed 'to take Parliament and the public with [it]'.[76] The message, in effect, was that legislation to introduce voting rights for prisoners was expected to be deeply unpopular within Parliament and in the media. The government's reluctance to be the responsible party for legislative changes can be understood in light of this.[77] Ultimately, the government was able to pass this political 'hot potato' on to its successors[78] and avoid having to deal with the political consequences of introducing remedial legislation.

As a result of this strategy, there was no serious legislative deliberation in the Houses of Parliament on remedial action, despite the range of options available, the need for some principled justification of continued restrictions on a central democratic right, and the fact that the UK was under an international obligation to remove the blanket ban. The JCHR continued to pressure the government to introduce a remedial order, or introduce changes through amendments to appropriate Bills.[79] But, according to the Committee's legal adviser, even members of the Committee were highly reluctant to pursue the issue in the House of Commons.[80] Even if remedial measures could be expected to be unpopular, the failure to introduce anything was a lost opportunity to provoke reflection on the instant negative reaction to a highly unpopular group—prisoners—having the right to vote, and publicly interrogate the aims and effects of the ban. One peer, criticizing the government's failure to introduce measures, captured it thus:

> [Removing the ban on prisoner voting] is a serious issue. Your Lordships may not find it attractive at first glance because it deals with prisoners, but were we able to have a full-scale

[73] JCHR (n 72) [108], [119].

[74] Liberty, Submission to the JCHR (n 73) Evidence 47. Lord Ramsbotham's speech to Parliament on 7 April 2010 presents a damning overview of the consultation process, in terms of the questions proposed, breaches of the government's own procedural rules, and comparisons to other consultations: Hansard HL vol 718 cols 1642–5 (7 April 2010).

[75] JCHR, *Sixteenth Report 2006–07* (n 70), Appendix 13 (Letter from Lord Falconer to the JCHR); Evidence of the Human Rights Minister to the JCHR, 2 December 2009, Q81–2 <http://www.publications.parliament.uk/pa/jt200910/jtselect/jtrights/uc112-i/uc11202.htm>.

[76] Evidence of the Human Rights Minister (n 75) Q84.

[77] Reference to the government's fear of the political reaction was made by Lord Ramsbotham, Hansard HL vol 718 col 1643 (7 April 2010); Lord Tyler, col 1646.

[78] For discussion of the response of the successor Coalition government, see Chapter 9.

[79] A backbencher amendment was proposed in March 2010, in the Constitutional Reform and Governance Bill, to draw attention to the fact that the matter should have been included in the Bill. It was withdrawn because of lack of time to develop the practical details of voting rights for prisoners, because the legislation was under a very tight timetable at the very end of the Parliamentary term. See Hansard HL vol 718 cols 1642–8 (7 April 2010).

[80] Interview with Murray Hunt, Oxford 17 March 2010. This sense that MPs did not want to raise the issue was confirmed by Baroness Vivien Stern, Interview, London 21 June 2010.

debate, I feel confident that we could convince your Lordships that this is something that needs to be done urgently for reasons quite separate from the need to abide by the law as established by the European courts. We do not have that opportunity.[81]

We can query whether, were it not for that fact that this case involved a binding ECtHR determination, this might have been one occasion where the government would simply state its disagreement with the DOI to Parliament. Even such a statement, for instance, subject to a parliamentary motion, would allow for closer examination of whether the issue here was principled disagreement over the scope of the right to vote, or simply hostility towards the beneficiaries of the judgment irrespective of the principled question of tailored restrictions on the right to vote. As it turned out, the matter was eventually subject to debate in the House of Commons after the study period, in February 2011, though only by way of a backbench motion supporting the ban and simultaneously criticizing the ECtHR. (This debate is considered along with other post-study developments in Chapter 9.)

It is worth considering whether, in this type of situation of popular hostility towards rights claimants, political actors may prefer that changes to the law did not emanate from them, but came from the courts. If the ban had somehow been removed by the court, rather than having to initiate the remedy of its own accord, the government could have introduced measures to Parliament reinstating partial restrictions on prisoner voting, and not face the same public hostility as if it were removing the ban. Indeed, it would not need to expend the same political capital as it would to garner the necessary support for removing the ban, if its proposed legislation instead reinstated a partial ban, a measure that could be expected to have wide parliamentary support. This is effectively what happened in the Canadian case of *Sauve v Canada (No 1)*.[82] There, the court struck out the same ban on prisoner voting as the UK because it was arbitrary and disproportionate, with no good reasons being advanced for its existence. The Federal Parliament then came back, within merely a year, to instate a new partial ban on prisoner voting, for prisoners serving sentences of two years or more.[83]

Had the courts in the UK made an intervention to change the law, the legislature could still have responded through new legislation and thereby made its own choice between different levels of restrictions on prisoners' voting rights. If, like Canadian courts, UK courts had the power to order delayed invalidity of the ban, this would have forced some responsive action, say, within 1 to 2 years. The legislative deliberation that the courts claimed was necessary to choose between different human rights-compatible outcomes would therefore actually have happened, as opposed to the years of delays and avoidance of the issue.

As I have noted at several points so far, evaluations of institutional capacity should not be abstracted from realistic evaluations of what different institutions are

[81] Lord Elton, Hansard HL vol 718 col 1646 (7 April 2010).

[82] *Sauve v Canada (No 1)* [1993] 2 SCR 438.

[83] This new restriction was then held to be invalid by the court in *Sauve v Canada (No 2)* [2002] 3 SCR 519.

willing and able to do. Even if we accept that certain remedial choices are ideally better made through full, legislative deliberation rather than court decree, in some instances, stronger judicial action may be needed to provoke that deliberation. The prisoner voting example in the UK suggests that this could be the case where public opinion is deeply hostile to the beneficiaries of legislative reform, and hence there are strong incentives for legislators to avoid remedial action if possible.

However, courts too may be unwilling to intervene in these types of circumstances. We saw in Chapters 4 and 5 that the UK courts were invited in the cases of *Smith v Scott* and *Chester* to use their power under s 3 HRA to remedy the incompatibility, or use the formulation of the DOI to indicate their view on the appropriate balance to be struck. In fact, the Court of Appeal in *Chester* refused to even take a strong stance on the ongoing delay, or add to the public record its own reasoning—as a national appellate court—as to why the state of the law was unacceptable. Rather, the leading judgment was carefully agnostic about the principled reasons underpinning the grant of a partial or complete right to prisoners to vote, citing the acute controversy surrounding the issue. Laws LJ gave brief mention to the arguments on each side, and concluded by saying that it was the law, according to *Hirst*, that the blanket ban was impermissible.[84]

The UK courts have, from the start, been decidedly reluctant to engage in the type of careful principled account of the right to vote that could contribute reasons to democratic deliberation, indicating either that UK courts are themselves unconvinced that the blanket ban is an infringement of the right to vote, or, more likely, courts are not immune from public outrage and preferred to keep a distance from such a controversial human rights issue. The deliberative failure in relation to prisoner voting is a sobering reminder that even if we may think a stronger judicial intervention—either in terms of clear and convincing reasons, or in terms of a stronger remedy—would be desirable, it may not be forthcoming from judges.

7.E. Conclusion

Open remedies have the potential to encourage legislative deliberation by inviting the legislature to participate in decision-making on how to respond to findings of human rights violations. The *Bellinger* example is one in which we see the political branches of government embrace this task and advance the case for change as a matter of ethical imperative. It demonstrates that the UK Parliament was capable of a form of human rights review that was distinct from simply 'court-proofing' legislation, in circumstances where legislative review was well supported by the government. It also illustrates how a broader approach to human rights than legal compliance is valuable because crafting remedial action may itself give rise to new human rights and other policy issues that merit a reflective legislative process.

[84] *Chester v Secretary of State* [2010] EWCA Civ 1439 [32]–[35] (Laws LJ).

In Chapter 3, when establishing the various dimensions along which this book would look at the performance of the legislature, I argued that the standards by which we assess deliberation in real-world representative assemblies ought to be realistic. In particular, they needed to be appropriate to the review (rather than law-*making*) function of the legislature in a parliamentary system. Within the parameters of a Cabinet-dominated, partisan legislature, the GRA debates were an example of good deliberation. Relative to the general expectations of political science accounts of the legislature (in Chapter 2), and fears of judicialization of the legislative process (in Chapter 3), this was a reflective and inclusive attempt to address a human rights problem. This example also serves as a striking contrast to the example considered in the following chapter, that is, the response to the *Belmarsh Prisoners* DOI.

Yet, there remain difficulties with employing the legislature to craft a human rights remedy in the first instance. From the perspective of remedial effectiveness for successful litigants, even when the political branches agree that the law violates human rights and needs to be corrected, legislators may overlook retrospective relief for past victims. There are also difficulties with the sheer permissiveness of the DOI device, which places no serious discipline on the executive or the legislature. This creates space for forms of resistance to judicial decisions that are not deliberative, namely, prevarication and a failure of public justification for the state of the law.

This suggests that there is a compromise to be struck in relation to open remedies when it comes to legislation. While the legislative process can support comprehensive and multifaceted reform of the law in response to identified human rights violations, it is difficult for this process to simultaneously fulfil the retrospective, corrective function of remedies. In some cases, this choice of an open remedy will be easier to make, for instance, where the wrong that the plaintiffs suffer is suffered by a broader group and can be corrected for all by prospective action. In cases where future legislative action cannot correct the wrong suffered by the plaintiff, then the trade-off is more acute.

The trade-off is less clear in relation to the deliberation-enhancing potential of open remedies. Here, the non-coercive nature of DOIs opens up the potential for delay even in the event of no disagreement (unnecessarily delaying relief for victims), and delay as a form of passive resistance or avoidance, when there is contestation. At a *practical* level, would a more coercive approach—for instance, the type of legislative remand mechanisms employed in the US, Canada, and South Africa, which give the legislature a set time period in which to act before the courts invalidate legislation—undermine legislative ownership of the human rights solution? It is not immediately evident that it would, for even coercive legislative remand allows the legislature to be the first mover and to devise its chosen remedial measures. The difference is only that there is an impetus to act in a timely fashion.

At a *symbolic* level, there appears at first to be a clear difference because these other mechanisms rely on the court possessing the power to invalidate legislation. The normative position underpinning the non-binding nature of DOIs was that any action to be taken would be the conscious choice of the political branches of government to agree with the courts and not the result of a judicial decision alone.

To give them this choice was to openly recognize that human rights decisions were not solely the preserve of judges, and the ultimate decision-maker was the legislature itself. Yet, a system, like the Canadian one, in which the legislature is given a set time to respond, and can within that time choose to expressly disagree with the judicial decision and formally reaffirm the impugned legislation, does not depart from this normative position. It simply places a different procedural burden on the political branches of government to justify their actions.

8

Belmarsh Prisoners and Dialogue over Control Orders

8.A. Introduction

Of all the DOIs issued from 2000 to 2010, the DOI in *A and Others v Secretary of State for the Home Department* ('*Belmarsh Prisoners*')[1] had, by far, the highest public profile. This declaration impugned a law passed by the government soon after its own human rights legislation, a law that the government had stated to be compatible with the HRA and which was at the centre of the government's anti-terrorist strategy. By contrast to almost every other DOI, *Belmarsh Prisoners* received significant attention, and was debated in both Houses, before the reply legislation was introduced into Parliament.[2]

This chapter begins by examining the parliamentary reaction to *Belmarsh Prisoners* and how this judicial statement was received by the legislature. Section 8.C then considers what type of deliberation occurred on the reply legislation, which introduced control orders to the UK, in the context of counter-terrorism and after such a high profile judicial intervention. Section 8.D turns to the ongoing dialogue over the control orders regime from 2005 to 2010, across the courts, executive, and Parliament.

We see in this episode a strong contrast between the initial portrayal of the *Belmarsh Prisoners* DOI by the leaders of the executive and the reaction of parliamentarians to it. The ensuing deliberation on the reply legislation was also very different from the examples in Chapter 7: this time, the Commons debate in particular was heavily concerned with judicial elaborations of human rights standards and the prospect of future challenges in the courts. Finally, the institutional interaction over the control orders regime provides a real-world illustration of how judicial and legislative review can be complementary to each other, but also how judicial review has the potential to suppress, not only provoke, legislative review on human rights grounds.

[1] [2004] UKHL 56.

[2] Hansard HC vol 428 cols 1911–18 (20 December 2004); vol 430 cols 305–23 (26 January 2005); vol 430 cols 1408–62 (8 February 2005); Hansard HL vol 667 cols 1586–96 (20 December 2004).

8.B. The Reaction to the *Belmarsh Prisoners* Decision

8.B.1. The *Belmarsh Prisoners* case

In 2001, the UK government responded to the terrorist attacks in the United States by making an executive order derogating from Article 5 ECHR (the right to life, liberty, and security) on the grounds of a 'public emergency threatening the life of the nation'.[3] It was thereby able to institute a system of detention without trial for foreign terrorist suspects under the Anti-Terrorism, Crime and Security Act 2001 (ATCSA). This legislation was passed quickly, with cross-party support and muted debate.[4]

In the *Belmarsh Prisoners* case, the House of Lords quashed the executive order purporting to derogate from the ECHR, finding that the measures were not strictly required by the exigencies of the situation and therefore the derogation was not lawful according to the criteria contained in Article 15(1). Without a valid derogation in place, the system of detention without trial clearly violated Article 5. Additionally, the regime violated the non-discrimination guarantee in Article 14 because it only applied to foreign terrorist suspects. Accordingly, the ATCSA was declared incompatible with Convention rights.

Unlike the decisions in *Bellinger*, *Anderson*, or *Smith v Scott* (but in common with the decisions in *Roth*, *Morris*, and *Gabaj*), the House of Lords was not driven to its decision in *Belmarsh Prisoners* by virtue of a ruling by the ECtHR against the UK.[5] In fact, this decision was heralded as a bold and important intervention by judges in holding up to scrutiny the reasons for powers of indefinite detention without trial,[6] and particularly so given traditional judicial deference in the field of national security and developments in the counter-terrorism field internationally since 2001.

8.B.2. The immediate reaction

In Chapter 6 we observed that DOIs were predominantly uncontroversial up until 2004. But the HRA itself was subject to public controversy in this period. In fact, in 2003, the then Home Secretary was vocally hostile towards a series of judicial decisions under the HRA and the resulting frustration, as he claimed, of government

[3] Article 15 ECHR.

[4] For discussion of the passage of the Act, see A Tomkins, A Jones, and V Bettinson, 'Legislating against Terror: The Anti-Terrorism, Crime and Security Act 2001' [2002] PL 205; D Nicol, 'The Human Rights Act and the Politicians' (2004) 24 Legal Studies 451, 462.

[5] In fact, the Court of Appeal had unanimously upheld the regime the previous year: [2002] EWCA Civ 1502.

[6] A Kavanagh, 'Judging the Judges under the Human Rights Act: Deference, Disillusionment and the "War on Terror"' [2009] PL 287, 288–9. See also A Tomkins, 'Readings of *A v Secretary of State for the Home Department*' [2005] PL 259; C Gearty, 'Human Rights in an Age of Counter-Terrorism: Injurious, Irrelevant or Indispensable?' (2005) 58 Current Legal Problems 25, 37. Cf: D Dyzenhaus, 'Deference, Security and Human Rights' in L Lazarus and B Goold (eds), *Security and Human Rights* (Hart, Oxford 2007).

policies.[7] Elements within the British media also took a strong editorial line against the Act.[8]

Hence, it is not entirely surprising that the government's initial reaction to the *Belmarsh* DOI was defiant. Immediately after the judgment was handed down, the Home Secretary delivered a written statement to Parliament forcefully asserting the principle of parliamentary sovereignty, and stating that the government would not revoke any certifications for detention under the impugned ATCSA.[9] He further stated that the government would ask Parliament to renew the relevant powers the following year. The only undertaking he made was to consider 'whether it was possible to address the judicial concerns' without any suggestion of immediate amendment or repeal of the ATCSA powers.[10]

The Home Secretary did not openly dispute the correctness of the House of Lords decision, but did argue that the existing legislation was 'based on a foundation of principle' which it was his duty to defend.[11] He also sought to emphasize to Parliament the complexity and controversy surrounding the decision, stressing that the judgment took eleven weeks to decide and that 'it would be a surprise if there were not deep controversy about the ethical, philosophical and moral issues involved'.[12] Likewise, in the House of Lords, Baroness Scotland (Minister of State) stated that the issue at stake was not only the compatibility of the law with the ECHR but the more fundamental question of how to 'balance the rights of the individuals against those of society'. She drew attention to the fact that the House of Lords had overturned the unanimous decision of the Court of Appeal upholding the legislation '[not] to find fault with the noble and learned Lords who made up the Judicial Committee, but simply to illustrate the complexity and the difficulties involved in the case'.[13] Hence, it appeared possible that, for the first time, the government would employ its power to disagree with a DOI, since leading Ministers were stressing to Parliament, and the public, reasons why one might have doubts about the conclusion reached by the House of Lords.

This early government defiance generated a broad parliamentary pressure, from members of all parties, for amendment or repeal of the laws declared incompatible.

[7] Home Secretary David Blunkett told the media that he was 'fed up with having to deal with a situation where Parliament debates issues and the judges overturn them'. When questioned about the right of judges to review his decisions, Blunkett stated 'I also have the right to say Parliament did debate this, we were aware of the circumstances, we did mean what we said and, on behalf of the British people, we are going to implement it': quoted in The Times 'Blunkett v the Bench: The Battle has Begun' 4 March 2003 <http://business.timesonline.co.uk/tol/business/law/article1115351.ece>.

[8] In response to the public unpopularity of the Act, the Department of Constitutional Affairs undertook a review to verify whether human rights protections were indeed having an adverse effect on government departments. It concluded that the HRA's provisions did not compromise the executive's ability to govern effectively, but that misinformation about human rights was rife, and more public education was required: DCA, *Review of the Implementation of the Human Rights Act* (July 2006).

[9] Hansard HC vol 428 col 151WS (16 December 2004).

[10] n 9.

[11] Hansard HC vol 428 col 1914 (20 December 2004).

[12] Hansard HC vol 428 col 1913. A similar point was made by Baroness Scotland in the House of Lords, Hansard HL vol 667 col 1590 (20 December 2004).

[13] Hansard HL vol 667 col 1588 (20 December 2004).

The court's decision was treated as an authoritative finding and not mere opinion or advice. The language adopted by MPs indicates the perceived force of the ruling. For instance, the matter was first brought to debate in the House of Commons with an Urgent Question on the legislative consequences of the judicial ruling 'that detention without trial under the anti-terrorism laws is unlawful'.[14] In fact, the affected provisions were described as 'unlawful' or 'illegal' by numerous parliamentarians[15] and there were also references to the law being 'overturned'[16] or 'thrown out'[17] by judges. The following response to the Home Secretary's stance illustrates the tenor of the debate:

> The Law Lords did not make what [the Home Secretary] described as an ethical, moral or philosophical judgment but a legal judgment . . . a statement of law regarding the relationship between human rights legislation and terrorism legislation. Since the judgment he has given the impression . . . of being rather contemptuous of it.[18]

MPs could not have been unaware of the fact that the relevant powers continued to have full legal status despite the *Belmarsh Prisoners* decision. The Home Secretary was careful to avoid the language of illegality and repeatedly drew attention to the power of Parliament to make its own legislative decisions, and in fact its obligation to do so.[19] However, the nuances of weak-form review under the HRA—that the judiciary may find primary legislation incompatible with human rights but not invalid—did not appear to have much significance for the majority of participants in the Commons debate. The approach taken by many MPs was that it was unacceptable or impossible to retain the existing law as a result of the judicial decision,[20] rather than that it was a valid choice to disagree with the highest court on the acceptability of the regime.

[14] Heath, Hansard HC vol 428 col 1911 (20 December 2004).

[15] Hogg, Hansard HC vol 430 col 317 (26 January 2005); Dismore, Hansard HC vol 431 col 405 (23 February 2005); Griffiths, Hansard HC vol 431 col 672 (28 February 2005).

[16] Hughes, Hansard HC vol 431 col 348 (23 February 2005).

[17] Johnson, Hansard HC vol 431 col 386 (23 February 2005).

[18] Baldry, Hansard HC vol 428 col 1917 (20 December 2004).

[19] Hansard HC vol 428 col 1918 (20 December 2004). The Home Secretary made a Statement to both Houses of Parliament that 'as the Human Rights Act makes clear, Parliament remains sovereign and it is ultimately for Parliament to decide whether and what changes should be made to the law': Hansard HC vol 428 col 1911 (20 December 2004); Hansard HL vol 667 col 1586 (20 December 2004). See also Baroness Scotland, vol 667 col 1592 (20 December 2004). The government similarly emphasized the non-binding status of the DOI in *Roth*, see text accompanying ch 6 n 70.

[20] For example, the ATCSA was referred to as 'law we would have to renew in March, but which we cannot, because of the Law Lords' judgment': Denham Hansard HC vol 431 col 778 (28 February 2005). See also Heath, Hansard HC vol 428 col 1911 (20 December 2004). Oaten drew attention to the cross-party consensus that the existing legislation was unacceptable, and added 'I think the Government have been forced to reach that agreement but in any event, they now agree with us that the current measures are not acceptable': Hansard HC vol 431 col 367 (23 February 2005). There were only two dissenters from this widespread parliamentary endorsement of the judicial declaration. One Conservative MP objected to 'the assumption that legislation should be conducted within the framework of the ECHR and the 1998 Act', and proposed that new legislation be enacted with a 'notwithstanding the Human Rights Act 1998' preamble that would prevent a finding of incompatibility: Cash, Hansard HC vol 431 col 346 (23 February 2005). Only one MP suggested disregarding the judicial decision: Trimble, ibid col 417; see also Hansard HC vol 428 col 1914 (20 December 2004).

In the upper House there appeared to be a better understanding of the nuanced position of the law: that the court had quashed the derogation from the ECHR as unlawful, but the operative provisions in primary legislation continued to have full effect. Instead, in arguing for the law to be repealed, peers relied on the government's assurances during and after the passage of the HRA that DOIs would meet with swift legislative action,[21] as well as the fact that this ruling could be upheld by the ECtHR as a violation of international law.[22]

The *Belmarsh Prisoners* decision also provides a clear example of members of *all* major parties employing the judicial declaration to put pressure on government. One early account of politicians' appreciation of the HRA, up to 2002, argued that the official Opposition (the Conservative Party) had failed to use human rights to pressure the government.[23] However, after *Belmarsh Prisoners,* a number of Conservative politicians argued that the declaration compelled repeal of the existing legislation and the introduction of a new legal framework for dealing with terrorist suspects.

The DOI was also used as a vehicle to restate *existing* calls for legislative change within the legislature, particularly from Labour backbenchers, Liberal Democrats, and parliamentary committees. In particular, the declaration was used to propel the recommendations of parliamentary committees into prominence. Half the speeches in both the House of Commons and House of Lords debates on the DOI referred to the views of either the JCHR or the specially formed Newton Committee (or both), and most of these specifically called for these Committees' recommendations to be considered, now that the DOI had confirmed the need for action. As one JCHR member made clear:

> The judgment not only endorses the findings of the very distinguished [Newton Committee] but also the findings of the JCHR, which represents both Houses and is cross-party . . . it is very urgent and important that the Government give careful consideration to the judgment because the institutions of Parliament have spoken, and spoken in line with what the judges have said.[24]

Overall, the parliamentary records indicate that this ruling from the courts captured the attention of parliamentarians, was taken seriously, and was used to challenge the government. The DOI was clearly a potent speech-act even though the judicial finding was controversial, was not clearly supported by a ECtHR decision, and went to the very core of a prominent government policy. Over a matter of weeks, the government revised its initial decision to renew the ATCSA and decided instead to replace the system with a new, HRA-compatible, scheme to deal with terrorist suspects.

[21] Lord Kingsland, Hansard HL vol 667 cols 1586–7 (20 December 2004); Lord Thomas, col 1588.

[22] Lord Tebbitt, Hansard HL vol 667 col 1549 (20 December 2004); Lord Kilcooney, col 1593.

[23] Nicol (n 4) 473–4.

[24] Lord Judd, Hansard HL vol 667 col 1595 (20 December 2004).

8.C. The Reply Legislation and Legislative Deliberation

8.C.1. The reply legislation: The Prevention of Terrorism Act 2005

In January 2005, the government announced that it would not renew the ATCSA regime. While continuing to assert that the powers were justified, the Home Secretary stated that he accepted the Law Lords' finding of incompatibility. However, the government's chosen response was more than simple repeal of the impugned scheme. Its proposed response was to institute an even wider set of counter-terrorism powers: replacing the ATCSA powers of detention with a system of control orders, to apply to existing detainees, and future terrorist suspects.

The new scheme was drafted with close attention to the letter of the ECHR. It provided for two categories of control orders, each involving a different procedure and degree of judicial involvement. 'Non-derogating' control orders placed restrictions on the liberty of an individual that, it was argued, would not constitute a *deprivation* of liberty and hence would not fall within the ambit of Article 5 ECHR. 'Derogating' control orders entailed greater limitations, including indefinite house arrest, which would violate Article 5 and therefore would only be issued if and when the government formally derogated from Article 5. The main argument supporting the scheme was that it allowed restrictions on terrorist suspects to be tailored to the threat posed by an individual, hence the regime was a proportionate response to terrorism; and it applied equally to foreigners and British citizens, hence it was non-discriminatory. The Home Secretary made clear the government's concern to comply with the HRA:

> The third motivating principle [of the Bill] is the need to meet the Law Lords' judgment... Their criticism of the regime was that it was disproportionate in character and discriminatory, and we should take that criticism incredibly seriously. The measures that I'm putting to the House in the Bill would address that question directly.[25]

The second reading speech given by the Minister in the House of Lords dealt in detail with how the government had constructed the scheme to take account of human rights law, particularly in making its distinction between derogating and non-derogating orders.[26] The responsible Minister stressed that the public would have liked the government to go further with its counter-terrorism powers, but that the HRA provided a template for a proportionate response to which the government was committed.[27]

The Prevention of Terrorism Act (PTA) is the UK's most prominent example of the executive responding to an adverse court decision by constructing a new legislative vehicle to realize its policy objective. It demonstrates dialogue-as-specialization in action: the impugned legislation was replaced with a new general scheme actively

[25] Hansard HC vol 431 col 345 (23 February 2005). See also Blears, Hansard HC vol 430 col 1420 (8 February 2005).

[26] Lord Falconer, Hansard HL vol 670 cols 122–3 (1 March 2005).

[27] Hansard HL vol 670 col 123 (1 March 2005).

argued to be a proportionate limitation on fundamental rights. However, the control orders regime raised a new, and expanded, range of human rights concerns.[28] While non-derogating control orders in particular may have been less liberty depriving than detention, the legislation authorized an incredibly wide range of restrictions on the liberty, freedom of association, privacy, and family life of controlees.[29] Being preventative, the making of an order was not based on the commission of any offence, but only on reasonable grounds for suspicion that a person may be involved in terrorism-related activity. Breach of any conditions imposed would constitute a serious criminal offence and could lead to imprisonment for up to five years. The regime could also be applied across the entire population. Additionally, the original Bill introduced into Parliament provided that all orders would be issued by the Home Secretary, with judicial review on points of law only. This presented serious concerns on due process and separation of powers grounds.

The ministerial statement of compatibility, required by s 19 HRA, and the accompanying explanatory notes, avoided these broad issues and instead focused carefully on the letter of the ECHR, particularly the rules surrounding derogation from Convention rights. Not only was the regime designed and justified with a clear view to compliance with human rights law, it was compliance with the *very minimum* standards of the Convention. The government placed heavy reliance on the rules surrounding derogation from Convention rights in making its case, and Ministers characterized a lawful derogation as rendering the legislation compatible with human rights.[30] Strictly speaking, it was correct that with a valid derogation in place, the law providing for derogating control orders would not be contrary to the provisions of the ECHR, but this would be because the relevant rights guarantees would be suspended.[31] To characterize derogation from rights as a form of human rights compatibility plays into the concerns of critics who argue that the formal legal protection of human rights distorts political debate, turning it away from substantive questions of whether new measures are legitimate, to whether they are technically legal.

[28] L Zedner, 'Securing Liberty in a Time of Terror' (2005) 32(4) Journal of Law and Society 507. Prior to any legal challenge, concerns were stated by the European Commissioner for Human Rights, 8 June 2005 Comm DH (2005) 6 with respect to Articles 5 and 6 of the ECHR.

[29] The PTA provided that the obligations imposed on the controlee may be any obligations that the Secretary of State considered necessary for the purpose of preventing or restricting the controlee's involvement in terrorism-related activity (s 1(3)) and included a *non-exhaustive* list of restrictions (s 1(4)). These included prohibitions and restrictions on movement, but also requirements to provide information to the government and to provide officials access to search one's residence at any time. The types of restrictions that were imposed in control orders from 2005 to 2010 go well beyond this list to include prohibitions on all forms of communication, prohibitions on contact with any persons other than those who were pre-approved, and even 'internal exile', that is, requiring the controlee to relocate to a different part of the country, away from all family and friends.

[30] E.g. Home Secretary, Hansard HC vol 430 col 1420 (26 January 2005).

[31] Tom Hickman distinguishes between the limitation model, where derogation provisions are understood as 'part of the network of limitations and qualifications on rights guaranteed in human rights instruments' and the 'derogation model' where a derogation releases the state from its human rights obligations, including its obligation to justify its conduct, and 'holds rights in abeyance'. He argues that the second model is the more persuasive understanding of derogation provisions: TR Hickman, 'Between Human Rights and the Rule of Law: Indefinite Detention and the Derogation Model of Constitutionalism' (2005) 68 Modern Law Review 655, 658–9.

At the same time, the legislation provided the vehicle for the government to impose wide-ranging restrictions on controlees under the cover of *non-derogating* orders. When aggregated, these restrictions could be characterized as equivalent to a deprivation of liberty.[32] However, any number and selection of restrictions other than house arrest could be imposed by the Home Secretary without making a formal derogation to Parliament.

Also, the new legislation did not address concerns over the right to a fair trial that arose in the context of the ATCSA, and procedures from the ATCSA relating to secret evidence were replicated under the PTA. When questioned on this, the government's response was that the Court of Appeal had affirmed these procedures and hence they were within the bounds of human rights requirements.[33] As such, the government saw no reason to respond to concerns that had been voiced about these procedures by parliamentary committees, and Special Advocates employed within the existing system for secret evidence.

The government's claim that its proposed legislative solution respected human rights was therefore open to question. How, then, was this reply legislation received in Parliament?

8.C.2. Legislative deliberation on the Prevention of Terrorism Bill

There were two notable features about the parliamentary debates on the Prevention of Terrorism Bill.[34] The first was that the debate was heavily concerned with legal arguments and judicial elaborations of what human rights require. This legislative episode provides an opportunity to explore the questions raised in Chapter 3.C as to whether, and why, legislative consideration of human rights may tend towards a minimalist 'compliance-oriented' form of review. The second feature was that the government exercised its powers to control the legislative process in the House of Commons in a way that prevented that House from engaging in meaningful review of the legislation. The Bill, though complex and controversial, was passed through all stages of both houses of Parliament in less than three weeks.

(a) The nature of legislative rights review

Chapter 3 raised the question of whether it was plausible that, even under a system of weak-form judicial review where courts cannot strike down legislation, the legislature will seek to 'court-proof' new laws and legislative debate will become dominated by legal argumentation.

[32] For the detailed argument on how not only house arrest, but an aggregation of restrictions of liberty, can amount to a deprivation of liberty, requiring due process protections to be followed, see H Fenwick and G Phillipson, 'Covert Derogations and Judicial Deference: Redefining Liberty and Due Process Rights in Counterterrorism Law and Beyond' (2011) 56 McGill Law Journal 863.

[33] Lord Falconer, Hansard HL vol 670 cols 551–3 (7 March 2005).

[34] For ease of reference, in this section '*Second Reading*' refers to the House of Commons Second Reading Debate: Hansard HC vol 431 cols 333–434 (23 February 2005) and '*Committee*' refers to Committee of the Whole House and Third Reading debates, vol 431 cols 644–788 (28 February 2005).

In the House of Commons debates on the Prevention of Terrorism Bill, MPs did employ a range of legal arguments in debate. In contrast to the debates considered in Chapter 7, MPs paid close attention to human rights compatibility of the Bill in the event of a future court challenge. For example, in Committee proceedings, MPs used the illegality of proposed measures under human rights law to put pressure on the government to accept amendments, and made forceful use of the JCHR's legal conclusions on the Bill.[35] There were also queries on the legal advice that the government had received[36] and whether the government had sought judicial opinions on the proposals.[37] The categories and exceptions in the relevant Convention rights and jurisprudence assumed critical importance throughout the Committee proceedings,[38] and the case law as well as individual judicial opinions in *Belmarsh Prisoners* were employed in argument.[39]

Does the absorption of legal argumentation here support the claims of judicial review sceptics that with judicial review comes the normative dominance of judicial viewpoints on what human rights require, impoverishing rather than enhancing political debate on the merits of a new law?[40] A careful look at the arguments made by MPs, and the underlying context of review, indicates a more subtle dynamic around the use of legal argument than such claims suggest.

First, it is important to recognize that a minimalist, compliance-oriented approach to human rights was initiated by the nature of the executive's proposed response and its justification of the Bill. By focusing on the technical interpretation of derogation and limitation provisions, the executive set the stage for a parliamentary debate that concentrated on the interpretation of these provisions. The argument was that (1) non-derogating control orders *restricted* liberty, but did not *deprive* the affected person of liberty, and (2) while the types of restrictions being introduced would affect a number of human rights of the controlee, these would be justified, proportionate limitations on rights in the pursuit of national security. This was a complex framework within which to assure human rights compliance, and hence it is understandable that the legislative deliberation was focused on interrogating the legal foundations of this framework. For instance,

[35] Win Griffiths, who led the main group of amendments, claimed that the existing law as well as the proposed laws violated the ECHR and that the proposals ought to be amended because the relevant Ministers had stated that they were keen to uphold the ECHR. These legal conclusions on the human rights compatibility of the proposed measures were drawn from the JCHR, and were said to render the proposed powers 'illegal': *Committee* cols 674–5. Another notable example was Richard Shepherd's speech (a Conservative MP and member of the JCHR) which was dedicated to the compatibility of the Bill with the requirements laid out in ECtHR jurisprudence, arguing that the Bill would again 'founder' on the basis of the HRA: *Second Reading* cols 390–2.

[36] Oaten, *Second Reading* col 372 also asking for this legal advice to be published.

[37] Hughes, *Second Reading* col 348: 'It would be far better for the authority of Government, of any party, for Ministers to have their proposal endorsed by the judiciary, rather than . . . have their decision overturned by the courts'. See also Cormack, *Second Reading* col 346, as well as debate over Lord Hoffman's opinion on the role and legitimacy of executive powers in this area, *Committee* col 675.

[38] For example, for an extended debate on what constitutes a deprivation of liberty, see *Committee* cols 692–8.

[39] E.g. Hogg, *Second Reading* cols 372, 402; Cash, *Committee* col 675; Clarke, *Committee* col 699.

[40] See the discussion in Chapter 3.C.

Committee proceedings were closely focused on the so-called 'Article 5 limit' on executive power, at which point derogation would be necessary.[41]

Second, the rights at issue were rights to due process in the deprivation of liberty and the right to a fair trial. Close attention to judicial standards here can be understood not as an abdication of independent political decision-making, but an understandable degree of advertance to and respect for judicial elaboration of *particular* rights which MPs may consider to be matters of judicial expertise.[42] In fact, it would be very hard for political actors to consider the requirements of due process and fair trial rights without reference to the way in which these rights have been developed by judges. Even though MPs may display a great deal of trust in judicial protections of these particular rights,[43] parliamentarians have been far less deferential to judicial statements in relation to, say, freedom of expression.[44]

Third, and most importantly, despite making legal arguments, MPs' speeches did evince concerns beyond future compatibility before a court. Hence, MPs employed conceptions of fundamental rights both as judicially determined legal standards and as ethical principles governing political conduct. Where arguments were made specifically on the basis that this legislation would fail to comply with human rights when tested by courts in future, these arguments were almost always advanced *in tandem* with arguments that the measures violated fundamental political principles and were morally unacceptable.[45] Hence, there were two responses to the government's arguments that the Bill complied with the minimum standards of human rights law. The first was to tackle the government's arguments on its own terms, and contest the Minister's interpretation of the case law;[46]

[41] See e.g. Vera Baird's speech, Hansard HC vol 431 cols 742–6 (28 February 2005).

[42] E.g. Cook, Hansard HC vol 431 col 713 (28 February 2005).

[43] This was illustrated throughout the Committee proceedings with numerous calls for greater judicial involvement in the control orders system. A number of MPs specifically defended the courts as well qualified to balance the public interest and individual liberty. E.g. Kenneth Clarke argued that 'Judges assess risk, and what is necessary, weighing the public interest on the one hand, against the need to protect the liberty of the individual on the other. Judges will be more conscious of the overriding national interest in the fullest sense': *Committee* col 729. See also Grieve, *Committee* cols 679, 707; Mackinley, *Committee* col 692; Denham, *Committee* col 698.

[44] An example here is another law introduced in 2005: the Racial and Religious Hatred Act 2005. This Act extended racial hatred offences to include religious hatred. A number of MPs were concerned at how judges would apply these offences with insufficient regard to freedom of speech, leading to repeated government assurances that judges would be required to pay sufficient regard to freedom of expression because it was required of them by s 3 of the Human Rights Act, and an eventual amendment strengthening freedom of expression protections. See HC Hansard vol 435 cols 668–767 (21 June 2005); Standing Committee E Proceedings cols 1–112 (28–30 June 2005) and HC Hansard vol 436 cols 597–671 (11 July 2005).

[45] This could be seen even in the most legally focused speeches, which also sought to ground their arguments in fundamental principles of natural justice. For example, Richard Shepherd, after dedicating his speech to why it was unlikely that the European Court of Human Rights would find the new laws to be compatible with the ECHR, stated further that 'The House is familiar with all that, because it has watched over these practices for centuries . . . [The Bill] goes against the spirit of this country, which has a powerful belief in liberty and freedom': *Second Reading* col 392. See also Davis, *Second Reading* col 364; Johnson, *Second Reading* col 387.

[46] For example, see Hughes *Committee* cols 773, 778; Bruce *Second Reading* cols 396–400.

whereas the second was to address the broader legitimacy of the measures, regardless of whether they were technically within the ambit of the ECHR.[47] The JCHR's review of the Prevention of Terrorism Bill illustrates this dual approach, expressing the prospect of failure in event of judicial review as a secondary reason for concern, with its primary arguments based on the substantive principles captured in the various Convention rights.[48]

The use of both types of arguments—arguments that the Bill would not survive judicial review ('we cannot do this') and that the Bill would make for bad law ('we should not do this')—suggests that the prospect of judicial review did not replace political with court-centred conceptions of human rights, but rather gave parliamentarians *additional* support for rights-based arguments in some circumstances. We should not assume that political actors only conceive of human rights as either legal limits or as ethical principles, when they can employ *both* conceptions of rights in reviewing legislation. Hence, the debates over the Prevention of Terrorism Bill provide only limited evidence of compliance-oriented review, where deliberation is reduced to legal vetting alone. They give us cause to question assertions from sceptics that debates that refer to judicial elaborations of rights are necessarily the poorer for it and involve an abdication of responsibility for making difficult choices about the scope of human rights.

In fact, regardless of what approach MPs took to human rights, the greater challenge to deliberation related to the practical conditions of deliberation, and executive control over the legislative process.

(b) *Practical challenges to legislative deliberation*

I have noted that an important feature of Cabinet-dominated Westminster Parliament is that the government of the day has considerable power over the basic conditions of deliberation, including setting the agenda and timetabling.[49] The principal challenge facing independent legislative deliberation on the questions raised by the control order regime was government control over two basic conditions of legislative deliberation: time and information with which to assess legislative proposals. It was not the case that MPs and peers did not take human rights concerns seriously—there were a significant number of parliamentarians who expressed grave concerns about the legislation. Rather, the Commons in particular

[47] Several Labour backbenchers argued that the debate ought to have been concerned with practical outcomes in terms of human rights and liberties, and democratic checks on executive power, rather than being concerned with 'legalisms': Denham, *Second Reading* col 375; Allen, *Second Reading* col 392; Palmer *Committee* col 697. Robin Cook observed (*Committee* col 716): 'I would be cautious about accepting a lawyer's point of view. In my experience . . . one can usually find a lawyer to support any possible point of view.' There were also arguments for a common sense understanding of the deprivation of liberty, after extended argument over the definition of deprivation of liberty and the threshold of a violation of Article 5 based on ECHR case law: Marris, *Committee* col 716; Garnier, *Committee* cols 720–1.

[48] JCHR, *Ninth Report 2004–05: Prevention of Terrorism Bill: Preliminary Report* HL Paper 61, HC 389; JCHR, *Tenth Report 2004–05: The Prevention of Terrorism Bill* HL Paper 68, HC 334.

[49] See 2.F.

was prevented by a strong and determined executive from giving the Bill anything more than scant scrutiny. This example illustrates how elected representatives in particular can be excluded from the process of striking a new balance between rights and government policy. The government constructed its legislative response to the *Belmarsh Prisoners* decision in a way that addressed judicial concerns, and was concerned to reduce the likelihood of a further DOI, but was less interested in parliamentary contribution or even the legitimation provided by a full parliamentary debate.

The PTA was passed on a rapid legislative timetable. The Bill was published one day before its Second Reading in the House of Commons, leaving MPs briefed with short reports hastily produced by the JCHR and a major NGO, Liberty. There were forty-three rapidly prepared amendments tabled in the House of Commons, with only five hours allocated to the amendment phase. Only a handful of these amendments were actually raised and they focused on only *one* of the many human rights implications of the Bill (the fact that the first instance decision on a control order was made by the Home Secretary rather than being judicially authorized). In fact, the government's open strategy, anticipating resistance to the Bill in the House of Lords, was to fast-track the legislation through the elected chamber. The Home Secretary announced that the government would make amendments to the Bill addressing concerns about the role of the judiciary, but would only do so in the House of Lords the next day. This strategy rendered the debate on proposed amendments futile, and meant that, despite the widespread sentiment that the Bill did not reach even a basic level of acceptability, the Minister was asking Labour MPs to pass the legislation in its unamended form.[50] The Minister sought to assure concerned MPs that the legislation would receive better review in the House of Lords than the limited time in the Commons permitted.[51] This was condemned as disrespectful to the representative chamber by not only members of opposition parties, but also frustrated government backbenchers.[52] Labour MPs in particular sought to stress that the legislation would be made better if greater time was given to the House.[53] There was also hostility to the idea that MPs should be satisfied with expected scrutiny in the House of Lords *as an alternative* to Commons

[50] 'Does [the Minister] recognise that his failure to accept amendments tabled by my right hon friend . . . and others puts many Labour Members in a difficult position, because we are extremely reluctant to vote for an unamended Bill?': Salter, *Committee* cols 677–8; 'Not a single speaker on Second Reading or in Committee has made an enthusiastically endorsing speech. Yet, in spite of that and grave misgivings, which are shared on the Government benches, we are not to have the chance to properly examine and scrutinise': Cormack, *Committee* col 748. See also Cook, *Committee* col 716.

[51] *Committee* col 667.

[52] For example, Vera Baird protested the 'hideous position' Labour backbenchers were being put in—'We will no doubt be asked to vote today against judicial involvement . . . The Lords will no doubt vote for judicial involvement . . . and this time next week we will doubtless be asked to vote for that. The situation is a complete nonsense and the shortage of time makes that nonsense greater and more obvious': *Committee* col 746.

[53] Graham Allen argued that proper and early scrutiny 'leads to better law that sticks': *Second Reading* col 394; see also Smith, *Second Reading* col 384: 'In response to the failures and flaws of the 2001 Act, which was introduced in haste, I fear we are introducing further legislation in haste.'

deliberation[54]—both from those who objected to the composition of the House of Lords[55] and those who were generally favourable to the House of Lords as a site of review.[56]

The types of arguments made by those Labour backbenchers seeking to give the Bill serious attention, relying on persuasion and unspoken limits on the extent to which the government could simply push measures through the Commons undebated, illustrate the weak position that such MPs are in when the government is not supportive of legislative review. Ultimately, the government was able to rely on its majority to pass its chosen response without real review in the Commons.[57]

The second major impediment to review, which affected both Houses, was the lack of sufficient information to assess the necessity and proportionality of the measures. Parliamentary briefing material was limited and produced very quickly.[58] The justification given on Second Reading of the Bill provided no more than a general argument that the threat of terrorism from al-Qaeda was different from former threats, implying that this difference alone justified control orders.[59] In terms of both why existing powers were inadequate, and how the new powers were expected to be used, secrecy and trust were the key motifs of the government's position. There were even suggestions that those seeking further evidence to justify the measures were being irresponsible.[60]

As with the lack of time, lack of information was explicitly identified by parliamentarians themselves as preventing a proper assessment of whether the new powers were proportionate in the circumstances.[61] There were, in particular,

[54] Fisher, *Committee* col 783; Cormack, *Committee* col 687; Garnier, *Committee* col 685. Similar arguments were made earlier, on the lack of time between First and Second Reading: Marshall-Andrews, *Second Reading* col 414; Allen, *Second Reading* col 393.

[55] '[O]bstruction from an illegitimate second chamber is not, frankly, a substitute for a sustainable strategy to defend our liberties': Allen, *Second Reading* col 395.

[56] 'When we leave the Bill, we will not have scrutinised it or discussed it in the House of Commons. Yes, it will have four days in the other place. Yes, there are many learned lawyers in the other place . . . However, we are the elected House': Cormack, *Committee* col 747; Oaten, *Committee* col 722.

[57] There were a number of Labour backbenchers who voted against the legislation, but not enough to affect the passage of the Bill.

[58] Dyzenhaus (n 6) 130 identifies this as a general institutional problem in the context of emergency powers, with the government's standard approach being that there is no time to debate measures.

[59] This trend has been identified by D Feldman, 'Human Rights, Terrorism and Risk: The Roles of Politicians and Judges' [2006] PL 364, 369, who argues that the qualitative difference between the al-Qaeda threat and the case of Northern Ireland was very limited. Parliament was also provided with briefing papers, but, again, in relation to the justification for the specific measures proposed, the information was limited to the general statements made in the Second Reading Speech on the general prevalence of terrorism.

[60] The following exchange (*Second Reading* cols 336–7) is illustrative:

> 'Does the Secretary of State understand the danger of proceeding on the basis of assertion, and the need to produce evidence to sustain support throughout the House and the country for these extraordinary measures? . . . I urge the Home Secretary to bring a detailed case to the House': Crispin Blunt
>
> '[The hon. Gentleman] simply does not accept the seriousness of the situation . . . [Hon Members—'He did not say that'] He did say that he could not accept it. He said clearly that he could not accept, without further evidence, that we face a threat of the sort that I assert. He should accept that': Charles Clarke (Home Secretary).

[61] The JCHR had previously noted this same problem in relation to the original derogation supporting the ATCSA regime. In response to the claimed need for secrecy, it had asked the government to consider at

statements of scepticism about the advice of the security services that key Ministers claimed to be acting upon, and unease about the disproportionate action recommended by national security institutions.[62]

David Feldman has argued that different governmental institutions advance different visions of the constitution to support their own claims to having greater importance and legitimacy than other institutions.[63] The interaction between the legislature and the executive over control orders bears out Feldman's thesis. The Home Secretary argued fiercely that it was the executive branch's constitutional responsibility to deal with terrorism, which it ought not abdicate,[64] and in relation to national security, the other institutions of government ought to properly recognize the executive's pre-eminent role.[65] Calls for trust to be placed in the executive were used not only to deflect demands for actual information upon which to evaluate the legislative proposals, but were also used as a strategy to undermine the need for parliamentary deliberation on the appropriate balance to be struck on civil liberties.[66] It was the role of the executive to strike the balance and Parliament was asked to give the executive what it had decided was necessary.[67] The Prime Minister in particular repeatedly stated, when asked to allow for greater parliamentary consideration of the Bill, that the powers being proposed were what the security services had decided were necessary, and it would be irresponsible of Parliament to deny them these powers.[68]

In section 6.F it was argued that legal standards may be relied upon by a parliamentary committee because arguments based on legal compliance are the ones which are taken seriously by leaders of the executive, and in the end, to achieve

least providing the gist of intelligence to Parliament: JCHR, *Eighteenth Report 2003–04: Review of Counter-Terrorism Powers* HL Paper 158, HC 713 (4 August 2004) [20]–[23].

62 *Second Reading*: Dalyell, col 361; Denham, col 376; Lilley, col 379; Sedgemore, cols 365–6. *Committee*: Clarke, col 727, Blunt, col 750. Many statements alluded to earlier supposed advice on weapons of mass destruction in Iraq as a reason for caution.

63 Feldman (n 59) 382–3.

64 E.g. 'Were I to surrender the responsibility of the executive to the courts, to take decisions on this matter, it would in the most real sense be a betrayal of the responsibility that I bear . . . for the security of the state.': Clarke, *Second Reading* col 318.

65 Regarding the courts: *Committee* col 695. Regarding amendments in Parliament: *Second Reading* col 339.

66 For instance, the statement from the Prime Minister on the lack of parliamentary review was: 'I don't think there is a lack of proper scrutiny . . . I would just urge people to bear in mind on this is that we do in fact face a terrorist threat, the security services and the police do believe we need these extra powers, and I am not being arrogant or railroading these things through, I am just trying to protect the security of our country.' Press Conference 25th February <http://webarchive.nationalarchives.gov.uk/20060715135117/number10.gov.uk/page7215> (Last accessed 23 July 2012).

67 This was prominent in relation to the calls that intercept evidence be permitted, so as to allow more prosecutions of suspected terrorists to proceed. This was sought by several MPs on the basis of the recommendations of the JCHR and Newton Committee: *Second Reading*: Jones, col 341; Davis, col 354; Smith, col 385. One MP noted that the only argument adduced against this proposal was that the security services were against it, even though 'pretty well everyone else is in favour of it': Smith, *Second Reading* col 384.

68 Blair, *Second Reading* cols 300–2; Hansard HC cols 1509–11 (9 March 2005). 'Should any terrorist act occur, there will not be a debate about civil liberties; there will be a debate about the advice that the Government received, and about whether they followed it. I have the advice, and I intend to follow it', at col 1513.

amendments, parliamentarians need to influence these Ministers. Likewise here we should consider how the structural features of the legislature which impede deliberation, namely executive dominance over the legislative process, may push parliamentary reliance on judicial standards to critique legislation. In introducing the Prevention of Terrorism Bill, the executive evinced a concern to comply with Convention rights and, accordingly, there were strategic reasons for parliamentarians seeking amendment to employ judicial standards to support their arguments.

The relative weakness of legislative scrutiny may also encourage parliamentary reliance on judicial scrutiny as a necessary supplement to Ministerial accountability to Parliament. The PTA conferred significant discretionary power on the Home Secretary, particularly in the choice and range of restrictions that could be imposed on controlees. The need for greater judicial oversight in the making of control orders was a principal concern of Labour backbenchers in particular,[69] in order to provide a check on whether this discretion was being exercised in a human rights-consistent manner. The Home Secretary argued against greater judicial oversight on the grounds that he would be accountable to Parliament. Given the way in which the measures were proposed and leading Ministers' attitudes towards parliamentary review, there was an understandable lack of confidence in parliamentary accountability as an adequate safeguard on the functioning of the control order regime.[70] In fact, in both the UK and Australia (where control orders were also introduced), the main changes to result from parliamentary scrutiny involved increasing the degree and effectiveness of judicial scrutiny of control orders.

This link between institutional weakness and reliance on judicial standards is further supported by contrasting deliberation in the House of Commons to the unelected House of Lords. Deliberation by the House of Lords was not beset by the same problems as the Commons. There was sufficient time for more detailed consideration of the Bill. Review of the Bill was also a more collaborative and (at least outwardly) respectful exercise, as has been noted about the House of Lords generally.[71] This allowed, for instance, legally trained members to explain the distinctions in the Bill to non-lawyers, as well as to probe the government on the soundness of their assurances on judicial oversight of control orders. Here too, there was some detailed reference to jurisprudence, but again this was in response to the Minister's reliance on jurisprudence in presenting the government's case.[72] One peer did concentrate on the spectre of another finding of incompatibility by the courts;[73] but on the whole, the debate did not display the same dynamic as the Commons debates of members pressuring the government with arguments about future non-compliance before a domestic or international court. Members even questioned the reliance on jurisprudence and whether the distinctions between

[69] Cook, *Second Reading* col 338, speaking for a group of concerned Labour backbenchers.

[70] E.g. Davis, *Second Reading* col 369.

[71] D Shell, *The House of Lords* (Manchester University Press, Manchester 2007) 88.

[72] For instance the debate over whether the judicial decisions on the special advocate system signified that this system was human rights compatible: see Hansard HL vol 670 cols 550–3 (7 March 2005).

[73] Earl of Onslow, Hansard HL vol 670 cols 497–8 (7 March 2005).

restriction and deprivation of liberty in ECtHR jurisprudence should be imported into UK law, particularly as the basis for allowing the Home Secretary the power to make non-derogating control orders.[74]

Peers interested in improving the Bill also faced a different task from concerned MPs. They were able to amend the legislation without government support, unlike their counterparts in the House of Commons, because of the different balance of party members and no controlling majority. In this case, House of Lords review produced significant amendments to the Bill, in relation to prior judicial authorization for all control orders, the burden of proof, and a one-year sunset clause. Rather than having to try to *persuade* senior Ministers, the House of Lords had the ability to refuse to pass certain legislative provisions. In this case, the Lords' use of this power resulted in a prolonged battle between the two Houses, ultimately producing a compromise between the demands of the Lords and the demands of the government. In the end, judicial oversight (albeit limited) was provided in relation to all control orders. The sunset clause was replaced with a requirement for annual renewal, ensuring that the law would return for further parliamentary consideration, which I consider in the following section.

8.D. Dialogue over Control Orders

Earlier I argued that the PTA illustrates dialogue-as-specialization: rather than refusing to change the law, by enacting the PTA the political branches of government continued to pursue the policy of preventative restrictions on terrorist suspects, through a different legislative vehicle that forged a new balance between human rights and security concerns. This legislation gave rise to a large volume of litigation, and several cases eventually reached the highest court (by then the UK Supreme Court). Cases where reply legislation returns to the courts for judicial evaluation have been referred to in dialogue scholarship as 'second look cases', emphasizing that these cases follow on from previous interactions between the courts, the executive, and the legislature over the requirements of fundamental rights.[75]

The PTA was carefully designed to avoid a second DOI on Article 5 grounds. Within the regime, the court could address itself to whether individual orders violated Article 5 (and quash them if they did), without putting the statutory regime itself into question. The legislation gave the Minister a wide discretion in the design of individual control orders, and invited the courts to tell the Minister just how far he or she could go with preventative restrictions on the liberty of

[74] Lord Britten, Hansard HL vol 670 col 500 (7 March 2005): 'It is fundamentally misconceived to found a distinction on the question of compliance or otherwise with the convention between cases where we have to go under the more onerous—if we may call it that—procedure and cases where we go under the simpler procedure subject to judicial review. If we are to have the public's consent, what matters between one procedure and the other is the gravity of the matter and not whether it is a breach of the convention'; see also Lord Forsyth, col 497; Baroness Hayman, col 498.

[75] See R Dixon, 'The Supreme Court of Canada, Charter Dialogue, and Deference' (2009) 47 Osgoode Hall LJ 235, 241.

terrorist suspects before Article 5 was engaged. In this way, the regime enlisted judges to police the line of what constituted a deprivation of liberty, rather than place limits on the Minister's power in statutory terms. This is not to suggest that the courts were free of any pressure from the executive to uphold control orders that were challenged. Rather, wide-ranging restrictions were applied from early on and appeals on control orders were strongly fought. Had the courts been activist in striking down individual control orders on an expansive view of the requirements of Article 5, they may have significantly frustrated the government's policy of placing preventative controls on terrorist suspects without derogating from the ECHR.

Indeed, the government's approach to the PTA has been described as a method of 'covert derogation', with the executive attempting, repeatedly, to place restrictions on controlees that arguably amounted to a deprivation of liberty, and waiting to then be told by the courts whether the orders were outwith the power to make non-derogating orders.[76] The courts ultimately allowed for wide-ranging restrictions to be permissible without violating Article 5, including curfews of up to sixteen hours.[77] The executive then adapted its control orders to these guidelines on the limit of Article 5 protections and never employed derogating control orders, with their more onerous procedural requirements.

The PTA did not invite the same kind of judicial role in relation to the Article 6 right to a fair trial. The legislation allowed for the use of secret evidence in establishing the grounds for a control order. These provisions were drafted on the assumption that the procedures involving secret evidence and the system of a Special Advocate (who was entitled to see the secret evidence and argue on behalf of the controlee), which was drawn from the immigration context and specifically from the ATCSA, would be found compliant with the right to a fair trial.[78] Chapter 4 considered the litigation on this matter and noted that the House of Lords overturned the DOI in *Secretary of State for the Home Department v MB* in favour of reading fair trial protections into the PTA. The Home Secretary's right to employ secret evidence was made subject to the requirement that the defendant receive a fair trial. However, the House of Lords laid forth a relatively permissive standard for secret evidence, concluding that in most cases it would be possible for the defendant to receive a fair trial without knowing the evidence against her.[79]

However, the lower courts had difficulty translating the judgment in *MB* into rules to guide the control order proceedings that were coming before them. As a result, the issue of the right to a fair trial where secret evidence was being employed returned to the House of Lords two years later. In the interim, the ECtHR had evaluated the former ATCSA scheme for its compliance with Article 6 and had held that Article 6 could not be satisfied if the case against a controlled person was made

[76] Fenwick and Phillipson (n 32).

[77] *Secretary of State for the Home Department v JJ* [2007] UKHL 45; *Secretary of State for the Home Department v E* [2007] UKHL 47.

[78] See n 33 and accompanying text.

[79] *Secretary of State for the Home Department v MB & AF* [2007] UKHL 46, [51]–[54] (Lord Hoffman), [74] (Baroness Hale), [90] (Lord Brown).

solely or primarily on closed material.[80] This ECtHR ruling limited the use of secret evidence more than the House of Lords had in *MB*. In 2009, the House of Lords in *Secretary of State for the Home Department v AF* considered this decision to determine the question of what the right to a fair trial required in relation to secret evidence,[81] in keeping with the mirror principle. Consequently, the gulf widened between judicial standards of a human rights-compatible control orders procedure and the procedure provided by the PTA. Nonetheless, this was again resolved by recourse to the section 3 HRA interpretative duty rather than a DOI, even though the operation of the regime would significantly depart from the original regime passed by Parliament.[82] The Minister did not seek a DOI, even after 'considerable provocation' to do so during the hearing.[83]

The judicial treatment of the PTA has generated significant criticism. The courts have been accused of advancing interpretations of Article 5 and Article 6 that strip them of much of their content, and clothing the PTA regime in apparent human rights compliance,[84] as well as excessive deference to the executive on the demands of national security.[85] Others have argued that these cases illustrate the institutional limitations under which courts operate, such that courts can make only partial or marginal gains when faced with draconian legislation.[86]

Understanding these cases as 'second-look' cases helps identify an additional reason why the courts have trodden carefully with the PTA. For instance, Lord Hope in *Secretary of State for the Home Department v AF* stated that the tension between protection of the public and fundamental rights was 'all the more acute' because the PTA had been introduced in response to the *Belmarsh Prisoners* decision.[87] Lord Hope expressed his concern that the government's attempt to protect the public in an alternative way that was compatible with Convention rights was to be 'rendered ineffective because another obstacle derived from the Convention is put in its path'.[88] Once the legislature has considered the court's opinion on the requirements of fundamental rights and chosen a new legislative path, courts may choose to take a cooperative approach (and according to some normative accounts of dialogue, they ought to).[89]

Even apart from normative reasons, I have argued that there are important strategic considerations supporting judicial restraint with DOIs specifically. Courts may hold back from issuing a DOI that risks being ignored, but conversely, where courts know

[80] *A v United Kingdom* (2009) 49 EHRR 29.

[81] *Secretary of State for the Home Department v AF* [2009] UKHL 28 [69] (Lord Phillips), [70]–[71] (Lord Hoffman), [80]–[81] (Lord Hope), [96] (Lord Scott), [98] (Lord Rodger), [144] (Lord Brown).

[82] n 81, [67] (Lord Phillips).

[83] n 81, [102] (Baroness Hale).

[84] Fenwick and Phillipson (n 32).

[85] K Ewing and J-C Tham, 'The Continuing Futility of the Human Rights Act' [2008] PL 668, 691–3.

[86] For this, and other criticisms of Ewing and Tham's futility thesis, see Kavanagh (n 6).

[87] *AF* (n 81) [77].

[88] *AF* (n 81) [77].

[89] For example, see Rosalind Dixon's argument that, once courts have brought a rights issue to the attention of the legislature, they ought to then respect the balance reached in reply legislation: Dixon (n 75).

that the DOI is a powerful statement of censure, it may precipitate public controversy over review powers given to judges.[90] Moreover, in these circumstances, a DOI may have prompted a formal derogation from human rights. In fact, in stating her argument for a section 3 HRA interpretation as the appropriate remedy in *MB*, Baroness Hale expressly raised the possibility of the court 'inviting' a derogation were it to make a DOI, which could have led to even further violations of rights.[91]

Yet, the danger of a 'cooperative' approach by courts is that it could serve to pacify legislative scrutiny of rights-limiting legislation, instead of supporting renewed deliberation on the balance struck by the control orders regime. Despite little support from the government, many parliamentarians attempted to subject the PTA to review and challenge on the grounds of Article 5 and Article 6 rights. However, the domestic courts did not follow through with interpretations of these rights that were as exacting as these parliamentarians had predicted. Hence, the interesting question, from the vantage point of legislative deliberation, is what impact the approach taken by the courts had on the impetus for amendment or repeal of the control orders regime. Was rights-based criticism of control orders pacified by the judicial decisions on the PTA?

The answer is both yes and no. From 2005 to 2010, the PTA was renewed on five occasions, suggesting that the measures came to be a normalized part of the legal landscape. The interest surrounding the initial passage of the legislation dropped away with time, and the debates on the annual renewal of the legislation were poorly attended, making them more a formality than an opportunity for robust review.[92] The government continued to argue that the regime was necessary and the main opposition party remained silent on any undertaking to repeal or replace the legislation.[93] However, we should bear in mind that the annual renewal debates were necessarily limited to two possible outcomes—renewal or repeal—without including the possibility of amendment. This was a further factor pushing annual review into becoming a formality because the scope for parliamentary input was limited and voting to repeal the entire regime was a fairly 'nuclear' option, particularly for government backbenchers, to voice dissatisfaction.[94]

In fact, one plausible reason for the government's constant preference for the use of section 3 HRA in litigation over control orders could lie in the political dynamics surrounding the legislation. On each annual renewal, the relevant

[90] Indeed, there were even critics of the legislation within Parliament who, though they may have wished for more robust interpretations of Article 5 and Article 6 by the courts, preferred that judges avoided a DOI and worked 'within the regime' against the most draconian uses of control orders, because a DOI would have led to unhelpful debate about the excessive power of judges: Baroness Vivien Stern, Interview, London, 21 June 2010.

[91] *MB* (n 79) [73]. See also text accompanying nn 60–4 in Chapter 4.

[92] The pattern of attendance was remarked upon by the JCHR, *Ninth Report 2009–10: Annual Renewal of Control Orders Legislation 2010* HL Paper 64, HC 395 [14], which called for the annual renewal process to be replaced with a sunset clause and a full parliamentary debate, to increase the burden of justification upon the government.

[93] The regime was eventually repealed in 2011, after the Labour party left office in 2010. The replacement regime is discussed below.

[94] As noted by Fenwick and Phillipson (n 32), 908.

Minister represented to Parliament that the House of Lords had found the regime to be compatible with human rights, and thus sought to neutralize human rights-based criticism of the regime. Had the courts issued a DOI, this stance would no longer have been tenable. This would have forced the issue of repealing or amending the legislation, something that the executive consistently sought to avoid.

On the other hand, despite the government's stance, human rights criticism of the laws continued in Parliament. The JCHR continued to argue that the legislation infringed a range of fundamental rights, and by 2010 stated their opinion in no uncertain terms that the regime was unsustainable.[95] Hence, legislative review did, on this occasion, clearly go beyond the application of judicial standards to make more exacting demands than the courts.

The JCHR adopted three different argumentative strategies in this field.[96] First, it argued that the government's depiction of the judicial decisions was misleading and that, despite the fact that no DOI had been issued, the laws raised serious human rights concerns.[97] Second, the JCHR again provided a conduit for evidence to be presented to Parliament on the way in which the laws operated, and conveyed the harsh effects of control orders on controlees and their families to the legislature.[98] Third, the JCHR extended its reporting to non-human rights-based arguments to attack the workability of the regime, in particular, the expense of the system relative to available alternatives such as surveillance.[99]

This further demonstrates how parliamentarians who seek stronger protections for human rights employ judicial decisions strategically, to attract greater attention to their concerns, but readily switch to non-legal arguments where needed. The JCHR did not stop pursuing amendments to the control orders legislation after the measures were subject to judicial review; if anything, its opposition strengthened. This is a further way in which judicial and parliamentary review can play complementary roles. In the litigation over control orders, courts' attention was focused on individual control orders. The courts were not asked to pass an evaluation on the regime as a whole: they were not asked, nor did they answer, the question of whether the control orders regime was 'a good idea or a bad idea'.[100] In fact, the

[95] JCHR (n 92) [22].

[96] The JCHR reported annually on the legislation: see *Twelfth Report 2005–06: Draft Prevention of Terrorism Act 2005 (Continuance in force of sections 1 to 9) Order 2006*, HL Paper 122, HC 915; *Eighth Report 2006–07: Draft Prevention of Terrorism Act 2005 (Continuance in force of sections 1 to 9) Order 2007*, HL Paper 60, HC 365; *Tenth Report 2007–08: Annual Renewal of Control Orders Legislation 2008*, HL Paper 57, HC 356; *Fifth Report 2008–09: Annual Renewal of Control Order Legislation 2009*, HL Paper 37, HC 282; *Ninth Report 2009–10* (n 92).

[97] A summary of these human rights concerns, as repeated across the reports is provided in JCHR *Fifth Report 2008–09: Annual Renewal of Control Order Legislation 2009*, HL Paper 37, HC 282 [9].

[98] The Committee in particular sought out evidence from lawyers representing controlees, and recounted often harrowing first-hand accounts to Parliament to challenge the official accounts given by the government and the official reviewer (Lord Carlile). See JCHR, *Ninth Report 2009–10* (n 92) [39]–[46], Ev 1 and Ev 6. It also drew renewed attention to the concerns of Special Advocates with the system: Ev 7–9.

[99] JCHR, *Ninth Report 2009–10* (n 92) [105]–[107].

[100] K Starmer, 'Setting the Record Straight: Human Rights in an Era of International Terrorism' [2007] EHRLR 123, 125.

House of Lords (Judicial Committee) made clear that the policy questions over introducing preventative action against people not charged with any criminal offence was a question for Parliament and not the courts. Nor did the courts address a range of human rights concerns raised by the regime that did not arise in litigation.[101] Over time, the JCHR confronted precisely these questions; making an overall evaluation of the regime, and the underlying policy, the centrepiece of its review. It continued to argue for reform, and demonstrated independent evidence gathering and judgment, well beyond simply applying legal precedent and predicting judicial evaluations.

The control order regime was eventually repealed in 2011 and replaced by a new scheme, entitled the Terrorism Prevention and Investigation Measures (TPIM) Act 2011. This willingness to change the label entirely came with a new government, which was happy to project the image of overhaul. However, the new measures were not fundamentally different, rather the change was a matter of degree. There was an increase in the threshold required for the imposition of an order (TPIM) from reasonable suspicion to reasonable belief, provisions for instituting measures which would require a derogation were removed,[102] and the restrictions that could be imposed under the new measures were more limited. In particular, there was no power to force suspects to relocate—the controversial 'internal exile' powers that had been heavily criticized by the JCHR and had led the Supreme Court to quash a control order in late 2010.[103]

These modifications were welcomed by the JCHR, but numerous concerns remained, not in the least because much of the PTA scheme remained effectively intact. The procedure for the making of orders remained largely unchanged, including the procedures in relation to secret evidence that had been subject to significant reading down in the courts. Significantly, the new scheme no longer required annual review, but was rather subject to a five-year sunset clause, itself inserted only as a result of parliamentary review. The Committee was concerned that control orders, rather than being a temporary and exceptional measure, had become a recognized part of the legal landscape, operating outside the rigours of the criminal investigative process. It remains to be seen how this new chapter in the ongoing institutional dialogue over counter-terrorism powers will be received by the courts.

8.E. Conclusion

Chapter 3 asked whether legislative debate may become oriented towards compliance with minimum legal standards even under a weak-form system of review such as the

[101] Kavanagh (n 6) 295.

[102] Instead draft legislation for emergency measures was prepared and held in waiting, to be passed in the event of an emergency need: *Draft Enhanced Terrorism Prevention and Investigative Measures Bill* Cm 8166 (September 2011).

[103] *Secretary of State for the Home Department v AP* [2010] UKSC 24, concluding that the forced relocation was unusually destructive of normal life, leading it to constitute a deprivation of liberty.

HRA, and if so, why. In this chapter, I have examined the attitude taken by Parliament to the DOI in *Belmarsh Prisoners*. It was mentioned earlier that the *Belmarsh Prisoners* judgment was, exceptionally, one in which judges specifically referred to the non-binding nature of the DOI, and drew attention to the DOI's status as 'political not legal'.[104] Yet, the DOI was perceived by parliamentarians as an authoritative legal pronouncement.

We have also seen the careful attention paid by the government to compliance with human rights law in devising its response. Yet, again, this was a legislative response that, in pursuing a policy in a new way, raised human rights concerns of its own. Legislative deliberation on this reply was poor on two main criteria: time and public justification. Within these constraints, what debate did occur on the Prevention of Terrorism Bill, in the House of Commons especially, was oriented towards whether measures met the bare minimum required for compliance with Convention rights.

I have suggested that executive dominance over the legislative process not only produced poor conditions of deliberation in this case, but was also a factor contributing to the highly legalized debate in the Commons, as it required MPs to orient their arguments to what was most likely to be taken seriously by government. Reliance on judicial standards may be a tool used by members of the House of Commons and parliamentary committees who oppose legislation on the merits, but are not especially empowered in the legislative process. A telling sign in the debates over the PTA was that a number of parliamentarians responded to the government's legal arguments on compatibility with more demanding substantive conceptions of what the relevant rights required, *irrespective* of judicial interpretations. This indicates that questions of legality did not *supplant* concerns about legitimacy, rather both concerns appeared to be important to most parliamentarians. This example gives us reason to reflect on whether heavy reliance on judicial standards in legislative review may be more a symptom of executive dominance than judicial dominance.

The performance of the House of Lords provides an interesting counterpoint to deliberation in the Commons. The upper House is a curiosity from the perspective of institutional design: a mixed hereditary and appointed house that has come to be favoured as a civic forum and a house of review.[105] It is notable that theoretical arguments based on the legitimacy and capacity of an elected assembly do not apply to the House of Lords, and in fact, being appointed 'guardians', providing independent oversight of the elected government, the House of Lords (Legislative) shares certain features with the judiciary. It does however suggest that unelected institutions of review need not only be courts and can be generalist, rather than legal.

Judicial review over the control orders regime was a continued source of friction from 2006, and did ensure that the government was held to account for its use of the powers that it pushed through Parliament. Here we see a further type of

[104] See text accompanying n 111 in Chapter 4.

[105] See D Oliver, 'The Modernisation of the United Kingdom Parliament' in J Jowell and D Oliver (eds), *The Changing Constitution* (OUP, Oxford 2004) 176–80.

specialization across the courts and the legislature. The courts directed themselves to individual control orders, upholding them or not depending on the concrete circumstances in the specific case. Legislative review, conducted principally by the JCHR, directed itself to an evaluation of the very policy underpinning the regime, and human rights concerns that were broader than those brought to the courts. The ongoing 'dialogue' over control orders also further shows that the use of legal arguments by parliamentarians did not signify judicial dominance over human rights discourse. Even when the courts did not follow through on predictions of incompatibility, members of the legislature continued to argue for reform on human rights grounds. The JCHR in particular has engaged, over time, in a form of rights review that evinces independent judgment beyond simply applying judicial decisions. Given the sheer latitude of discretion that the executive possess in drafting reply legislation, and the realistic pressures on courts not to issue repeat DOIs, we see here that the existence of a parliamentary institution that takes evidence, records human rights concerns, and demands greater justification from the executive is a healthy and important element of a deliberative system of weak-form review.

9
Epilogue

The main case study in this book concerns the operation of DOIs from the commencement of the HRA until May 2010, spanning three Parliamentary terms, and the full period of the Labour government. However, it is worth briefly noting recent developments, during the early period of a new government, in light of the conclusions drawn in the study. This is not because a significant new body of DOIs has come into existence—in fact, only one new DOI has been issued to the time of writing.[1] What is interesting is the impact of a significant change in the political landscape—with the long-standing Labour government replaced by a coalition between the two other major opposition parties—on outstanding DOIs, or even outstanding human rights concerns over legislative schemes such as control orders. While the dominant dynamic between courts and legislatures over DOIs has not departed from the specialization model of interaction, in 2011, the House of Commons held the first parliamentary debate dedicated to open disagreement with a judicial finding of incompatibility. This debate was nested in a broader context of escalating criticism, not of national courts, but of the European Court of Human Rights, and the creation of a commission to investigate a new UK Bill of Rights.

9.A. The Dominant Dynamic

We saw in Chapter 6 that the early phase of the HRA was characterized by quick and willing legislative responses, and most DOIs were uncontroversial. It was only over time that DOIs began to relate to policies that the government sought to defend, and were met with forms of resistance.

For the Labour government, the HRA was one of its own initiatives. However, the Coalition government came into power with an ambivalent position towards the Act. The larger Conservative party was opposed to the Act and had made election pledges to repeal and replace it with a new 'national' Bill of Rights. The smaller Liberal-Democrat party supported the Act and had pledged to retain it.

[1] *R (on the application of Royal College of Nursing & Ors) v Secretary of State for the Home Department* [2010] EWHC 2761 (10 November 2010) ('*Royal College of Nursing*'). This DOI was in fact a 'second look' case, as it related to provisions of the Safeguarding Vulnerable Groups Act 2006 that were claimed to remedy the earlier DOI in *Wright & Others v Secretary of State for Health & Anor* [2009] UKHL 3.

Against this political backdrop it is interesting that there was a return to relatively prompt responses by the new Parliament, in contrast to the long delays characteristic of the 2005–10 period.

The only fresh DOI since the study period (*Royal College of Nursing*) was addressed by primary legislation within a year. Remedial measures were included in the Protection of Freedom Bill 2011, which sought to roll back a number of limitations on civil liberties (including further regulation of camera surveillance, a reduction in the available pre-charge detention of terrorist suspects to fourteen days, and modification of stop and search powers). The remedial order mechanism was revived as a means of addressing DOIs. The long-standing DOI in *Baiai*,[2] relating to religious discrimination in requirements for marriage certification, was addressed by a remedial order in April 2011 repealing the Certificate of Approval scheme.[3] The outstanding DOI in *Thompson*,[4] relating to the absence of a mechanism to review inclusion on the Sex Offenders' Register was dealt with by a remedial order introduced in June 2011 and passed in May 2012.[5]

One reason why a new government may quickly respond to DOIs with legislative changes is that they relate to policies of the previous government and the new administration may not be wedded to these policies nor particularly troubled when they are criticized. This would explain the readiness of the Coalition government to repeal the entire Certificate of Approval scheme impugned in *Baiai* rather than to extend it to the Church of England and therefore make it non-discriminatory. It would explain why the *Royal College of Nursing* case was a 'quiet' case and the DOI was not appealed nor subject to debate, even though it directly contradicted the Labour government's contention in 2009 that it had remedied the DOI in *Wright*. Similarly, it would explain the Coalition government's readiness, after many years of back and forth between the courts, the executive, and parliamentary bodies over the control orders regime, to replace the scheme with the new TPIMs regime.[6] Here, the Minister was eager to send the message of replacing the previous government's flawed scheme with a new, wiser legislative solution, even though the TPIMs regime was not remarkably different in substance. The politics of replacing legislation may therefore be entirely different based on *whose* legislation it is perceived to be.

However, not all prompt responses have been accompanied by a spirit of agreement with, or even necessarily respect for, judges. The Supreme Court decision in *Thompson* upheld a DOI which stated that the absence of any possible review of continued inclusion on the Sex Offenders' Register was a disproportionate limitation on the privacy rights of those convicted of sex offences. This was a DOI

[2] *R (Baiai & Ors) v Secretary of State for the Home Department & Anor* [2006] EWHC 823 (Admin).

[3] Asylum and Immigration (Treatment of Claimants, etc) Act 2004 (Remedial) Order 2011.

[4] *R (Thompson & JF) v Secretary of State for the Home Department* [2009] EWCA Civ 792, upheld by the Supreme Court at the very end of the study period (*R (Thompson & JF) v Secretary of State for the Home Department* [2010] UKSC 17).

[5] Sexual Offences Act 2003 (Remedial) Order 2012.

[6] See discussion in 8.D.

drawing attention to the procedural rights of an extremely unpopular group of criminal offenders and was appealed by the government up to the Supreme Court.

MPs and the Prime Minister himself were openly critical of the Supreme Court's decision, as, for example, 'fly[ing] completely in the face of common sense'.[7] The Home Secretary, when stating the government's intention to respond by way of remedial order, was clear that the government was 'disappointed and appalled' by the decision, because it prioritized the rights of sex offenders over the protection of the public, yet, since no further appeal was possible, the government would do the absolute minimum to comply with the judgment.[8] Simultaneously, assurances were made to strengthen other aspects of the Sex Offenders' Register, e.g. increasing the reporting requirements for those on the register. This response evinces the features of passive resistance that were considered in Chapter 6: reassertion of the policy underlying the impugned law, criticism of the judicial conclusion, and minimal changes to the law to comply with the judgment.[9]

What is interesting, however, is that the government nonetheless responded promptly, using the remedial order device. It did not propose that Parliament avail itself of the ability to disagree with the courts formally and state that the legislation was not a violation of human rights. The misalignment between the rhetoric accompanying the statement of the government's response and use of a prompt remedial order is more noteworthy when we consider the timing of the statement made in Parliament, which was ten months after the Supreme Court judgment was handed down, but only days before the announcement of a Commission to investigate the creation of a UK Bill of Rights. The Home Secretary used her statement on the DOI to inform Parliament that this Commission was about to be announced, stating that

> It is time to assert that it is Parliament that makes our laws, not the courts; that the rights of the public come before the rights of criminals; and, above all, that we have a legal framework that brings sanity to cases such as these[10]

—quietly failing to mention that in fact it was entirely possible for Parliament to refuse to comply with the *Thompson* DOI within the existing legal framework of the HRA. The Home Secretary was evasive when the question was put to her that it was lawful for her to leave the impugned regime unchanged.[11]

Hence, it can be suggested that the bluster and vocal opposition surrounding the *Thompson* DOI had less to do with disagreement over the correctness of the

[7] Prime Minister David Cameron, quoted on the BBC News website, 16 February 2011 (<http://www.bbc.co.uk/news/uk-politics-12482442>).

[8] May, Hansard HC vol 523 col 959 (16 February 2011).

[9] In fact, the JCHR argued that the review procedures introduced by the remedial order were insufficient to remedy the violation of human rights because review was to be conducted by the Chief Police Officer rather than a court: JCHR, *Nineteenth Report of Session 2010–2012* (HL Paper 200/HC 1549) 11 October 2011. However, the government maintained its position that review ought to be police led and that its measures would remedy the violation of Article 8: Proposal for the Sexual Offences Act 2003 (Remedial) Order 2011, Cm 8293 (March 2012).

[10] May, Hansard HC vol 523 col 960 (16 February 2011).

[11] Straw (n 10) col 963.

decision itself, and more to do with the broader Conservative policy of replacing the HRA.[12] It was convenient to use this outstanding DOI, which related to sex offenders, to support the message to the public that the HRA itself was flawed and ought to be replaced wholesale. This message would not have been served by a refusal to change to law within the terms of the Act. If we look at the debate over the DOI in the House of Commons, where the decision was criticized, this was not grounded in any consideration of the judicial reasoning, or even opposition to the scope of the procedural rights in question. Rather, opposition was couched in general statements on judges placing the human rights of 'bad people' above public protection,[13] without specific arguments being made as to why excluding the possibility of any review was necessary for public protection. The view that the courts were putting the rights of perpetrators above the rights of the public and victims was explicitly encouraged by the Home Secretary herself.[14]

Therefore, despite the tenor of this short debate, it provides little evidence of principled disagreement over the conclusion reached on the proportionality of the interference with human rights in question. But it does point to an underlying political dynamic of discrediting the HRA, promoted by the Conservative Party, despite their practice of prompt remedial responses. Later in the same month, however, we see the first debate dedicated to open refusal to change the law subject to a DOI, in relation to the one exception to the Coalition government's record of responding to DOIs.

9.B. Prisoner Voting Revisited

Prisoner voting has proved to be the most intractable issue over the life of the HRA. In Chapter 7, I argued that resistance through delay tactics had amounted to a failure of due deliberation in relation to this limitation on a central democratic right. The matter was finally subject to debate in the House of Commons in 2011.[15] This eventual debate was not ideal. For one, rather than being oriented to a piece of proposed legislation, involving debate on its policy and provisions with possible adjustments over multiple stages of debate, or even oriented to a motion capturing government policy not to change the law, it was simply a single debate on a backbench motion, oriented to a statement of opinion. Moreover, the motion contained two statements, one supporting the ban on prisoner voting and the other asserting that whether to retain the ban was a question for the UK Parliament not the European Court of Human Rights. Hence the debate had a split purpose, one of which was to express opposition and frustration at the ECtHR's jurisdiction and interpretation of the Convention more broadly. However, given the absence of any

[12] This 'neat segue' to the Bill of Rights Commission was not lost on at least one commentator in the media: L Brooks, 'This is not the way to keep us safe from sex offenders', The Guardian 18 February 2011.

[13] See, for example n 10, Burley, col 965; McCrea, col 968; Hollobone col 969.

[14] May (n 10) cols 962–3.

[15] Hansard HC vol 523 cols 493–582 (10 February 2011) ('*Prisoner voting debate*').

Commons debate on the voting ban to that point, the four-hour debate was one step towards the reasoned justification from legislators that ought to accompany limitations into fundamental rights.

From a broader perspective, this was the first instance of parliamentary debate leading to open disagreement with an outstanding DOI (the motion was passed with a majority of 234 votes to 22).[16] It may seem surprising that this first instance of open disagreement relates to one of the subset of DOIs that was based on a binding determination by an international court, rather than in relation to a DOI with which Parliament could indeed disagree without defying any legal obligation. That being said, this was only a backbench motion and not a case where the executive has openly stated that it will not change the law; the executive could not do so without being in violation of the UK's obligations under the ECHR. In fact, in December 2010, the Coalition government announced its intention to remedy the violation and its chosen response, namely a modified ban on the voting rights of prisoners sentenced to a custodial sentence of four years or more. This was justified on the grounds that the government was under a legal obligation to act, had been given an August 2011 deadline by the ECtHR, and failure to meet that deadline would lead to compensation awards for prisoners.[17]

In Chapter 7, I suggested that, were it not for the treaty dimension to this particular incompatibility, this would be the type of situation in which it was politically feasible for the political branches of government to openly refuse to address a DOI. The relevant Minister would have the weight of public opinion behind them and an apparent consensus across the two major parties on the desirability of maintaining the ban. The backbench debate is therefore one, albeit limited, example of what open legislative disagreement with a judicial conclusion on human rights compatibility looks like. It allows us to examine, in this specific case, what type of reasons were offered by MPs who supported the ban on prisoner voting, and whether this represents the type of careful deliberation on the meaning of human rights that we would seek to encourage in a deliberative democracy.

In Chapter 3, when considering the theoretical justifications behind empowering legislatures to decide on the scope and limitation of human rights, I noted the arguments from proponents of legislative decision-making that the balancing of rights against the needs of society was not something that judges were necessarily better equipped at than legislatures, and indeed, that the proportionality inquiry is more like a policy judgment than a legal one.[18] However, in this particular example

[16] Less than half of the House of Commons voted on the motion.

[17] Statement by Parliamentary Secretary, Cabinet Office, Mark Harper, Hansard HC 150–151WS (20 December 2010). At the time of writing, no further action had been taken. Subsequent litigation at the ECtHR in *Scoppola v Italy (No 3)* Application No 126/05 (GC, 22 May 2012) in which the UK intervened, allowed the UK to delay its deadline further to November 2012. The UK sought, unsuccessfully, to have the Grand Chamber overrule its decision in *Hirst v United Kingdom (No 2)* (2006) 42 EHRR 41 but the Grand Chamber did however affirm its position in *Hirst* that a variety of lesser restrictions on prisoner voting rights may be permissible and the choice between them was for the UK authorities. The government's stated position has remained that it will do the minimum required to secure compliance with the judgment in *Hirst*.

[18] See text accompanying nn 76–9 in Chapter 2.

of legislative rights review in action, where MPs did in fact openly disagree with the judicial conclusion, by and large they did not do so by engaging in an open balancing of the right of prisoners to vote against a pressing social need to limit that right. Rather, the dominant reasons offered for retaining the ban were, first, that prisoners did not deserve to vote, second, the sheer public unpopularity of giving prisoners voting rights, and third, general attacks on the ECtHR.

On the first type of argument in favour of the ban, several MPs questioned the status of the right to vote as a right, preferring to see it as a matter of policy or a privilege, and one which convicted criminals lost by virtue of their actions.[19] Many others simply stated their opposition to modifying the ban in terms of an objection to advancing the rights of prisoners in any way, arguing that the law should protect victims' rights.[20] In relation to the second type of argument, one of the clearest repeated reasons against removing the ban was that the public would be appalled or would find the move to enfranchise criminals baffling.[21] Earlier chapters have posed the question of whether DOIs, by bringing matters to the legislature, can introduce marginalized viewpoints—indeed, act as 'door-openers' for the questioning of discrimination that has long been socially acceptable. However, a prominent justification for not modifying the ban was that it was the duty of MPs to represent the public sentiment. This type of agency approach to representation will be resistant to any attempt to challenge the treatment of deeply unpopular minorities. In fact, those who supported changing the law were challenged on whether they had the support of their constituents.[22]

Neither of these types of arguments in favour of the existing law fall within a human rights framing of the prisoner voting issue. The basic contours of human rights, as an ethical approach, on this issue would be that, where a fundamental right is withdrawn from a particular group or person, that limitation on society's protection of the right must be justified by an important social need and tailored to that need. There is room for disagreement on the scope of the right in the first place (for instance, the right may not extend to those below a certain age), what counts as a social need, and whether the extent of the limitation corresponds with the social need being claimed (that is, is proportionate). However, deliberation within a human rights framework is bounded in the sense of beginning with the

[19] This tone was set by the MPs who introduced the motion, Jack Straw and David Davis. Straw, for instance, argued that 'the issue before us today—is by no stretch of the imagination a breach of fundamental human rights. Rather it is a matter of penal policy' (*Prisoner voting debate* col 502) and Davis stated 'there is an important point about not confusing the rights that are *properly held* by everybody who is a British citizen . . . with those much more circumscribed rights that are *given* to prisoners' (col 493, emphasis added). This approach resonated with MPs opposed to the ban, for example, 'Does my hon. Friend agree that it is extraordinary that we should allow judges in Strasbourg to tell us that voting is not a privilege but a right? . . . Privileges can be conferred on those of us who contribute to our communities as law-abiding citizens': Bray, col 537.

[20] A typical example was 'I find it extraordinary that we are talking about the rights of convicted criminals—people in prison—rather than the rights of those who are the victims of crime': Patel, *Prisoner voting debate* cols 575–6.

[21] E.g. Davis, *Prisoner voting debate* col 495; Paisley, col 518; McCann, col 529; Main, col 531; Hollobone, col 536; Harris, col 548; Coffey, col 558; Vickers, col 561; Binley, col 568; Patel, col 575.

[22] See the exchange between MacShane and Davidson, *Prisoner voting debate* col 509.

presumption that all persons are entitled to their fundamental rights irrespective of moral character or popularity alone.

These types of contributions based on the revocation of a privilege or sheer unpopularity were dominant, but not the universal approach. MPs were in fact urged by the Attorney-General and some others to articulate the reasons why the current ban was a proportionate limitation on voting rights.[23] Some participants did articulate their reasons for believing the ban as it stood was a justified limitation on rights—principally, that if an offence is serious enough to warrant imprisonment, it is serious enough to justify deprivation of the right to vote alongside the deprivation of freedom of association, for the period of imprisonment.[24] However, others openly rejected a proportionality approach, arguing that this was a simple matter of 'right and wrong', 'common sense', or instinct.[25]

There were a minority of contributors who argued against the motion, and that the UK should remove the blanket ban on prisoner voting, both because of the importance of complying with the UK's international legal obligations[26] as well as because the blanket ban was unjustified on the merits.[27] Hence, there was a diversity of arguments put forward, as well as reference to comparative practice in other countries, the views of prison governors, victim support groups, and prison reform groups.[28] In this group of contributions, we do see greater engagement with the reasons for incarceration and whether those reasons justified the deprivation of voting rights, alongside arguments around the importance of the UK adhering to its international obligations irrespective of the popularity of the ECtHR's decisions. One MP even argued, in face of considerable opposition, in favour of the ECtHR ruling pushing the UK to reconsider what it believed to be human rights compatible, as a form of external pressure that helped to ensure that the country did not become locked into a static understanding of human rights protection.[29] Overall, the debate did serve the purpose of putting a range of arguments onto the public

[23] Attorney-General (Dominic Grieve), *Prisoner voting debate* col 514: 'I appreciate that [whether it is the right of the ECtHR to decide] is what my hon. Friend and many others believe the issue for debate to be. I recognise that it is going to be a major topic for debate this afternoon, but, if he will forgive me, I will suggest that hon. Members might also wish to focus on why they consider the current ban, or some variant of it, to be reasonable and proportionate in our own national context.' See also Bottomley, col 565.

[24] This was an argument advanced by the UK in *Hirst*. Bryant, *Prisoner voting debate* col 518; Main, col 531; Davis, col 494.

[25] For example, McCann, *Prisoner voting debate* col 529, who went on to state that, when he asked his constituents whether it was right or wrong, they expressed disbelief at the very thought of giving prisoners the right to vote. These types of contributions followed in the vein of David Cameron's statement during Prime Minister's Questions in the House of Commons months earlier that it made him 'physically ill even to contemplate having to give the vote to anyone who is in prison'; Hansard HC vol 517 col 921 (3 November 2010)

[26] Brake, *Prisoner voting debate* col 542; Corbyn, col 537–9; Reevell, col 554–5.

[27] Long, *Prisoner voting debate* cols 532–3; Qureshi, col 535–6; Brake, col 544; Bottomley, col 564–5.

[28] MacShane, *Prisoner voting debate* cols 507–8; Corbyn, col 538; Brake, col 545; Burt, col 576 (who had previously been a prison officer).

[29] 'My point is that this external pressure is useful, as it repeatedly questions what our understanding of human rights should be. It is too easy for us to get locked into a narrow definition and understanding of those rights that constantly looks to the past. That is what will happen if we simply sit

record, even if the relative emphasis of the debate was not considered justification of the ban within a human rights framework.

What the eventual parliamentary debate on the blanket ban does reinforce from the debate in response to *Thompson* is that engagement with human rights in the legislative process can be compromised by deep-seated unpopularity of certain minorities. This is a difficulty facing legislative deliberation on human rights: how to ensure that MPs disentangle the unpopularity of beneficiaries from reasons for the limitation on rights in question? The debate in the House of Commons did engage with the reasoning of the ECtHR in *Hirst*, but what was missing was any contribution from the UK courts to the reasons why the law as it stood was incompatible with the right to free and fair elections. This was the consequence of a domestic judicial position that, prior to the ECtHR decision, did not review the ban on the grounds of deference, and after the ECtHR decision, affirmed that the law was incompatible with human rights but did not add its own reasoning as to why the ban was unacceptable and the conclusion in *Hirst* was the correct one (as discussed in Chapter 7).

The third type of reasoning offered for not changing the law was to attack the legitimacy and competence of the ECtHR as a decision-maker. This was a major focus of debate, and for some, the actual rights issue at hand was less important.[30] MPs were no doubt cognizant of the popular media coverage of the matter, which was deeply hostile and had cast the issue as a matter of European institutions overriding UK lawmakers. Many of the MPs present were Conservatives,[31] and there is a long-standing debate within that party on the broader question of the UK's involvement in European institutions. Hence, the debate was not solely, or even principally, about the merits of the ban.

Yet, even while several MPs used this opportunity to discredit the ECtHR, many other MPs displayed a deep discomfort with the idea of non-compliance with a judicial decision. Even some MPs sympathetic to the ban believed that, irrespective of their feelings on the merits, one could not 'pick and choose' which judicial decisions to comply with, for this would send entirely the wrong message about the importance of respecting the law. Instead these MPs argued that the UK Parliament should take heed of and 'moderate' the judicial decision[32] (or 'shape the dialogue')[33] and make limited changes to the law, as was its proper and lawful role.[34] This reasoning was in the context of a binding international judgment. However it is interesting to note the sentiment, which endorses the specialization model of interaction as the preferable way for the legislature to react when faced

within our own jurisdictional context and fail to look at what is going on in the wider world': Green, *Prisoner voting debate* col 546.

30 '. . . the rights of prisoners to vote is relatively unimportant. . . . The motion invites us to address a much more fundamental issue': Streeter, *Prisoner voting debate* col 505.

31 Grieve, *Prisoner voting debate* col 510.

32 Reevell, *Prisoner voting debate* col 555.

33 Grieve, *Prisoner voting debate* cols 512–3.

34 Baldry, *Prisoner voting debate* col 551.

with a controversial decision—expressing its reservations through its choice of the new legislative position, not by rejection of the judicial decision itself.

9.C. Reforming the Institutional Settlement on Human Rights?

Above, I noted how the new government has taken an overall approach to DOIs of relatively prompt remedial action. At the same time it has taken a hostile approach to the institutional settlement reached over human rights in the UK, with escalating public claims about the need for a national approach to human rights which repudiates unpopular stances taken by the ECtHR in relation to, particularly, the deportation of terrorist suspects and prisoner voting.

Any reforms that may be taken are still in early phases: the HRA is likely to stand at the very least until the next UK general election in 2015. The Conservative and Liberal-Democrat parties agreed in their coalition agreement to investigate replacing the HRA with a UK Bill of Rights, but that any changes would not reduce the protection of human rights in the UK. In 2011, the government established an expert commission, staffed almost entirely with prominent barristers, to inquire into the possibilities of a UK Bill of Rights as well as advise on reform of the ECtHR. The commission is due to report at the end of 2012. In 2011, it conducted a public consultation into whether the UK needed a Bill of Rights, to which a significant response was that it already had one in the HRA.[35] The discussions that the Commission has held in Northern Ireland, Scotland, and Wales, have indicated relatively little support for a UK Bill of Rights.[36] It remains to be seen if the commission will recommend incremental or fundamental changes in its report. In early 2012, one member of the Commission resigned, citing dissatisfaction that the Commission was not taking proper account of the inability of the UK Parliament to override the decisions of the ECtHR, and thereby was not taking due account of the Prime Minister's stated desire to assert the sovereignty of the UK Parliament over the decisions of the ECtHR.[37]

Being staffed with barristers, the Committee will be well aware that a UK Bill of Rights is not the vehicle to institute major changes to the UK's international obligations under the ECHR. If the UK government seeks to modify the role of the ECtHR, it must do so directly and alongside other member States. The UK government has pursued reform of the ECtHR itself as part of its Chairmanship of the Council of Europe, initiating what will necessarily be slow reforms if they are accepted. The Strasbourg court has demonstrable problems with its case load and severe delays in processing claims, many of which do not constitute new matters of principle. The measures that the UK has proposed to reduce this case load have

[35] The Guardian, 'Majority verdict: we already have a bill of rights', 22 November 2011 <http://www.guardian.co.uk/law/2011/nov/22/already-have-uk-bill-of-rights>.

[36] Commission on a Bill of Rights, Meeting Minutes 14 December 2011, [2.2].

[37] BBC News, 'Sunday Politics', 12 March 2012 <http://www.bbc.co.uk/news/uk-politics-17338629>.

focused on limiting the role of the ECtHR relative to national institutions, particularly courts.[38] Its recommendations have been to formalize the margin of appreciation and principle of subsidiarity, to ensure sufficient national discretion. It has also proposed making claims to the ECtHR inadmissible where a matter has been considered by a national court unless the national court had 'clearly erred', and giving the court the power to issue advisory opinions on the interpretation of the Convention, at the invitation of national courts, but leaving national courts to apply the law to the facts in specific cases. Some of these recommendations were adopted in the 2012 Brighton Declaration of States Parties. However the introduction of additional admissibility criteria was not, and the proposals around advisory opinions were heavily watered down.[39]

From the perspective of the HRA, and specifically the role of DOIs, reforms in this direction would not only increase national latitude in applying the ECHR rights, they could in fact *strengthen* the position of the UK courts. The focus of reforms has been on the powers of national courts as an alternative to the Strasbourg court and a stronger margin of appreciation would make it more likely that domestic DOIs will be affirmed by the Strasbourg court as part of its respect for national institutions. It seems possible therefore that, over the long term, rather than disappear, DOIs will only be strengthened.

38 *High Level Conference on the Future of the European Court of Human Rights—Draft Brighton Declaration* (circulated by the UK government 23 February 2012).

39 *High Level Conference on the Future of the European Court of Human Rights—Brighton Declaration* (adopted 19 April 2012).

Conclusion

This book has been an investigation of the project of engaging institutions beyond courts in human rights protection—in the twin tasks of deciding what human rights principles require of public action and acting to uphold human rights. This investigation has focused on an institutional innovation in human rights adjudication: a remedial mechanism with the potential to enhance the protection of human rights by enlisting the legislature in crafting responsive action and to enhance deliberation within the legislature on the fundamental rights commitments of a democracy.

Institutional design is generally unpredictable until tried, perhaps even repeatedly tried, and this is one reason why test cases are valuable.[1] In this conclusion, I offer some reflections on DOIs from the perspective of institutional design, drawing on this first experiment with them.

Of course, there are limits to our ability to generalize from a single example. Even over the study period of ten years, there was development over time. There was greater controversy and strain on cooperation in the later phase from 2005 to 2010, as well as a learning process in the political branches of government. The HRA may have now settled into a stable mode of operation, but this is not certain: recent developments present a mixed picture, with the continued operation of the dominant specialization model of interaction, yet with questions over the institutional settlement in relation to human rights over the long term.

Background conditions are also important and will differ in other jurisdictions. In particular, we have seen that the status of the ECtHR has been an important factor in the operation of the HRA. Also, in other jurisdictions, there may generally be higher levels of conflict or intransigence between the different branches of government; this may mean that the type of cooperative interaction that has occurred in the UK would not occur if this type of open remedy were transferred elsewhere.

DOIs in the UK provide one example of the fact that innovations in constitutional design may not necessarily translate to different *practice* or different *behaviours* in the ways one might expect. Despite the novel non-coercive nature of DOIs, they have operated similarly to other open remedies, insofar as the respective functions of courts and legislatures have been fairly distinct and

[1] For discussion, see A Vermeule, *Mechanisms of Democracy: Institutional Design Writ Small* (OUP, New York 2007) 17.

specialized. This book has identified some reasons for this. Courts have been careful in their use of DOIs, despite their non-binding status. The political branches of government have played an important role in translating findings of violation into new legislation and policy. The mechanism has allowed space for political actors to resist decisions, but they have done so through their ordinary powers of legislation, rather than taking the more sensational route of refusal offered by the HRA. As a result, the interaction between courts and legislatures over the meaning to be given to human rights has operated similarly to how a more coercive form of legislative remand would do.

Over the study period, we do not see the more radical vision of dialogue-as-dual review in action. We do not generally see a differentiated approach to judicial determinations as less authoritative because of the structural features of DOIs. The UK experience suggests that accepted notions around the respective roles of courts and legislatures may be difficult to displace in the way that this model of dialogue would seek to do. In the most open expression of disagreement with a finding of incompatibility, the willingness of a number of MPs to advocate non-compliance with the ECtHR's decision on prisoner voting was accompanied by arguments discrediting that court itself, rather than simply respectful disagreement on the merits of a particular decision.

This is not evidence, however, that the political branches of government in the UK will never use their power to disagree with the courts: only that they have declined to use it so far. The nature of interaction has generally been cooperative rather than conflictual; a large number of cases have not been controversial, and a significant proportion of DOIs have been supported by direct Strasbourg rulings. There were cases in this period where the courts did *not* make a finding of incompatibility where a DOI was sought—such as in relation to the ban on political advertising[2] and the ban on fox hunting.[3] Perhaps DOIs in relation to these types of laws would be more likely to result in open, principled disagreement. At this stage of the HRA's development, the power to refuse to change the law appears to have assumed the place of a 'safety valve': an option in the event of a type of rare finding of incompatibility that has not yet occurred at the national level.

At the same time, we see that a significant latitude may exist in devising a response, which may throw up varied human rights and other policy concerns. In select examples, the UK legislature was engaged in delivering a systematic response to a human rights problem, negotiating new rights and policy issues that arose, bringing to bear information and views from a number of groups and even engaging in continued review of the concerns raised by a legislative reply beyond the ability or willingness of the courts to do so. Therefore, the case study does demonstrate some of the posited benefits of legislative remedies and how legislative review and judicial review can be complementary in holding executive power to account.

[2] *R (Animal Defenders International) v Secretary of State for Culture, Media and Sport* [2008] UKHL 15.
[3] *R (Countryside Alliance & Ors) v Attorney-General & Anor* [2007] UKHL 52.

In terms of drawing lessons for institutional design to support a deliberative democracy, it is useful to think of DOIs in terms of Adrian Vermeule's concept of mechanisms of 'institutional design writ small'.[4] Here, instead of considering the grand questions of constitutional design (such as, say, the parliamentary system versus the presidential system), institutional design is directed to how we can improve the functioning of existing democracies even while certain large-scale background features remain stable. The motivation of 'institutional design writ small' is that even small-scale changes can lead to significant improvements in terms of democratization.[5] The very idea of weak-form review is that the process of judicial review of legislation can be tailored to better achieve democratic values and human rights protection. Indeed, the conclusions that I draw from the UK study suggest that seemingly small matters of design are significant to better realizing these values.

Three related lessons for institutional design emerge from the UK experience. The first is that, in designing a system of human rights protection that takes into account the powerful concept of reasonable disagreement over rights, we should be careful not to assume that reasonable disagreement is an ever-present feature of human rights adjudication in practice.[6] Where DOIs are not met with dispute, because it is accepted that the legislation is harsh or unfair, we see gains from judicial oversight, without any corresponding loss to principles of self-government. Moreover, we should not neglect the possibility that judges will prefer to limit use of their powers where opinion is highly divided, to avoid having their decisions perceived as 'mere opinions' rather than authoritative rulings. Weaker judicial powers may not therefore lead to judicial activism, but prudential self-restraint on matters of divided opinion.

Yet, the 'default' result where a DOI is employed (that is, the result in the event of inaction, or institutional inertia) is that there is no legislative change. By disabling judges from invalidating or suspending legislation and imposing no timetable for action from the legislature, the design of the mechanism anticipates open disagreement with the judicial decision on human rights. In order to preserve the symbolism that courts cannot invalidate Acts of the legislature on the grounds of human rights unless the legislature agrees, DOIs are designed in a way that fits exceptional cases, rather than routine cases in the UK. This is not to argue that it is *never* a good idea to design institutional mechanisms to best suit exceptional cases; only that we need to reflect on whether this is, on balance, the best approach to take.

This bring us to the second lesson that can be drawn from the case study, which is that there are some concrete problems with setting the default result as no legislative change. Where judges are playing a valuable checking function—identifying human

[4] Vermeule (n 1). [5] Vermeule (n 1) 3.

[6] For a recent open statement of this assumption, see J Allan, 'The Victorian *Charter of Human Rights and Responsibilities*: Exegesis and Criticism' (2006) 30 MULR 906, 914–16: 'What, in fact, happens [in the UK] after the judges issue [DOIs]? Does the elected legislature ever dispute what almost always amounts to a highly debateable line-drawing call, one over which sincere, reasonable, well-informed, even nice people can and do disagree?'

rights violations that are not controversial—the design of DOIs has a cost in terms of human rights protection. Victims may miss out on effective remedies if this requires some retrospective measure to be taken, even if the executive/legislature are in agreement that the impugned law was unacceptable. Even where DOIs are controversial, the sheer permissiveness of their design under the HRA has a cost in terms of deliberation. One, presumably inadvertent, aspect of the design of DOIs is that, in the short term, they leave open the possibility of neither remedial action nor principled refusal to comply. Prevarication and a failure of public justification or legislative deliberation are made possible by the lack of any formal obligations. In these ways, DOIs are *too permissive*, and I suggest that it would be a better balance to impose, at least, procedural duties following a DOI, if not to secure for courts greater powers over primary legislation (for instance, the power to provide a time period within which the legislature must act or the courts will institute a remedy). This would preserve the legislature's ability to reach even a radically different answer on human rights to courts, but ameliorate some of the routine practical difficulties seen in the study of DOIs.

Some may take issue with the argument that DOIs are too permissive in their design, given that all DOIs have met with compliance. Judicial review sceptics have already tried to use the UK example to illustrate why judicial powers should be more limited, and that even granting HRA-style powers reproduces the juridical paradigm of rights protection.[7] However, there is little in the UK's experience with DOIs to suggest that more limited judicial powers would have provided any benefit to either legislative deliberation or the protection of human rights. The HRA has brought gains for human rights protection, as well as some modest gains for legislative deliberation, primarily through the JCHR. Rather, the third lesson to be drawn from this study of the UK experience with DOIs is that, if we are concerned to improve legislative engagement in human rights matters, then future efforts would be best directed to strengthening support for independent deliberation in the legislature. Mechanisms through which information is introduced into Parliament, forums in which the executive is required to answer questions and justify its actions, and whether time and support are provided for consideration of legislation are all examples of important practical steps to support independent legislative review. In terms of the substance of deliberation, as UK courts develop experience in their human rights jurisdiction, they may start to actively seek not simply to speak to lawyers, but to write human rights judgments that speak more broadly and provide persuasive reasoning that legislative and public debate can engage with. As public scrutiny of human rights judgments increases, this need will be greater. Insofar as the system of government concentrates power in the leaders of the executive, a focus on weakening or even removing judicial powers is misplaced; in fact, we have seen that parliamentarians, and through them the civil society

[7] Examples include Allan (n 6) and T Campbell and N Barry, 'A Democratic Bill of Rights for Australia: Submission to the National Human Rights Consultation' [2.1], available at <http://www.humanrightsconsultation.gov.au>

organizations and others who input into the legislative process, may rely on the prospect of judicial review as a way to extract information and justification from the executive. This is not to discount the symbolic importance of weak-form review, only to say that *more* is needed than to give the legislature the formal last word.

The JCHR gives us a good example of how attempts to positively support legislative review are more important to encouraging deliberation than attempts to limit judges. The Committee has begun to gain international attention: in 2012 the Australian Parliament established a parliamentary joint committee modelled on the JCHR; Adrian Vermeule has called for a similar institution to be developed in the United States Congress on constitutional issues;[8] and the Council of Europe has cited the Committee as a model for other European parliaments to follow.[9] We have seen that it has taken the Committee some time to develop its own 'voice'. Yet, while the JCHR has begun to build its own expertise and become a site of independent review and civic engagement, it has not had a great deal of effective power, and has not managed to 'mainstream' human rights concerns across Parliament.[10] This suggests a puzzle for further consideration: whether there is a compromise between effective power and quality deliberation, and whether attempts to make the JCHR stronger would compromise its ability to steer outside party politics and place a burden of justification on the government. Broader research on the legislature and other sites of human rights deliberation could helpfully draw on the idea of a 'deliberative system' in which various parts of the system are designed to satisfy different criteria of a deliberative democracy, rather than attempting to achieve ideal deliberation in one forum.[11]

This book began with the recognition that, beyond fundamental human rights as law, fundamental human rights exist as ethical claims on the exercise of power, and these claims may evolve in a different way and at a different pace from the law in a given country. Academic work on these rights has dedicated significant attention to theoretical debates over democracy and judicial review. Without attention to the sometimes less exciting day-to-day operation of various forms of rights protection, there is a danger of these debates becoming self-referential, and losing sight of how power is exercised and justified *in practice*. Democratization is an ongoing project of striving to increase participation, reflectiveness, and reason-giving in public decision-making, and both the protection of human rights, and debates over what they entail, are important components of this project. Overall, the research in this book suggests that our efforts should be directed less to pulling courts out of these debates, and more to building the institutional foundations for drawing other actors in.

8 Vermeule (n 1) Chapter 7 'Optimizing Deliberation: Constitutional Issues in Congress'.

9 Council of Europe, Parliamentary Assembly Resolution 1516 'Implementation of judgments of the European Court of Human Rights', 2 October 2006, [8] <http://assembly.coe.int/Main.asp?link=/Documents/AdoptedText/ta06/ERES1516.htm>.

10 For the beginnings of research into this see M Hunt et al, 'Parliaments and Human Rights: Redressing the Democratic Deficit' (AHRC Public Policy Series No 5, 2012).

11 J Dryzek, *Foundations and Frontiers of Deliberative Governance* (OUP, Oxford 2011).

APPENDIX 1

Table of DOIs

	Case Name, citation, date (court)	Subsequent litigation	Incompatible legislation	Affected human right (ECHR Article)	Legislative response
1	*R (H) v Mental Health Review Tribunal for the North and East London Region & the Secretary of State for Health* [2001] EWCA Civ 415; 28 March 2001 (Court of Appeal)	No appeal was made.	ss 72–3 Mental Health Act 1983	Right to liberty (Article 5)	The legislation was amended by the Mental Health Act 1983 (Remedial) Order 2001 (SI 2001 No 3712), which came into force on 26 November 2001.
2	*R (Alconbury Developments Ltd) v Secretary of State for the Environment, Transport and the Regions* [2001] HRLR 2; 13 December 2000 (Divisional Court)	Overturned by House of Lords: [2001] UKHL 23.	ss 77–9 Town and Country Planning Act 1990	Right to a fair trial (Article 6)	No action taken.
3	*Wilson v First County Trust Ltd (No 2)* [2001] EWCA Civ 633; 2 May 2001 (Court of Appeal)	Overturned by House of Lords: [2003] UKHL 40.	s 127(3) Consumer Credit Act	Right to a fair trial (Article 6) and right to property (Article 1, First Protocol)	No action taken.
4	*McR's Application for Judicial Review* [2002] NIQB 58; 15 January 2002 (Northern Ireland Queen's Bench)	No appeal was made.	s 62 Offences Against the Person Act 1861	Right to a private and family life (Article 8)	The legislation was repealed in Northern Ireland by the Sexual Offences Act 2003, which also repealed similar offences in England and Wales.

(*continued*)

	Case Name, citation, date (court)	Subsequent litigation	Incompatible legislation	Affected human right (ECHR Article)	Legislative response
5	*International Transport Roth GmbH v Secretary of State for the Home Department* [2002] EWCA Civ 158; 22 February 2002 (Court of Appeal)	No appeal was made.	Part II Immigration and Asylum Act 1999	Right to a fair trial (Article 6)	The legislation was amended by the Nationality, Immigration and Asylum Act 2002.
6	*Matthews v Ministry of Defence* [2002] EWHC 13 (QB); 22 January 2002 (Divisional Court)	Overturned by Court of Appeal, and this decision was upheld by House of Lords: [2003] UKHL 4.	s 10 Crown Proceedings Act 1947	Right to a fair trial (Article 6)	No action taken.
7	*R (Anderson) v Secretary of State for the Home Department* [2002] UKHL 46; 25 November 2002 (House of Lords)		s 29 Crime (Sentences) Act 1997	Right to a fair trial (Article 6)	The law was repealed by the Criminal Justice Act 2003.
8	*R (D) v Secretary of State for the Home Department* [2002] EWHC 2805 (Admin); 19 December 2002 (Administrative Court)	No appeal was made.	s 74 Mental Health Act 1983	Right to liberty (Article 5)	The law was amended the Criminal Justice Act 2003.
9	*Blood and Tarbuck v Secretary of State for Health* (unreported) 28 February 2003 (Sullivan J)	No appeal was made.	s 28(6) Human Fertilization and Embryology Act 1990	Right to a private and family life (Article 8) and right to non-discrimination (Article 14)	The law was amended by the Human Fertilization and Embryology (Deceased Fathers) Act 2003.
10	*R (Uttley) v Secretary of State for the Home Department* [2003] EWHC 950 (Admin); 8 April 2003 (Court of Appeal)	Overturned by House of Lords: [2004] UKHL 38.	ss 33(2), 37(4)(a), and 39 Criminal Justice Act 1991	Non-retrospectivity of criminal law (Article 7)	No action taken.

11	*Bellinger v Bellinger* [2003] UKHL 21; 10 April 2003 (House of Lords)		s 11(c) Matrimonial Causes Act 1973	Right to a private and family life (Article 8) and right to marry (Article 12)	This was remedied by the Gender Recognition Act 2004.
12	*R (M) v Secretary of State for Health* [2003] EWHC 1094 (Admin); 16 April 2003 (Administrative Court)	No appeal was made.	ss 26–9 Mental Health Act 1983	Right to a private and family life (Article 8)	This was remedied by the Mental Health Act 2007.
13	*R (Hooper and Ors) v Secretary of State for Work and Pensions* [2003] EWCA Civ 875; 18 June 2003 (Court of Appeal)	Decision upheld by House of Lords, though the court declined to issue a DOI: [2005] UKHL 29.	ss 36–7 Social Security Contributions and Benefit Act 1992	Right to property (Article 1, First Protocol) and right to non-discrimination (Article 14)	The law had already been changed at the date of the judgment by the Welfare Reform and Pensions Act 1999, s 54(1), which came into force on 9 April 2001.
14	*R (Wilkinson) v Inland Revenue Commissioners* [2003] EWCA Civ 814; 18 June 2003 (Court of Appeal)	Upheld by House of Lords: [2005] UKHL 30.	s 262 Income and Corporation Taxes Act 1988	Right to property (Article 1, First Protocol) and right to non-discrimination (Article 14)	The law had already been repealed by the Finance Act 1999 ss 34(1), 139, and Schedule 20.
15	*R (MH) v Secretary of State for Health* [2004] EWCA Civ 1609; 3 December 2004 (Court of Appeal)	Overturned by House of Lords: [2005] UKHL 60.	s 2 Mental Health Act 1983	Right to liberty (Article 5)	No action taken.
16	*A and Ors v Secretary of State for the Home Department* [2004] UKHL 56; 16 December 2004 (House of Lords)		s 23 Anti-terrorism, Crime and Security Act 2001	Right to liberty (Article 5) and right to non-discrimination (Article 14)	The provisions were repealed by the Prevention of Terrorism Act 2005, which put in place a new regime of control orders.

(*continued*)

	Case Name, citation, date (court)	Subsequent litigation	Incompatible legislation	Affected human right (ECHR Article)	Legislative response
17	*R (Morris) v Westminster City Council & First Secretary of State* [2005] EWCA Civ 1184; 14 October 2005 (Court of Appeal)	No appeal was made.	s 185(4) of the Housing Act 1996	Right to a private and family life (Article 8) and right to non-discrimination (Article 14)	The law was amended by Schedule 15 to the Housing and Regeneration Act 2008.
18	*R (Gabaj) v First Secretary of State* (unreported) 28 March 2006 (Administrative Court)	No appeal was made.	s 185(4) of the Housing Act 1996	Right to a private and family life (Article 8) and right to non-discrimination (Article 14)	The law was amended by Schedule 15 to the Housing and Regeneration Act 2008.
19	*R (Baiai and Ors) v Secretary of State for the Home Department and Anor* [2006] EWHC 823; 10 April 2006 (Administrative Court)	Article 12 DOI upheld by Court of Appeal, [2007] EWCA Civ 478; but overturned by the House of Lords: [2008] UKHL 53. The Article 14 DOI was not appealed.	s 19(3) Asylum and Immigration (Treatment of Claimants, etc.) Act 2004	Right to marry (Article 12) and right to non-discrimination (Article 14)	The law was amended by the Asylum and Immigration (Treatment of Claimants, etc) Act 2004 (Remedial) Order 2011, which was made on 25 April 2011 and came into force on 9 May 2011.
20	*Re MB* [2006] EWHC 1000; 12 April 2006 (Administrative Court)	Overturned by the Court of Appeal, and this decision was upheld by the House of Lords: [2007] UKHL 46.	s 2 Prevention of Terrorism Act 2005	Right to a fair trial (Article 6)	No action taken.
21	*R (Wright and Ors) v Secretary of State for Health and Anor* [2006] EWHC 2886; 16 November 2006 (Administrative Court)	Overturned by the Court of Appeal, but was reinstated by the House of Lords [2009] UKHL 3.	s 82(4)(b) Care Standards Act 2000	Right to a fair trial (Article 6) and right to a private and family life (Article 8)	This Act was replaced by the Safeguarding Vulnerable Groups Act 2006, which included changes to the affected scheme.

22	*R (Clift) v Secretary of State for the Home Department; Secretary of State for the Home Department v Hindawi and another* [2006] UKHL 54; 13 December 2006 (House of Lords)		ss 46(1) and 50(2) Criminal Justice Act 1991	Right to liberty (Article 5) and right to non-discrimination (Article 14)	The affected provisions had already been repealed by the Criminal Justice Act 2003, but continued to apply to offences committed before 4 April 2005. The Criminal Justice and Immigration Act 2008 therefore amended the Criminal Justice Act 1991 to remove the incompatibility in the transitional cases.
23	*Smith v Scott* [2007] CSIH 9; 24 January 2007 (Registration Appeal Court Scotland)	No appeal was made.	s 3 Representation of the People Act 1983	Right to vote (Article 3, First Protocol)	The Labour government launched a consultation on this matter in 2006, the second stage of which concluded in September 2009. No action was taken in time for the 2010 UK general election. The Coalition government announced its proposed remedy (a modified ban) in December 2010, but at the time of writing no measures had been presented to Parliament.
24	*Nasseri v Secretary of State for the Home Department* [2007] EWHC 1548; 2 July 2007 (Administrative Court)	Overturned by the Court of Appeal: [2008] EWCA Civ 464. The House of Lords upheld the Court of Appeal's decision: [2009] UKHL 23.	Paragraph 3, Schedule 3 Asylum and Immigration (Treatment of Claimants) Act 2004	Prohibition on torture and inhuman and degrading treatment (Article 3)	No action taken.

(continued)

	Case Name, citation, date (court)	Subsequent litigation	Incompatible legislation	Affected human right (ECHR Article)	Legislative response
25	*R (Wayne Thomas Black) v Secretary of State for Justice* [2008] EWCA Civ 359; 15 April 2008 (Court of Appeal)	Overturned by the House of Lords: [2009] UKHL 1.	s 35(1) Criminal Justice Act 1991	Right to liberty (Article 5)	The affected provisions had already been repealed by the Criminal Justice Act 2003, but continued to apply to offences committed before 4 April 2005. No further action was taken.
26	*R (F and Thompson) v Secretary of State for the Home Department* [2008] EWHC 3170; 19 December 2008 (Administrative Court)	Upheld by the Court of Appeal, and then upheld by the Supreme Court: [2010] UKSC 17.	s 82(1) Sexual Offences Act 2003	Right to a private and family life (Article 8)	The draft Sexual Offences Act 2003 (Remedial) Order 2012 was laid before both Houses of Parliament on 5 March 2012. That Order seeks to introduce a mechanism for reviewing the indefinite notification requirements under section 82(1) of the 2003 Act.
27	*R (Royal College of Nursing) v Secretary of State for the Home Department* [2010] EWHC 2761; 10 November 2010 (Administrative Court)		Part I, Safeguarding Vulnerable Groups Act 2006 (Schedule 3)	Right to a fair trial (Article 6) and right to a private and family life (Article 8)	The government included provisions in the Protection of Freedoms Bill to amend Schedule 3 to the SVGA 2006 (on introduction these provisions were contained within clause 66(2) and 66(6) of the Bill).

APPENDIX 2

Empirical Data

The primary empirical data relied upon in Part III are public records: parliamentary transcripts, reports of parliamentary committees, official correspondence, and evidence to parliamentary committees. There are limitations in looking to the public record for political analysis, for one may miss behind-the-scenes bargaining and other private interactions. However, reliance on public records was justified in this study for three reasons. First, examination of the legislature is uniquely assisted by the existence of official transcript records of all debates and all materials put to debate, as well as all evidence available to parliamentary committees and their reports to Parliament. The public record is a rich data source on the legislature. Second, the purpose of this research was to evaluate democratic deliberation in the aftermath of a judicial decision, and publicity is a component of this deliberation. Third, reliance on the public record is useful to guard against difficulties in relying on personal interview evidence, such as partial or selective accounts of the past.

The research has however been assisted by interviews with certain key figures for an insight into the Joint Committee of Human Rights (JCHR), the Ministry of Justice, the Opposition, and Labour backbenchers interested in strengthening Parliament. Interviews were conducted with:

Dominic Grieve MP, *then Shadow Attorney-General, subsequently Attorney-General—23 May 2008, Beaconsfield*

Tony Wright MP, *Labour Backbencher, subsequently Chair of the Wright Committee—10 June 2008, London*

Evan Harris MP, *then member of the JCHR—1 August 2008, Oxford*

Rob Linham, *Head of Litigation, Human Rights Unit, Ministry of Justice—22 February 2010, London*

Murray Hunt, *Legal Adviser to the JCHR—17 March 2010, Oxford*

Baroness Vivien Stern, *former member of the JCHR—21 June 2010, London*

Index